Talking Poetry

Conversations in the Workshop
with Contemporary Poets

Talking Poetry

Conversations in the Workshop
with Contemporary Poets

Lee Bartlett

UNIVERSITY OF NEW MEXICO PRESS
ALBUQUERQUE

LIBRARY OF CONGRESS CATALOGING-IN-PUBLICATION DATA

Talking Poetry.

  Interviews held at various workshops at the
University of New Mexico from 1983 to 1985.
  Bibliography: p.
  Includes index.
  1. American poetry—20th century—History and
criticism. 2. Poets, American—20th century—Interviews.
3. English poetry—20th century—History and criticism.
4. Poets, English—20th century—Interviews.
5. Poetry—Authorship. 6. Poetry. I. Bartlett,
Lee, 1950–
PS325.T3 1986   811'.54'09   86-16163
ISBN 0-8263-0911-9
ISBN 0-8263-0912-7 (pbk.)

Designed by Joanna V. Hill

Contents

feather to feather added
(and what is mineral, what
is curling hair, the string
you carry in your nervous beak, these

make bulk, these, in the end, are
the sum

—Charles Olson

Preface

In his preface to the *Collected Poems,* Ed Dorn writes, "From the beginning I have known my work to be theoretical in nature and poetic by virtue of its inherent tone." This attitude holds generally for the whole range of poetry in English in this century—from the imagists to the Language poets—as for better or worse our verse has been a working out of a complex of issues as much as anything else. Obviously, one of the continuing attractions of the literary interview is the sense that we are overhearing a fascinating kind of gossip, with passing remarks on contemporaries, trends, and literary politics. But more important, and perhaps the reason that we attend to interviews at least as seriously as to poets' prose, is the feeling that to get a poet to comment on craft will both provide a kind of map for reading that particular work and open up the larger geography of the art itself.

In a way, I would hope that this book makes no specific attempt to argue for anything beyond the variousness of contemporary poetry in English, but in a discipline which has been suffering a split sensibility since at least Emerson and Poe, such a claim would be either dissembling or naive. As Helen Vendler's recent *Harvard Book of Contemporary American Poetry* makes clear, even if we assumed various poetics had somehow finally managed to reconcile themselves (or at least stand in the same room together) after the frenetic and often destructive "anthology wars" of the fifties and sixties, such is not the case. That book, edited by a critic many regard as the eminent arbiter of the fashion of current verse, and carrying Harvard's imprimatur, charts a rather reactionary and one-dimensional territory. While Vendler's collection of contemporary writing contains selections by Wallace Stevens (born 1879), Theodore Roethke, and Elizabeth Bishop, there is nothing by Ezra Pound, William Carlos Williams, H.D., George Oppen, Louis Zukofsky, Charles Reznikoff, Denise Levertov, Charles Olson, Robert Duncan, or Robert Creeley. And, needless to say, none of the poets speaking here is represented as, like Williams and Pound, for Vendler and Harvard they seem somehow not to exist.

I would hesitate, however, to offer this gathering as a kind of coherent "countertradition," for obviously a writer like Thom Gunn (who, were he American, might be the one candidate from this selection to find his way into Vendler's anthology) has little in common with Tom Raworth, or William Everson with Michael Palmer. Further, a countertradition implies that the work is not only out of the mainstream, but also perhaps less immediate, less influential, and frankly of a second order. Reputations rise and fall like so many winds, yet even a cursory glance through the following pages should convince the most skeptical reader that many of these writers do more than hover on the margin of significance, that their contributions to our poetry continue to alter our aesthetic landscape both vividly and profoundly.

It is unnecessary to argue that somehow all of these writers are "major poets," though, and that term can mean little when speaking of contemporary writing. Set against Vendler's canon of the current (I'm thinking here of Amy Clampitt, Frank Bidart, Robert Pinsky, Dave Smith, Louise Glück, Albert Goldbarth, Michael Blumenthal, and Rita Dove), however, figures like Theodore Enslin (with his sense of the music of the line), Clayton Eshleman (with his movement into the cave of the paleolithic), William Everson (with his lifelong commitment to the sacred and bardic vocation of the poet), Michael Palmer (with his emphasis on the potential of "intertextuality"), Nathaniel Tarn (with his sensitivity toward the multicultural), and Diane Wakoski (with her insistence that poets need to relearn the Dionysian embrace, that they are first, and finally, human beings) do seem to offer us a body of work with far more at stake, continually prodding us further into both the contradictions and the possibilities of poetry.

While I would not want to overstate the case, then, there are various interesting points of convergence among these poets. The Pound/Williams/Olson influence (more or less Donald Allen's "New American Poetry") is as pervasive here as both the New Critical and the newer academic are muted. A number of these writers have either edited influential magazines (for example, Coolidge and Palmer's *Joglars*, Eshleman's *Caterpillar* and *Sulfur*, Reed's *Y'Bird*) or a whole series of books (Tarn's Cape Editions, Raworth's Goliard Press); many have worked at translation seriously (Eshleman, Palmer, and Tarn are primary here); and while all frequently give readings and occasionally do workshops in university settings, most don't currently teach regularly or full-time. Further, work by most of the poets here (with Gunn and Reed being, it seems to me, the only exceptions) has found publication through the network of smaller magazines and presses rather than the large New York publishing houses or university presses.

Over the past decade good collections of interviews with poets have appeared: the ongoing *Paris Review* series, the *Contemporary Literature* series, and the University of Michigan's *Poet's Prose* series, as well as such individual volumes as Richard Jackson's recent *Acts of Mind,* are just a few. This collection differs from those projects, however, in that rather than the traditional one-on-one interview, the conversations here are between working poets and groups of apprentice writers, graduate and undergraduate members of various workshops in poetry and poetics which I led as part of the Creative Writing Program at the University of New Mexico from 1983 to 1985.

In a note published a decade ago, Ron Loewinsohn pointed out that "the interview is an attractive form, but some of its strengths are also its weaknesses, particularly its spontaneity and immediacy. One weakness is that the form tempts you into a too easy and actually specious formal coherence." A common result is that early on "a key signature or a theme song gets established, and from then on both people will unconsciously relate questions back to that theme song." Such a process happens here often—Ted Enslin on music and the long poem, Kenneth Irby on the notion of place, William Everson on the poet's vocation, along with frequent reference to Language poetry, are just a few examples—though I hope this is not at the sacrifice, as Loewinsohn warns, of "a greater complexity and possibly comprehensiveness." Certainly the desire is that this collection will provide a range of fresh perspectives on postwar poetry in English and its concerns (the relation of theory to practice, translation, the small press situation and the politics of publishing, and so on) from poets who, as Clark Coolidge says, are "doing it."

Thanks go first of all, of course, to the poets who agreed—in every case with enthusiasm—to meet with students to discuss their work. Once I had prepared the initial transcripts from these meetings (often reworking the questions for greater concision and coherence), the writers read through them, clarifying and correcting. Additionally, they generously allowed me to choose representative selections from their work for reprinting.

A number of workshops and seminars were involved in this project, and I'd like to thank the countless student writers who participated. A few, who attended nearly all these meetings over two years, include Jane Suzane Allyn, Alan Baehr, Mara Gould, Mary Rising Higgins, Sharon Lewis, Kathleen Linnell, James Mackie, Robert Masterson, Susan Miller, Bayita Garoffolo O'Rourke, Carl Peterson, David Putney, Billie Schimel, Cassandra Sitterly, Robert Stonecipher, Steven Sullivan, John Tritica, Cynthia Vogt, and Devi Wilkinson. Faculty and staff who have been particularly helpful include

Rudolfo Anaya, James Barbour, Jon Bentley, Lynn Beene, Paul Davis, Gene Frumkin, Barry Gaines, Patrick Gallacher, F. Chris Garcia, Sam B. Girgus, Hamlin Hill, David Johnson, Joel Jones, David McPherson, Louis Owens, Patricia Clark Smith, James Thorson, Hugh Witemeyer, and Peter White, as well as K. T. Martin, Joanne Tawney, and Denise Warren. Additionally, Gus Blaisdell, Larry Godell, and Jeff Bryan of The Living Batch Bookstore have provided much support, as has John Randall.

Robin Tawney continually set aside his own work to coordinate writers' visits; Beth Hadas of the UNM Press gave early support to this project, and Dana Asbury served as an intelligent and enthusiastic editor; Marta Field not only typed and retyped versions of these transcripts, but in the process made innumerable and perceptive editorial suggestions, always with great cheer. Further, selections from this collection previously appeared in *American Poetry, Another Chicago Magazine,* and *Poetry Flash.*

Finally, I'd like to inscribe this collection to my wife, who, like the writers here, believes what she says.

1. Clark Coolidge

"A constant retrogression, and this is not memory"

Clark Coolidge was born in Providence, Rhode Island, in 1939. He attended Brown University, and between 1964 and 1966 edited *Joglars* magazine with Michael Palmer. His many books include *Space, The Maintains, Polaroid, Research,* and most recently *Mine: The One That Enters the Stories* and *Solution Passage: Poems 1978–1981;* a play, *To Obtain the Value of the Cake Measure from Zero,* written with Tom Veitch, was published in 1970. Coolidge received a National Endowment for the Arts grant in 1978, and the New York Poets Foundation Award in 1968. An issue of *Stations* was dedicated to an analysis of his work.

"The context of my works is the Tonality of Language (seen, heard, spoken, thought) itself," Coolidge has written, "a tonality that centers itself in the constant flowage from meaning to meaning, and that sideslippage between meanings. We are free now to delight in the Surface of Language, a surface as deep as the distance between (for instance) a noun (in the mind) (in a dictionary) and its object somewhere in the universe."

What I have in mind is a phrase, a sentence actually, from Maurice Blanchot, the French writer. At the moment he's not too well known here, though he's starting to become part of the academic procedure. He examines the writing act, the actual state of mind while writing, and a lot of his work is abstract and a headache to read, but once in a while he gets in a great phrase. He said, "One can only write if one arrives at the instant towards which one can only move through space opened up by the movement of writing." It's an incredible paradox in a way, but that word *movement* is for me the key.

I started out as a musician playing drums, which transformed eventually into jazz and be-bop. If I don't get a certain kind of movement, a literal moving forward in time in my work, I don't feel like it's really happening. That's the kind of carrier frequency that I work with. This is not to say that my work is what they call "sound poetry" that you don't have to care about the meaning, which I care about very much. I just thought I'd like to begin by getting that into the record, Blanchot's phrase.

What does it mean?
That you have to be writing in order to write. The poet Philip Whalen, when he teaches, says the first thing is to write down the words on the paper. Now that sounds dumb, but it's a great secret because you start the transformation process from outside to inside to back outside, something you can see. You can't carry it around in your head forever.

It seems to me that you are more than anything else preoccupied with the meaning between words.

Well, at an early point in my writing I really tried to separate all the language out into its basic component, which seemed to be the word. Some poets take a syllable, others a single letter, but that atomizes it too much. But the words—trying to put them together from scratch. Language didn't come that quickly to me when I was young, and the idea of speaking in front of a group like this in school would have terrified me. I couldn't write letters to relatives or friends. It was awful. So I think had to go back to the beginning and tear it all to pieces to find out where I could start. I did some works in 1966, which appeared in *Space,* where I was even trying to see the resistances. They were little constellations of words, maybe five or six, spaced out rather than in vertical structures. To see what kind of resistance words had against going together, to somehow tap that energy. In that sense, I guess you are right.

To what degree are you conscious of the process while writing?

While writing at the best heat I'm not. Nevertheless, I think there is something in your mind that is doing that all the time. I just came from Boulder, Colorado, where I was teaching a course on Samuel Beckett. If you've ever read *The Unnamable* there is an incredible pronoun shift that goes on continually—he's thinking of himself, voices tell him things, he sees himself talking to himself, amazingly reflexive. Once you've had the experience of a book like that, it's very hard not to be involved with that consciousness. I don't want to say that it's an historical imperative of Modernism, like the sixties in painting, where everything was reduced down to the point where there was no incident on the canvas, nothing reflecting the picture frame. I don't believe that, and in fact tend to think of it as good old American consumerism. But after reading Beckett you can no longer think of yourself as simply telling a story. I have an impulse where I'd really like to do that, but it has to get filtered. If you've looked at my book *Mine,* you'll see that it is really an attempt to write a novel, but I can't. It always returns to me at the desk writing and looking out the window. Little threads of stories come seemingly out of nowhere, and it was fascinating for me to follow those threads through to see what would happen. I had no plan, and in fact almost gave it up after a few pages when I realized it wasn't going to be a novel. There is this poet's thing—you want to write one of those big books that tells a story. But I can't just decide to throw out all this different kind of stuff I've done and become a different writer.

You mentioned music as an influence.

Yeah. I had a lot of nonliterary influences. The music. I was involved in looking at the painting in the fifties in New York, the Abstract Expressionists especially. Merce Cunningham's dance. Movies from Stan Brakhage to Godard to last week's whatever.

The prose pieces in Mine *seem very cinematic.*

Sure, if you think of things being framed in certain ways, or a movement through one thing to another. I am really a hodgepodge writer, coming from all sorts of directions. I'm still catching up on various great works of literature which everyone else has already read.

You didn't study English in college?

No, I had just one English course. I hated it and walked out after a few meetings. I was majoring in geology, which was another mistake. Because I had started collecting rocks when I was six years old I thought it would be a wonderful thing to do with my life. But as it turned out, I looked around at the guys who were doing it and teaching it, and they were some of the most boring human beings I've ever seen. There was one terrific guy, but his form of geology was getting phased out. I went to college when geology was changing from a natural, descriptive science to things like geophysics. It was moving into an awful lot of math and lab science, and I realized that I'd be stuck in a lab all my life. The irony is that now I'm stuck at a desk in my basement.

Anyway, I had one freshman English course, a seminar actually. They were trying out this thing called the IC Program at Brown in 1956; the IC stood for "Identification and Criticism of Ideas." As a result, none of the teachers really knew how to teach it. It was a freshman course, and they'd never tried the seminar format with underclassmen. My teacher had the idea that he'd stay completely out of the discussion, give no information or opinions. We were freshmen trying to read things like *The Sound and the Fury* and it was a joke. The whole class kept trying to figure out what the plot was. There was also a division between the guys like me who came from public school and the guys who came from, say, Andover—they had *read* Faulkner. Of course they didn't understand any more than we did, but they looked down on us. Finally, we got on to *Moby Dick.* Now this was a book that meant a lot to me; I first tried to read it when I was about twelve years old. It turns out that my family on my mother's side relates to the Coffin family in Nantucket, one of the big whaling families. If you know the story of how Melville got the story, it was from a boat called the *Essex* which actually was stove in by a sperm whale. A lot of people were killed immediately, while others got into open boats and made for the west coast of South America. They thought that the islands they were near were full of cannibals, but this wasn't true. So they tried to cross this incredible stretch of water, and to survive had to eat each other. There was a cabin boy who was eaten who was a Coffin. So you see how that works. My parents wanted me to read the book, and I tried and tried and finally made it. It became a favorite, so that by the time I got to this guy's course I knew the book inside and out. He seemed to be taking the novel very casually, and we got into this raging argument. He asked me my religious ideas, and I replied that I'd tell him mine if he'd tell me his. He said no, so I asked myself why I was in that room with that person and decided to walk out.

Do you feel that you've missed out in some way?
Not really. That's not the way to read literature, at least the way they were doing it. You've got to start the threads going and follow them out through a lifetime of reading. Start anywhere and pick up a thread.

You mentioned earlier "planning," and reading your work I often wonder how much planning you do. Or is much of it spontaneous?
It's pretty spontaneous. Whenever I've written anything that I feel works, it's been pretty quick. I'm not one of those people who do a lot of revision. I might change a word or two, but that's about it. If something isn't working, I just throw it out and start over. Many of my writer friends really do work their way back through a manuscript and change it all around so that it eventually ends up really different from where they started, but I can't do that. I've got to keep it going. To make a kind of figure of it, it's like a carrier frequency on a radio, picking up the pitches. Or maybe it just means I don't have any patience.

What about your shifts?
I spent a lot of early time working with cutups, like Burroughs, chance generation of words, things that ultimately didn't satisfy me very much, but they were good practice. I remember getting very upset once that I was stuck with my own vocabulary. If I just wrote from out of my head, the same words would keep coming. I thought that it was really a small body of words. A painter uses all the colors, a musician all the scales. So I'd tried to purposely feed in random words, and went through about five years of

that kind of thing, mostly unpublished. As people have said about spontaneity, you can practice so that you are ready. You get your instrument
working, get your chops as jazz musicians say. Write every day.

You say you know when something works. What clues do you have to that?
A feeling, and that it keeps on going. Otherwise it stops, sags, loses energy,
and I've got no desire to proceed. It's a feeling, but how can I describe it?
It may involve so many synesthesiac circuits that it's impossible to explain.
There is a psychologist named Anton Ehrenzweig who wrote a book called
The Hidden Order of Art. He had this idea he called "de-differentiation." The
theory is that very little children and artists have a place in their heads where
they can keep many, many different particles in suspension, all ready to drop
into place. When you are really working well you've got all that stuff
suspended and ready to go, and this is mainly unconscious.

Is this a kind of muse?
Well, if I can say I hear voices in my head without sounding certifiable,
that's it. I can hear certain tones of voice saying certain words in certain
line lengths. I don't know what that is exactly, and I don't want to get all
that mystical. But it feels like it's coming from outside, something not me.
Beckett talks a lot about that too. He wrote a play called *Not I,* which is
all spoken by just a mouth—everything else is blacked out. He said that he
was in Tunisia and he saw this Arab woman waiting for a child to come out
of a building, and for some reason that image struck him. She said nothing
at all, but it struck him and he got the whole play. What do you make of
that?

***Do you find that when you read from your own work aloud, that it sounds
like a very different voice than you've imagined, and that maybe you
don't even like it?***
Well, I don't know about not liking it, but sure. There is a funny thing
that happens: even when I hear what is identifiably *my* voice, reading my
own work to myself without speaking, that voice is not the same as the
voice I hear out loud when I give a reading. There is a frequency difference,
something wrong. Reading it aloud is always a scramble for me to get the
two to line up. I used to play with a pianist who had perfect pitch, and
we'd go around and play in little clubs where the pianos were always out of
tune, of course. Sometimes the top would be out of tune with the bottom,
or whatever. He said it was like physical pain for him. One split second

before his hand went down he'd hear it right, then the hammer would strike and he'd hear it wrong. He said it was like little headaches for him. The real friction between the imagined pitch and the real pitch. It's the same kind of thing between my speaking voice and the voice in my head when I wrote it.

Getting back to spontaneity, in order to maintain it is there a certain ritual or procedure you use when you write?
At this point, it's just writing. Originally, I would do the kinds of exercises I mentioned. I'd take a magazine article—the kind with two columns on a page—and start most anywhere. The rule was that you'd connect one line to another in the piece, but the syntax had to work, had to make complete sense.

Do you work for a certain length of time each day?
Well, I try to, but that can't always be done.

And do you take off from the work of others?
Sure. Other writing, music, visual things, conversation. Some kind of receptivity is necessary, I suppose, but I wouldn't say anyone should do *this* to get *that*. It's just a way of being awake intellectually. What gets me to the desk these days is simply the desire to keep writing. At the moment I've got a lot of projects going, and if I miss a day I'm dying to get back to them. Recently this last winter I wrote a long work called *The Crystal Text*. There is a quartz crystal on my desk and I just look at it. I tried to make that the focus of the thing. It may sound too limited, but believe me, after six months it wasn't. If you look at anything that long you are going to get some way to argue it out.

So you work on several things at once?
Well, sometimes somebody will ask you for something and you have to interrupt what you are doing to write it. I'm always writing letters to friends, and they can get very involved. I find that I might write short poems in the middle of working on a longer piece, and there seems to be a space available for that. These activities go on simultaneously and don't seem to have anything to do with one another, though maybe they do.

One thing that I've finally learned how to do, which I never felt possible, is to write in a bad state of mind. I've found out that even if I'm depressed or something, if I just push a little bit, just start, I can sometimes get amazing things written. I can't give up and say, "Not today, I'm too down." After all, your mood is not all of your mood. There is something else going on below it that you might not identify until you are writing.

And then other times you can't stop it from coming.
Yeah. Sometimes I feel that I just can't write fast enough. You're really charged up and thinking about three or four words ahead, and then by the time you get there you forget. I still can't believe that happens—it's such a short space of time—and yet it happens to me all the time. This leads me to believe that that space where you are working with words in your head must be really vast. One word may be miles away from another word, and that's why you lose it. If that's not true, then I'm simply losing my memory. Think about it: a tenth of a second ago I had a particular word, and now it's gone, interrupted by these words.

This is going to sound dumb, but can you spell?
Not at all, and I think this is because I'm ear-oriented. Some writers are very visual, like William Burroughs. He says he sees the words in his head in the air above the typewriter. If you can do that you've got no problems with spelling because they are all right there. But in my case, when I type up a final manuscript I keep looking in the dictionary for the spelling of very simple words.

I'm intrigued with your mention of music. Might you talk about that a bit more? Why did you stop playing?
Well, the problem with a musical group is really trying to find the people with the right chemistry. I was never able to do that. All that other stuff kept coming up—personal problems, clash of life-styles, and so on. I was filled after a number of years with a lot of frustration.

Another thing is that for a while I was writing and playing music at the same time, and I began to feel that I couldn't do both. I may be wrong about this, but I felt I had to choose. So I spent the next twelve years without playing any music. Interestingly, just a little while ago I started playing again. I ran into somebody who asked me in the right way at the right time. He said, "Look, if you can play music, you should. It's stupid to waste that talent." So I've been playing my drums in the basement with the earphones. Not with anyone, because all the old problems are still there. But on my own.

Do you think the performing of music predisposed you to think about "hearing" your poetry?
I don't know. I once asked a class a similar question and the split was about 50–50. Do you subvocalize when you write? When you read anything, even the phone book, do you hear it? It's something that seems to happen on its own for me, and it horrified me to find out that some people don't do it. What does it mean for a poet if his or her readers aren't hearing off the page? My God, that's what you're doing.

In speed reading they emphasize that you just flash the line across.
Yeah, that's a horror show. As I get older I read more and more slowly. It can be anything—even a pulp mystery.

Since you've made the decision to move from music to poetry, would you say that poetry addresses more levels somehow?
No, I wouldn't compare music and written art that way. In a way, music has an incredibly enviable quality. As somebody said, "It's completely inexplicable, but perfectly apprehendable." You try to do that in words and you run into hassles immediately—what do you *mean?* Music is just in the air, it is air.

Would you say, then, that the intellect is central to your poetry?
Well, how do you define intellect? I'm interested in what words are that other things aren't. Once you get into the sound of words, then you've got music coming up pretty quick. When you get the visual side you get into paintings and movies. But somehow in the center you've got a system of these "things," I don't know what to call them. It's like a very thin membrane between the inside and the outside that feeds both ways. You've got something where the word *saw* means a number of entirely different things. English is so rich that I don't understand how anyone can learn it as a second language.

By intellect I meant "meaning." I noticed a review connecting your work to Ashbery's. The reviewer speaks of two phases in Ashbery's work—the analytic and the synthetic. Does that make sense to you?
I couldn't use those terms, though I think I know something about what Ashbery went through. If you know his work, his first book *Some Trees* was chosen by Auden as the Yale Younger Poets winner. The poems were written in quatrains and so forth, real *verse*. After that, Ashbery went to Paris to

work for the *Herald Tribune,* and he just got tired of everything he had been writing. He says his breakthrough had a lot to do with music, but I always see it as the painting he was looking at, with its shifts and collage effects. When I was younger and I looked at a poem like his "Europe," I thought that it was wonderful and crazy. Now I look at it and see that there is a narrative running through it. But he was trying to knock himself out of a habit pattern with poems like that.

Well, I think the critic was trying to say that in his earlier work he was dismantling language, and in his later work trying to put it back together. That's easier for critics to say than for poets. I don't think John would agree. He probably reads his work with as much puzzlement as anyone. In fact, there was an interview recently in which he was asked about winning all these prizes and being taken up by people like Harold Bloom. He was talking to a Polish interviewer in Warsaw. John said that he feels like a "poetical football," and of course the guy didn't understand because they don't have that phrase. There is a great removal from what he thinks he is doing as the critics throw his words back and forth. Some are building their careers on the interpretation of his work, some on saying it's trash.

I just don't find that much difference between his early stuff and the late. I just remember what a shock it was, and how wonderful, to see that work in 1962. Someone was doing something that was somehow related to all that new music and painting. There just wasn't much of that kind of poetry around. Interestingly, John rejected that book (*The Tennis Court Oath*) himself for awhile. Until a couple years ago, he wouldn't read those poems at readings. Of course poets do want to read their newest work, so maybe that was it. A kind of hell for me personally would be to go around reading my old poems. I always feel that the first time I read something it's the best. Some poets practice their poems, but that would drive me nuts.

A while ago you said that the writer had to take meaning into primary consideration. I don't know if I'm speaking for anyone else, but reading your work I often have a very difficult time picking up a paraphrasable content. This leads me to believe that perhaps you have another notion of meaning than the ordinary.
I don't know which work you are talking about, but first I'm talking about the meaning of individual words. It might look as though in some of my earlier work—where everything is fragmented—that the meanings of the words might not be valuable, but they are. Everything that I could possibly

bring to my mind about those words was there. After all, it isn't considered so weird visually to make a collage of two completely disparate images in painting, but in writing you're not supposed to do that. For me, there is a kind of sense that comes from jamming those words together, and that involves what those words mean and what they might suggest. Part of Pound's logopoeia was that some words lead you to expect certain words following others, and so you should as a poet try to disrupt that habit.

I don't try to write paraphrasable poetry, but what good poetry is paraphrasable? Something like Beckett's *Unnamable* is the most unparaphrasable book I can imagine, and that's its great worth and beauty. It actually is those words, and it can't be other words. You can talk endlessly around it, but that's not what it is. You can say that it's about a guy who isn't sure that he's got anything more than a mind. He makes up a few stories and they don't quite work out, and he ends up saying, "I can't go on, I'll go on." That's the plot. Unless you want to talk very elaborately about the way the pronoun shifts work, that's about as close to a paraphrase as you can get.

So do you notice any shifts in your work between Space *say, and* Research?
Sure, there's been the kind of development I've already alluded to. A lot of the work in *Space* was influenced by what was going on in Ashbery's *Tennis Court Oath,* and what that led to in the New York School around the early to mid-sixties. In my case, that meant an interest in single words to generate a larger structure. From there, it's kind of funny. In some ways my syntax got more "normal," while in other ways more complicated, but maybe that's for someone else to say. All I know is that I got more interested in sentences about ten years later, which led to a big prose book which I proposed to be a thousand pages long. I managed to write about six hundred pages of it, which led to the writing of *Mine.*

What kind of book was it?
It has various sections that deal with areas of interest that I've had pretty much throughout my life, like geology, music, movies. There are other sections that have to do with writers who've meant a lot to me. The whole thing kind of accumulates. It's written in sentences, though some of the sentences have a nutty syntax. Basically, I suppose I think of the sentence as something like the key center in a piece of music. That work occupied me for five or six years, though I got tired of its structure and put it aside for awhile. I guess that's a simple change from the earlier work.

The earlier poetry seems to border on minimalism—
I never thought of it as minimalist. That was a term that was used in the visual art scene in reference to people like Robert Morris, who I was interested in. Particularly Robert Smithson—his writings continue to interest me. I was trying to figure out how to do some work that would interest me, that would be my own. My feeling was that I had to start small and generate a language of my own. I think I always had some notion of making it larger and more complex.

There was a period where I was very close to Aram Saroyan, and you certainly might call him a minimalist. He was literally writing one-word poems. I remember having a lot of arguments with him at the time because I couldn't understand how there could be just one word. One word always led to another in my mind, helplessly. So even in those days when someone might be looking at a poem of mine of ten seemingly separate words, I was thinking of larger structures. And maybe their perceptions had something to do with the ground of poetry they were used to.

Do you read much poetry?
Yeah, I do, but I think I probably read less of what I perceive to be the amount of poetry that is being published now than I used to. There was simply less of it being published twenty years ago, or at least it seemed that way. Also, as you get older you tend to follow your own threads of interest, rather than being so worried about covering the waterfront.

Who do you find interesting?
Two of the basic ones, since I've known them both for a long time and have always followed their work, would be Michael Palmer and Bernadette Mayer. The changes they've gone through in their work I've found fascinating. The other day I read John Godfrey's new book; it was impressive. He's a poet living in New York who has published two books, *Dabble* and *Where the Weather Suits My Clothes*. He's someone who should be better known, but that's the way it goes. The books aren't distributed well. He's interested in Rimbaud, Baudelaire, Céline, and people like that, bringing in a kind of symbolist strength that you might not associate with someone of the "New York School." I don't like that term much, though, *New York School*.

Speaking of terms, are you a Language poet?
Well, I think almost helplessly I'm involved with that term; I'd be seen to be involved with it even if I denied it. Some of those poets have said that

my work has been an influence, and I can see how in certain cases that's true. Of course they've taken it in directions that I sometimes can't follow, or don't want to. Some of them write a great deal of method essays, theory, which isn't native to my procedure. I'm thinking here of Barry Watten and Ron Silliman in particular. I find their emphasis on the word fascinating, though I sometimes feel that they want to describe a poetry almost before it exists.

Have you seen Watten's *Total Syntax*? It's certainly a very focused trip into that work, the most thorough one thus far. There is one sentence that stands out to me that really describes the difference between our approaches. He is talking about a poem of Kit Robinson's: "The transformation in Robinson's poem is not the coming into being of the image but of something even deeper—the perception of mind in control of its language." I wrote that in a notebook and underlined "mind in control of its language." I don't have much faith in the possibility that one's mind *could* be in control of one's language. Or at least in *total* control, as that's the implication of his title, *Total Syntax*. My procedure is more open; I often feel pushed around by things, at least more than Barry's methodology would allow. I tend to think that some of those writers want that kind of control, and I don't.

What about Ron Silliman's Marxism? Does it hold any attraction for you?
No. One difference between myself and writers like Ron and Barry is that I don't read a great deal of semiotic or political writing. I just don't see the connections they make so easily between the analytic or political point of view and the art form. It may be generational.

You mean because you are generally older than these writers?
Yeah. I'm not sure that it's true in every case, but generally. Thinking of the early stimulus I had in the arts, it wasn't ever a political text. I came out of a situation in the fifties where the things that were going on were Abstract Expressionist painting, John Cage's work, the so-called free jazz revolution. Those are some of the things that still keep me fascinated. Thus I tend to come out of a more purely artistic procedure, rather than political. Or at least rather than from the texts of politics.

I know that John Cage has said that the syntax is the army—if we destroy the syntax we'll destroy the control of language over us. I just don't see it as that simple. I remember when Ron Silliman read one of his long works on Market Street in San Francisco at rush hour as, I believe, some kind of political act. I never understood how it could work in that sense; people passing by would take it as some sort of goof or irritation, passing by after work, rather than having their syntax freed.

Have you ever tried translation?
Very little, mainly because I don't have other languages. I do know a little German, and I've been struggling with Rilke for years. He is supposed to be one of the most difficult German poets, but he does fascinate me. With a dictionary I can work it out to some extent, just to the point of seeing how it may finally be impossible to get it into English. But this is nothing that I would consider publishing.

One thing that I'm sorry about in my education is that while I had German in high school I didn't have French. I've been interested in French poets a great deal, and I'm sorry that I have to work with translations on that level.

Which French poets?
Rimbaud. Of the Surrealists, particularly Paul Eluard, especially his early Surrealist love poems. Also, lately I've been interested in the German writer Peter Handke; I don't know his plays, but lately he's been publishing a lot of interesting prose. There are probably many more of interest—Beckett is obviously a great source, and I like Marguerite Duras—but they escape me at the moment.

What about teaching? Have you ever taught full-time?
No, I haven't. I've always thought that I really wouldn't want to. I like to do it every couple years when I feel that I've got something to say that might be useful. I wouldn't want to get stuck in the situation of teachers who have to do the same thing over and over again every semester. I like my writing to be the primary thing, and if something spins off from that so that I feel like I've got something fresh to say to someone else, fine. I want to do more of it, but interspersed with time between.

What do you think of "creative writing" workshops?
I tend to have doubts about them, although I did teach a writing workshop last month while I was at Naropa. I was doing the Kafka/Beckett course at the same time, and I thought that would go over best, but it turned out that the writing workshop worked better than I'd thought. Though I do

find it hard to read people's manuscripts and make quick comments. Maybe it's just that I doubt my own ability to help much.

What attracted you to Naropa?
Anne Waldman and Larry Fagin, both of whom I've known for a long time. That friendship allowed me to go there, and I'm thankful for the freedom there. They allow me to pretty much do what I want in terms of courses. Probably Naropa and the New College in San Francisco are the only places like that. The first time I went to Boulder was in 1977, and I've been there four times. Now there seem to be fewer students than before, but they are more serious. That's a help—if the student is really writing, it doesn't make much difference whether you are there or not.

Richard Kostelanetz once wrote of you that, "None of the young experimental poets in American has been as various, intelligent, and prolific as Clark Coolidge." Do you think of yourself as an "experimental writer"?
Not really. I understand that category in a general sense, but "experimental" always sounds like you are trying to do something rather than doing it. But if the term does mean what it could mean—pushing things beyond various limits—great!

---

from *Quartz Hearts*

I could use the map book that pages fall out.
Pilaster under a sun. Gumbo till. The clock
comes around. The wind rises. Culpables.
Inroads. The seven caves. Noontime earth place.
A spoon let down. Going to the drawers.
The roll turned up. Closing that brain can.
Stalactical ooze. Might dreams. Supposed
soda. A brief march closed the case on
what may do. Pacific sun paper. Oxymoron.
Gullible pak. Getting the slant on
mid America. Book shelving over tube.
The guide I could consult. The screen aslant.

Marvelous tucks. Clip birds. Hot
locust clicks. The butterfly I saved
dried out and disappeared. The volume
of an English dictionary. Light motions
on a wall. Attention happens on a door.
The wind discs opening the slate.
Just a slate too big. Copious prods.
Eyelet dines. Green wheat below the air.
A fan nailed shut. Folders that allow
the caves around the country. Since
I was ahead I opened the door.
Lighting on the grave of Sacajawea.

from *mine: the one that enters the stories*

X

The Khaki plastic soldiers had been placed on a green plasticene board molded
into two facing ridges with a river of blue poster paint between. Sentences
of description tend to loss of kilter. A few of the model men had had their
legs cut off so that they appeared to be standing hip-deep in the water. This
comprised a project that my daughter had been assigned to make for school.
The teacher had decided the time had come to fill time with a battle. There
seemed to be no other rationale. An evening had been spent in silly con-
templation of plastic men's postures. The time had dried.

Outside a snow had finally come to weigh the bare board January. The two
articles could exchange positions without disturbing the balance of that
sentence. In that way a perfect equation is assured, as with a tuning fork.
I have no problem with that. I'll leave as planned for Nantucket by night.
The file drawer was shut on the spilled can of coffee or tobacco. No meaning
is perfect.

The question of night had come up. Night had arrived with certainty. The
lock on the lay of the land was secure. There was no limit to the manners
in which the land could be laid out. A cough was heard from the upper left
dormer window. In the town car in a word the function of moth-free bats
was the topic. At evening most of the constituents tended to be silent. What
is needed in words? What is mated in other words?

XIII

I wonder about things and the people between us. The currents, the feedback, and the whelms. The sharp cracks between trees, and the tolling between the knees. The world is sharp, narrows, and perhaps lost. But I was born on an avenue, though perhaps too short for the name. Now I skip the yard plots and end up in these wood lots. Do you wish me to tell plots, to pronounce names. A walk in the woods would last a while longer than some of its beings. They die loose since they never came up with time. Step over by and around and sometimes on the small things being a history of this world. Shout, as you're shutting the books on the roles.

Nobody has said to me Stop when it mattered. And I go on doing what I had been doing in a manner that keeps its lights trimmed. Push the finger into the woman at the point of lash control. As in sleep we lose lives in ourselves. Time to matter. Time to cancel the fly-over. Time to fur the wand. Is there time for control of the slowest, as we know there might be in the fast. From which we speak we are hidden, as the lines of the walls have the parallel power of candles. I lie down abed and imagine your body in all its positions at once. This is a speech from which, as in gnarl of chemicals, an act will proceed. Time seems insistent on the singular. If not mere alone one is next.

The woman rises, her breasts never the same. A man's wife's body is the greatest mystery. Each time it is revealed. Do you know me? Each glimpse a start, each stare another. And the removal of tight silks is a peeling away of skin to expose the more sensitive flesh beneath. What was your name before you were born? I wish that only I will know it. Standing unclothed across the room you are sensitive only to my eye. And when I cross to you and enter you I will infuse you with my sources. A kiss of my extremity speaks with you inside. Then is the world shut down for awhile.

The world is coming up to us all the time. It has its chicken and lands. I see a greatness in dull whacks, light boards and snooze. The buckle on one's carapace, who can assemble it? Pirates have stormed the land from the north down to the cove. The new lights on your itching wrists are the sealed product of rice. A nova occurred at the black rim and brought them. There will be a ruby soon, it will be the robber of dense.

I have no call to say this but I think you should store my place. Needles are required and a shut solution of darkness. The chickens will chime then and the warts on a pickle rise adroit. You have no sun here but often a

moon, it curdles the wicks that singe dreams. And the constant drawing
toward and away limns a hotness. The man stands on his own hands in the
backwards, a land of longness and told gaps. Buzzings in the nose the toes
and the penis. Lights that at night are holes in pitch, turning you each
center whichway. Each one writes a novel which is a stream at the bottom
of the yards behind the houses. In the way that no one can hold in the mind
what is constantly on the move. And the hero will be kneeling in the turns
on his mind. He will be the Borealis of the Wheatrows in brown corduroys.

Brass Land I Live In

The avenue's too long for howsoever phased a song
rather a truncheon the thing that eats by itself is eaten
by the very one the gables are lit in a teething monsoon
sorted and vented in a happenstance cribbage
you take your time with, lose no matter

The water the rhythm, rooted in a kilter
an exit over which no red spot hangs
I'll steep you boys some tea, diluted far from harm
a dilemma of loading you'll label as language
and farm off all boats in one leakproof lot

Stark as mention, at all at trying-out wall
all that's either bricked or soapy dries
and neckties act in a pinch as throttles
will guard you off a sky too thin a ground too slow

I've come to the tiniest of conclusions: rice
and you keep putting your first foot forward
perhaps to cancel the phosphorous forest faster than a breeze
we'll coil all hell into a forcing hand and head

2. Theodore Enslin

"The work itself, the place at either end"

Theodore Enslin was born in Chester, Pennsylvania, in 1925. Educated in both public and private schools, he studied music and composition for many years, working with Nadia Boulanger. When he turned to writing poetry seriously, Cid Corman discovered his work and published a number of his poems in *Origin,* as well as his first book, *The Work Proposed,* in 1958. Enslin has published a number of volumes of shorter poems, many collected in 1974 in *The Median Flow* (Black Sparrow), though his main energies have gone into writing the long poem. To date he has published three long poems—*Forms* (Elizabeth Press, 1970–73), *Synthesis* (North Atlantic, 1975), and *Ranger* (North Atlantic, 1979–81)—with a fourth, *Axes,* in progress. Additionally, Enslin has edited *The Selected Poems of Howard McCord* for Crossings Press. Enslin was awarded a National Endowment for the Arts grant in 1976; he has lived on a farm in Maine for many years.

Of his work, Theodore Enslin has written, "I suppose I would classify as a nonacademic, and have been allied with those who broke with the New Criticism in the early fifties. Perhaps, as Cid Corman said, I write more 'you' poems than anyone else alive. . . . My formal structure is based on sound, and I feel that my musical training has shaped this more than anything else. The line breaks/stresses are indicated as a type of notation, something which concerns me, since I believe we have no adequate notation for poetry, and I conceive of any poem as requiring a performance. It should be read aloud. I would say that Rilke, W. C. Williams, Thoreau, and latterly Zukofsky, were influences. The rest must be said in the poems themselves."

If you have all read that autobiographical essay *Chapters* which appeared in *American Poetry* and which, as I understand it, was given you in advance, you've found me out. If it raised any questions, maybe we can start from there.

You say that you don't like to be called a "nature poet," but on the other hand the wilderness, the nonhuman world figures prominently in much of your work. Can you delineate how place is important in your poetry?
Well, I think it figures primarily because that happens to be where I live. I live in the country where nature is obvious. I've often said that while there would be certain differences, if I lived in a city I'd probably use city objects, the urban milieu, in much the same way; it would be my experience. That is the important thing as far as my writing is concerned, what my experience is. What I have not experienced I don't feel competent to use. This doesn't mean that you must be right in the middle of experiences of various sorts,

just. . . . Look, no matter where I lived I think the poetry would be similar—it's just that the furniture would be different. And that is why I object to being called a "nature poet." There are, certainly, a lot of trees and rocks and water—things that I love very much—in my poems, but they are my familiars, things that I experience day by day. I don't think, however, that I have too many illusions about them. I'm not interested in theorizing about them or trying to blow them up into something that they are not.

You said in an interview that the poet writes what he does not know.
He does.

How do you carry this idea over into your writing? Do you bring it with you each time you sit down to write?
No, I hope not. I am sometimes far more surprised at the results of a poem than anyone else who reads it. Writing, particularly writing voluminously, which I guess I do, reveals a great deal of yourself, probably more than you'd like. So I don't really even like to think about such things.

As I said in the essay you read, regarding music, for many years I was simply not aware of how much I was using my early musical training. Of course the temptation as you get older, and people sort of encourage you to do it, is to theorize about it. I'd much rather not. Now I sometimes use my musical background far more consciously than I used to; I was using things like various sorts of cadences in much the same way as one might in a musical composition for years. When I really became aware of this I went back through older work and found that I'd been doing it all along.

Well, do you ever begin a poem thinking, what am I going to find out?
Not very often. I know what you mean and it has happened a few times, but that is not usual for me.

Then what triggers you?
Anything. In my particular case a great deal goes on subliminally most of the time. I'm a little wary of saying *subconscious* or *unconscious,* but it is on another level. I find that again and again, once I begin a poem it seems as if I'd already known that a long time before, and thus I do relatively little revision. Usually the poems that I have to revise, really revise, are the poorest ones. I know that that does not apply to many people; there are all kinds of ways of working, as many ways as there are people doing it. But I talked with Denise Levertov and Robert Duncan about this, and they both agreed

completely that it's so. My poems have been revised, but they've been going on for long, long periods of time, sometimes for years, and suddenly they surface and appear to come very quickly. It's just like other forms of gestation. Some animals require very little attention at all after they are born—the foal struggles to its feet and pretty soon it is running around. The human baby takes a long time.

Can you discuss the particular problems involved in getting the long poem published?

I'm afraid all I can say about that is that I've been supremely fortunate. People have *been* there at the time I needed it done. I had absolutely no idea at all when I was writing *Forms* that it would ever be published, and I wasn't actually interested in that for about ten years. But then Jim Weil simply said one day that he would be interested. I didn't believe that anyone would. I don't think it's as hard to publish the long poem now as it might have been twenty years ago. It seems that most of us have some sort of long, working thing going on, even if many people don't admit it easily. I guess there is a limited audience for it, but on the other hand the long poem does seem to be of interest now.

What are the problems of composition of the long poem? How do you go about writing it?

Well, I think Pound said it direct, and Olson used to say it too—a long work is long all over. Again, you'll have to forgive me if I seem to make many references to music, but it's so much a part of the way I think about these things. The situation of the poet writing the long poem is like that of the composer who conceives of something and then, if he is at all sensitive and knowledgeable as far as sound is concerned, will know exactly what instrumentation to use, and he will also know whether the germ of the thematic material is capable of development.

When I was a kid I wrote many, many short poems, and it always bothered me that that's the way it seemed to come out. And then I got interested in the sequence, taking off particularly from Rilke—things like *The Book of Hours, Sonnets to Orpheus,* the *Duino Elegies.* There are parts of my work which can stand by themselves, but in aggregate make a whole which is really quite different from the emphasis on any one part. So I discovered for myself an *inclusive* type of writing in which I could use all sorts of disparate materials. I was tremendously interested at the start in Williams's technique in *Paterson;* there all of a sudden it becomes obvious that you can incorporate anything into a poem. You have to discriminate and know what you are doing, but it can be done. If you are including things in great number, it implies length.

There is of course no rule of thumb for this. Years ago I got mad with Donald Hall when he said that for a long poem you've got to have a long line, for shorter poems you don't. This seemed to me sort of pat. Of course sometimes that is true, but not always. I don't know if any of you know the work of Frank Samperi. He's one of the original *Origin* people, and he's a very severe and difficult poet to get into. Zukofsky had a very high opinion of him. He wrote a tremendously long poem called *Lumen Gloriae,* about four hundred pages. And yet the lines are often simply one word. It works.

Do you compose at the typewriter?
No.

Well, when you are working in the long format, don't you get tired, or bored?
It's a funny thing. It goes back to what I said before about the subliminal. Many times I'll break off—sometimes even in the middle of a word—and I won't get back to it for six months, and then maybe I won't have the fragment with me that I left off from. The numbers of times that these things will fit or join with no break whatsoever is amazing. It goes on all the time. I don't work at a desk very often. Now I have for the first time in my life a decent study, and I love it and spend a lot of time there. But it's a place to spend time rather than a place to work. So most of what I do I do on the sort of notepaper I've got in my shirt pocket right now, just walking around.

Ginsberg says that the size of the piece of paper dictates the length of the line.
If I realize that what I start to work on, maybe on a small slip of paper, won't sustain the line, then I'll get mad and take something bigger. I do carry around larger notebooks in a leather pouch when I go for walks. So I agree with Allen completely. The size of the paper has a great deal to do with the line, and I just wouldn't feel comfortable working on a long poem in a small notebook.

The section of Synthesis *we read—17—seems like a meditation on pure*

form. I'm not really sure what you are driving at there. Does "pure form" exist, or is it more like a sculptor chiseling out some kind of form?
What I was thinking of was the freeing of form from the natural object, like Bergschneider. Michelangelo did it too, but Bergschneider made a big deal about it—picking up a rock and looking at it, freeing the form.

Does that mean that you don't think there is really anything new in art?
I guess it does. There are infinite ways of combining, and infinite ways of being contemplative. But I don't think there is anything new. That's just one of those catch phrases. There are a few things that make me want to reach for Goering's gun—you know, when people speak of culture I want to reach for a gun. One is when people speak of nature poetry. Another is when people talk about something being new.

I want to ask you something about another subject that gets you upset. . . .
There are many.

Through the sixties you deliberately chose not to write political poetry. Do you see any role for politics in poetry?
Well, in total, yes. What I objected to in the sixties was the fact that everyone felt he *had* to write a political poem—you know, now it's time for *me* to write *my* Vietnam poem. For those who were sincerely moved to do that I have no criticism whatsoever. It's simply that there are so many "bandwagoneers" that get involved with these things. There is a place for political poetry, sure: Vallejo, Neruda, George Oppen. *That* is wonderful. There was an anthology, however, about a third of the way along. *Where Is Vietnam?* I reviewed that savagely. It was supposed to go into the *New York Herald Tribune,* but with my usual luck the *Tribune* died at that point. It did appear in the *Washington Post,* though I can't figure out why. Anyway, so much of that anthology was simply worked up. You'd read these poems and certainly would have no objection to the righteous anger, but *Vietnam?* You might have a few stone lanterns in a poem, or something of that sort, but if you took that imagery out it was simply a universal rage at man's stupidity. That is why I've felt through the years the way I have. I guess I am prickly. When people start talking about the present time as "now more than ever before," that's another time I reach for my gun.

If I can change the subject a little, I want to ask you about your sense of time. You seem in your poetry to be obsessed with the question of time and duration. Is that so?

That is so. It's because I'm always worried by our artificial divisions of time, and I've been trying to find something that is not "cut up" in the usual way. One reason that I like living on the coast is because of this question. I live in a fishing town, and the hours in the day in the traditional sense mean very little to these people. Nine to five, no; it's from high tide to low tide— that's how you divide your day. This is something that is not arbitrary, not something that we have superimposed upon the natural world. That's a very simplistic way of talking about it, but it has always concerned me, and in my writing I've been shaking the concept of time like a terrier a dead rat.

What is it that governs your feeling that a poem, especially a very long poem, is ended?

I never feel that it is ended. The long poem is essentially a long walk, and I'm using the same material again and again, though from different focuses. At the end of *Synthesis,* for example, I simply get up and go on. It's not a conclusion, but a turn, where a particular procedure is no longer viable. Finishing *Ranger* bothered me a great deal because I loved it, but it became too easy to do. Maybe my feeling is the remnant of the Puritan ethic. *Axes,* the long poem I am writing now, has been a beast the whole way, *hard.* And that's good. When it starts to get easy, I think I've got one more turn in me.

When I finished the first book of *Forms,* which took me ten years, I became aware of these various turns and levels simply by fooling around with a piece of graph paper. I began to see how my material really did demand other workings.

Can you talk a bit about the genesis of Axes? *Is it part of* Forms?

Yes, it's all part of the same thing—*Synthesis, Axes, Forms, Ranger.* As a matter of fact, *Axes* is a little strange in one way, because it overlaps. The others were more or less a continuum. I'd leave one and go to another. But *Axes* I started in 1976–77, the winter we lived in New Mexico, and at that time I had not yet finished with *Ranger.* There was an overlay of nearly a year.

In your essay "Chapters" you say that you hope the reader will come to your work as an individual. This puzzles me. How does a reader go to a poem as anything other than an individual?

Well, I think that many come with the recommendations of others. There are certain things for which I do plead. That is one. Another is this: in both *Ranger* and *Forms* there appears to be a great deal of intimate autobiographical detail, but I am not Sylvia Plath. The reason for the use of the autobiographical material is a sense of scale. It's like some of those old photographs of Teddy Roosevelt standing against a sequoia. It's not a photograph of Teddy Roosevelt; he's there simply to give a sense of how big this thing is. The autobiographical details really have no more importance than that.

Also, if you have looked at *Synthesis* or *Ranger,* you will notice that there is a marginal gloss. That is an integral part of the poem, and it is also a key in some cases to suggested "other reading" and identification.

Do you think it helps?

Yes, I do. I think it really works. I've always felt very good about the technique ever since Robert Kelly told me that it was a brilliant thing to do. He had later thought of doing it in his long poem *The Loom,* but changed his mind for one reason or another.

Does your feeling about individual response, then, mean that you wouldn't want one of your books used as a college text? Read with a little guidence in a group like this?

That really would depend upon the way in which it was done. The so-called explication of the text gives me a severe pain. I've often said—and I realize that this is rank heresy, and has to be qualified—if we were suddenly to lose 95 percent of all criticism written in the last thirty-five hundred years, we would lose *nothing.* This would include the commentaries on the *I Ching,* the Bible, and so forth. As long as we have the texts and people come to those texts as individuals, that is what is important. You can go through a formal or informal education without ever reading a book. All you do is read books about books.

Don't you think, though, that without some kind of model you tend to reinvent the typewriter?

No, I don't think so at all. If I want to experience a work of art, I have no interest whatever in what somebody else has experienced. I'll discover things for myself, thank you. Now there is a kind of criticism in which the critic reveals far more about himself than his text. That's the only valid criticism—

the other is bullshit. Maybe one of the reasons I feel this way is because my father was a textual critic, and a very good one. His exegesis of the *New Testament* is pretty impressive. His text is still in print and I get the royalties.

Why do you write poetry?
Why do I breathe?

I get the impression from your work that you feel creativity to be a special vocation, somewhat removed from other vocations.
I'm sorry if I've given you that impression. It's not quite it. I believe in a high seriousness, but I certainly do not believe that simply because I have taken this path that it's the only way. *A* way is not *the* way. For me, it's the only way that I find life tolerable, this kind of vocation which certainly does in many cases shut out things that I probably would have found of great value, if I had examined them in the same way.

That's what I'm curious about. It seems as if you feel a peculiar sense of responsibility that might not adhere in other vocations.
I would go even further. I think that a high seriousness should apply to anything. This doesn't mean that there can't be a lot of playfulness and fun.

Well, before in talking about politics I found myself agreeing with you— because you have a public voice you are not obliged to deal with a popular issue. But exactly what kind of responsibilities do you feel?
To simply keep at what I am doing. If any of it is of any value, maybe it'll be of use sometime. I'm not really concerned that it is, at least at this moment.

Is the poem that you write more a record of the life of the artist or is it a piece of work in and of itself?
I'm not sure that it's the life of the artist, exactly. It's more a kind of continually evolving *source* of life. It is presupposed that much of this can be very boring—life is boring at points. But out of that boredom will sometimes come something such as you can get with raga. It's not repetition, but cumulative. The story has it that when John Cage was teaching at the New School and raga was relatively unknown, he brought some recordings of it into a class. There were two reactions. One student said, "Stop it, stop it, I can't stand it!" So he did. Then another student asked, "Why did you stop it? It was just getting interesting."

Do you have an idea of the ideal reader?

No, I don't, and I hope I never do. There's another place where I reach for my gun. When I see a book of poems with a jacket blurb that says so and so is a "poet's poet," I'm very suspicious. Hopefully it's the stupidity of the guy who wrote the blurb. But I have absolutely *no* sense of an audience. There is nothing when I'm writing save for the materials. I'm not writing for myself, exactly, but to solve a problem. Only the materials, myself, and the working out of the problem. If afterwards the problem is not imperfectly resolved and I want to keep the work, *then* I am very much concerned with an audience. I want an audience, but a very wide one. I'm much more pleased to hear from a druggist in California than from another poet. Sure, I like to talk shop with other writers and have fun, but after all my writing really is for people; hopefully we can somehow widen the audience.

Can we return to music for a moment?

Sure.

Does it enter your work as an imposed structure? When you talk about a rondo or the twelve-tone scale or serial composition, is this a subliminal situation, or something very conscious?

I think about it quite a lot when I have the feeling that something may come, but during the actual composition I try to forget that stuff as much as possible. There is *not* an *imposition* of form. Again, you have to be fairly conscious of what the material you have at hand is fit to do. I had wanted at one point to write a rondo, but I did not have the material.

A piece of music or a poem?

Both. A thematic structure that is composed of words but on one level is close to a piece of music, one that is strong enough to sustain under these conditions of continued repetition, even though it isn't quite a repetition, the bridge passages. Finally I got such a thematic structure, though I wasn't particularly looking for it. I certainly didn't try to think of the form itself. The earliest big poem of this type I did was a passacaglia. The classic passacaglia implies a base theme of eight measures; there are eight parts to this structure, which can be used infinitely in performance or they can be simply read straight. Now I'm talking about a poem—you would not have that choice musically. Still, I'm satisfied that passacaglia is a genuine title for that work.

In "Chromatic Fantasy" I actually did work through a step-by-step half-tone rising up the scale. There was a very simple thing behind that. I took a walk along the road where there are twelve old houses, which might correspond to the twelve tones of the scale. And then I realized that these houses were all built on knolls, high ground. Here these twelve houses are, and they are very prominent, and they are all more or less of the same period—late eighteenth, early nineteenth centuries. But the relationship among them is as distant as a modulation, say, from C sharp to C. Those are the hardest to do as they are the closest together. If you are going to modulate smoothly without preparation, the easiest thing to do is to go to a dominant, which would be C to G, or subdominant C to F—go down the scale until you get to C to D. The houses seem to do the same thing, so instead of writing another simple and nice poem about a walk past the houses on my road, why not build this into that kind of a structure? That was the genesis of that particular poem.

Have you ever thought of writing any kind of musical score for your readings?
No, I don't think that would work very well. I'm always wondering about this, however; there are magnificent examples of the wedding of music and words. But there is always the very great danger that one might overshadow the other. I will make a confession here. There is a group of poems of mine called "Ayres" which I dedicated to a lifelong friend of mine who happens to be a composer. I thought that if I dedicated something to him he might pay enough attention to score it, and he did.

You spoke earlier about the finishing of a long poem. Since you say you do do some revision, how do you know you've finished a shorter piece?
It's not only in the long work that I feel there is not a finish, but in all the work. In the end if any of it amounts to anything it is all one poem. I am not much of a friend of the isolated masterpiece. They are so many blocks of granite and look like just what they are—gravestones.

Perhaps I should rephrase that: how do you know *when a given poem is finished?*
That to me is a mystery. And of course, sometimes there are miscalculations, I make mistakes. Sometimes it works just right, sometimes it has gone too far. But there is an intuitive feeling that is a mystery. There are, after all, so many ways of working. My dear friend Keith Wilson—between us there is the most tender bond—can sit down and work on a word processor. God!

If anything would drive me up a wall, it would be that. Yet he can do it, and he does it very well.

I think we make mistakes, particularly in workshops, when we begin asking "how to?" There is no method, and the answer that anyone gives you is his personal answer. It must be qualified. You may be able to pick up something that may be of value, and that's fine. But you must realize that it is a limited application. It is not like a blueprint for putting together an automobile.

Back once again to the long poem, are you trying to contribute something new to the form? Do you have, when you work, predecessors in mind?
Of course I do. That came up at a class I did at the University of Maine where I admitted that while my material is not original, maybe the way I use it is. The process itself is very often the work. I've said this in so many words in section 14 of *Ranger*—"When I had the process / fully in hand / I was no longer living— / I had gone / into another place— / a place not believed in. / There was no need / for belief. / I found, on this plane, / the town of other dimensions. / It does exist, and people walk there." That is, I would say, as close to an original contribution as I get.

Of your contemporaries, whose work do you find especially valuable?
Well, of course that's something that is liable to change in some ways, depending upon how or at what I'm working on at a particular time. I would say, however, that certain people stay at a constant. Two of the generation just before me—Objectivists—Louis Zukofsky and George Oppen. . . . If I had to make a choice, which I'd hate to do, I guess I'd give it to Oppen. There I go out just about as far on a limb as I'd dare. At one time I'd probably written more about Oppen than anyone else—in an early *Ironwood* I got pretty superlative. I think about George Oppen, I think about his work, and that is something that just does not change.

What about younger poets?
I must plead guilty to getting older. I try to keep up with what comes along, but I'm afraid I absorb much of it by osmosis. There just isn't time. I particularly admire John Taggert. We are both interested in the same kinds of things, particularly the serial composition. Among the very young ones is George Evans, a really impressive talent. He is featured in the new *Origin*, fifth series. He is Cid Corman's discovery. I don't know—I range through a lot of material which I like and enjoy. I'm probably not as touched by other people's work as I should be. I think that's a penalty for spending a

lifetime doing it. Certainly if you'd asked me that question twenty years ago I'd have been able to fire off fifty names. Maybe sometimes I just prefer reading Sherlock Holmes.

You said earlier that a poem is a solution, a working out. Can you expand on your sense of the poem?
Well, I'd say it's that, a solution. Further, as Williams said, it's a machine, and you can think of it in terms of efficiency; that is, it attempts to reach 100 percent, though it doesn't often. A poem can be a great number of things, and we have to remember that it *is* rather than is *about*. We must not think of it as ancillary to this or that, but let it be an object. One poem can be many things for many people.

But for you, the poem is primarily a working out.
That is an idea that is highly attractive to me. I think that is the way that Mozart approached composition. He never does the same thing, or quite the same thing, twice.

But you said that there is never anything new.
Let me clarify that. He never gives anything the same emphasis twice. The materials may be exactly the same. In fact, Mozart is a good example. There is an Alberti bass figure at the beginning of the G Minor Symphony, Number 40. That was the most hackneyed thing that every composer of his period used. There is nothing different, apparently, in Mozart's use of it from half a dozen other people using the same thing. Yet you listen to it and it's unmistakably Mozart! Again, you can't analyze the thing and explain why— believe me, we tried to discover the key to that particular one as music students. It just doesn't work.

There is plenty that can be learned, that can be passed on, but we are all so eager to be told how to do it. You simply pick up things from other people because there are elements there which can be of use to you. One of the most valuable lessons that I ever learned, and it is the reason behind that rather grandiloquent dedication at the beginning of *Synthesis*—"To the Memory of Igor Stravinsky / from whom the first and final precepts"—was something Stravinsky said to us at a dinner. He was sitting at the head of the table, and he leaned back and said, "Beethoven is a rotten composer!" I was about eighteen at the time and of course I thought what sacrilege! It took me a long time to figure it out, but it was of great value to me. When I finally did figure it out it made a lot of things easier. What he was actually saying was that at the present time I, Igor Stravinsky, am so much involved with the composition of "The Rake's Progress" that I cannot *hear* Beethoven. Beethoven is unavailable to me. This is in a way my curse. I have to be prejudiced in this way and I have to put on blinders.

The only trouble with statements like that for the followers of a great man is that they tend to accept what he says at face value. There couldn't have been anything more stupid than for twenty people to be walking up and down the street the next day with placards reading "Down With Beethoven!" But that happens. That pointed out so many different things to me. When I become extremely prejudiced, which I often am, I have to realize that I need to be there; if a person doesn't have a definite bias, he really isn't going to accomplish very much. He'll just be sitting around all the time saying well yes, but on the other hand. . . . If you are going to do something, there are limitations. The well-rounded connoisseur of art is not an artist. He can't be.

Many young writers have nightmares wondering whether or not they'll ever publish anything. Did you at the start of your writing career?
Yes, I certainly did. Hindsight is always much better—now I wonder why I worried so much about it. But I don't think you can tell anyone that. You will all worry about it, and worry about it a lot. I think that I have been incredibly fortunate in that there always seemed to be someone like Jim Weil standing around more or less urging me to give him something. With the exception of a couple places where I really wanted to be, I've not sent anything out unsolicited for a long, long time. Almost all of my work has been solicited from the days when I met Cid Corman on. He certainly was very helpful, and I probably don't know till this day how much he did.

But you two are almost exact contemporaries.
We certainly are—within three months of each other.

And as you both were young at that time, maybe the lesson for a group of writers like this . . .
Would be instead of looking to *Poetry* or the *Partisan Review* or even *Origin* to look among themselves. That is really something that is worth thinking about. For a while, though most of it was garbage, there were all kinds of magazines and some were quite good. At the present time I don't know of very many that are worth much. For one thing, the money from CCLM is pretty much gone, and thus there isn't much patronage. In one way that's good because a lot of people got money who shouldn't have, but in another

it's very bad because now there seem to be only a very few serious and sustained magazines.

Which are you thinking of?
Well, certainly *Origin,* which is the elder statesman. Brad Morrow's *Conjunctions,* which is just about as good as you can possibly get. Clayton Eshleman's *Sulfur* which, while there are things about it I don't like, must be acknowledged. And of course Michael Cuddihy's *Ironwood.*

Many of the magazines we are supposed to aspire to in terms of publication don't seem very exciting, like the American Poetry Review.
You can't have just discovered that! No, they are not very exciting. *APR*—good Lord. It was such a good idea, but then they got off the track and now . . . *Kayak,* while it is rather provincial in that it is not open to a wide range, within its range is very good. *Conjunctions* obviously has prejudices, but it does try to be inclusive. Morrow is a first-rate editor. And good old Cid Corman is still open to new writers. He will very rarely not answer letters, and he can be of great value in both what he accepts and what he rejects. With Cid there is just no middle ground.

One thing about publication that can't be dismissed—a certain amount is very valuable for the ego early on at a time when the ego is vulnerable. But by the same token too much is made of it so that people feel they must rush into print. Publication is nice, but if I didn't publish another thing, life would go on.

There are certain practical elements here also, aren't there? It is a little difficult to fill out Poets in the School applications in Santa Fe saying that you have a drawer full of poems that you will eventually send out. How do you make a living? Chop wood?
Yes, that's exactly what you do. Because here you are talking about a *use* of poetry, and I don't think you use it. I think Denise Levertov put that very well in the first sentence of an essay years ago: "To use poetry is to abuse it." If you think of it in terms of making a living, then. . . . There is nothing wrong with making a living from poetry—don't misunderstand me. But if you think of it in terms of something you can put in a resume only, I think you are in trouble. Life in art is poor and it always will be. If you can keep the relationship together, marry a rich girl . . .

Or a rich boy . . .
Or a rich boy. Or for that matter, one of each.

The View Towards Black Nubble

The wind thins blood,
still,
   the sun is rich enough
for dozing under the trees.
A bed of herbs—
spearmint
    is it?
We do well to rest,
and better, to walk north.
(The road will freeze tonight.)
Tomorrow, the first snow.
I see
   only between the trees,
an opening.
      If some night
the air would clot!
      Now only
what travels in a
      vein
against the day.

Ballad of the Goodly Company: Birds

They were singing a grey song
of flat words
    made dull
as the sun between clouds
      wading
down the afternoon
    now
this morning the rain
     makes
such a racket between
     the eaves
and discarded metal
     in the dooryard

I can't tell what song
                from
the color of the day
                I would say
some shadings
                up
from green.

Axes 82

The seat of power will destroy us,
not the power—for we never held such power.
It lies beyond us, and our folly
has made us old.
Old men are fondest, and foolish.
They believe in the strength of their wisdom,
but they have never flexed the muscles,
and they prate.
Along the river, at low tide,
there is a bar that hardens
into form, and it seems a solid ground.
Seabirds take refuge—fish for food.
A solitary crane stands further, in
an almost silent water.
All that will change and wear away
whenever the tide reforms.
It does,
                and makes and breaks and makes
again.
                The birds will scatter and return.
There will be no sense of holding back,
or letting go.
                Things are as they are.
We are the only ones
                willing to hamper
or destroy for our own ends,
and curse the high water breaking through the dikes.
It is not 'fair' to us. We must have

a permanent security, but
the middle ground—the pivot—
was passed and overweighted long ago.
We are on another swing.
It may not return.
Our laughter and assurance are
the shrillest desperation.
                              We believe in nothing
but ourselves, and vaunt the privilege.
We lie before we take each breath.
But we have changed nothing but our thinking,
seeing what was never there,
was never possible—
have taken shadow for the form;
and if that bar impedes us,
we will dredge it out.
The only law observed is
one we write ourselves,
                              not so much
foundering in it as the shifted sand.
Seizing what we think is power,
we will find no source.
It shrivels at a breath.
The vacuum which is its seat
will not support our lives,
or life in any thing.
It seems a window framing our illusion.
Once through it, we will not return.
We seem and seem to be,
we do not grasp the sense of
what is ours, or once was possible.
There is never any reason,
there will never be.
So careful of our axioms, we build
elaborate fancy that cannot stand the light of day.
It thaws at any point when touched
by living.
                  A small child, one not thinking,
overturns the ages.

We have gathered dust,
and molded what will not cohere.
Too long ago we moved beyond
the small things needed for content,
and there is only contents.
To question sanity is simple.
We do need to laugh or cry,
or go about those things we once found

                                        simple.

It is easy to give indictment,
leave it hopeless at that.
It does not do.
                        There are other qualities:
We share them, however much we squander.
It is not a patrimony—
old money accruing interest. There are smiles,
brightness in recognition, and the same
who tempt the sources of power
are those who recognize their own

                                        off hours.
They will walk into the sunlight—or
a distilling of it (their own making)
which will destroy them.
                                It is not pride
that forces any man to admit that he is one.
It could have been better, if he had not been.
He is, and he is flawed from the start.
The birds on the river need only the luxury
of being there.
                        We think we need more,
and that ambition has destroyed a greater:
simply to live.
                        Not to go back to Eden,
or think that was paradise.
Not to have left—not a place in geography—
but to have risen naked among good things,
stayed,
            naked among good things.

The hardest is the simplest.
We will not get around them—
                              most of us
will not try. We will attempt to go through,
using a mailed fist, invoking righteousness
which none of us possess.
We are used in our own usury.
There is no hope, but it is not hopeless.
It may not be a hope for us.
                              Why should it be?
We've moved over a long stretch.
At the beginning
It would have been better to leave it,
or stand with the crane in the river,
waiting for the return of the tide.
Not certainty but more certain than we are.

Yet, in the fields,
I have heard girls singing.
I have seen them walking,
and the light surrounded them.
An aura that did not leave them,
together or alone.
I have seen that light in faces
turned to love,
or learning what it was surrounded.
It is not often.
The usual is grey
as a winter's morning,
silent and preformed for snow.
The movement is hurried,
furtive,
         busyness
to fill up spaces;
but the spaces are not ever filled.
Sealed off, complete,
they seem the core.
One sound of joy would shatter them.
It rarely comes.

The chance is all we have.
A man stands poised,
looking at the water, seeing what he never sees again,
and calls it constant.
He writes his deeds 'forever.'
Any season. Any tide.
Any year.
                    Only the records.
Sealing them up, he hopes for what he cannot have.
Nor can these, his artifacts.
It is all too much for us.
We will never learn to look to
those things that are simple,
accepting their transience,
finding them enough.
                            It is too easy.
We think of worth as struggle,
and there is no struggle that succeeds.
The parts, dismembered, lie everywhere.
And then?
We pay no attention to them,
or at most give burial,
a clump of wilted grass the monument.
No wonder, and no wondering.
The wondering
                    only for the things we cannot have,
and think we want.
A place? All is the place.
The seat of power, fire,
that we cannot sense—too bright, and
too complete.
Such seat of power that destroys.
Come, rise again and naked.
Things that are good surround the bed.

3. Clayton Eshleman

Photo by Nina Subin.

"Into the moonlight of his own holdings"

Born in Indiana in 1935, Clayton Eshleman is one of his generation's most prolific poets, editors, and translators. Over the past two decades he has published forty-two books, thirty-seven of which are collections of poetry and essays; his two most recent books are *Fracture*, 1983, and *The Name Encanyoned River: Selected Poems*, 1985, published by Black Sparrow Press. His volumes of translations include *Cesar Vallejo: The Complete Posthumous Poetry*, with José Rubia Barcia (for which they won the National Book Award), *Pablo Neruda: Residence on Earth*, and *Aimé Césaire: The Collected Poetry*, with Annette Smith. Since 1981, Eshleman has edited *Sulfur*, a literary tri-quarterly featuring work by some of America's most interesting avant-garde writers. Between 1967 and 1973 he edited the literary quarterly *Caterpillar*, publishing such poets as Charles Olson, Gary Snyder, and Paul Blackburn.

Eshleman's many awards include a National Endowment for the Arts Poetry Fellowship, a National Endowment for the Humanities Translation Fellowship, a Witter Bynner Grant-in-Aid, a Guggenheim Fellowship, and the P.E.N. Translation Prize. He has traveled extensively, living for a year in Mexico, three years in Japan, and two years in France. For the past decade, the poet has been doing fieldwork and research on what he calls "Upper Paleolithic imagination and the construction of the underworld."

"As species disappear," Eshleman writes, "the paleolithic grows more vivid. As living animals disappear, the first outlines become more dear, not as reflections of a day world, but as the primal contours of psyche, the shaping of the underworld, the point at which Hades was an animal. The new wilderness is thus the spectral realm created by the going out of animal life and the coming in, in our time, of these primary outlines. Our tragedy is to search further and further back for a common nonracial trunk in which the animal is not separated out of the human while we destroy the turf on which we actually stand."

To begin with a rather unintelligent question, what kind of advice can you give us for becoming better poets?
Do you know Gary Snyder's poem called "What You Need To Know To Become A Poet"? It's a bit pat, and perhaps too clever, but nevertheless a serious one-page statement in *Regarding Wave*. There Snyder gives you in a Poundian and jaunty fashion what could be a curriculum for an M.F.A. program that would be meaningful. Snyder's poem is a statement that one must become as aware as possible of the things that impinge upon one, taking oneself outside usual life and studying such things as the *I Ching*, tarot, mystical and magical systems, which in a sense become source ma-

terials. You'd become involved with a certain mythology; you'd need to know at least a bit about other mythologies that don't relate to your own background; you'd become intensely involved with language.

I think it's very important to try to cultivate areas of information that have not yet been brought into poetry. For the last ten years, for example, I've been doing work on what I call "Paleolithic imagination and the construction of the underworld." This means going to the French caves and looking at them as, say, Charles Olson in the early fifties went to Yucatan and literally started picking up pot shards and looking at them, getting a real feel for them, rather than sitting in a library. Of course you can do that too, but one of the things that has made poetry meaningful and complex in the twentieth century is that the lyric has opened up and begun to include a lot of material that was the prisoner of various disciplines and departments sixty years ago. So that would be one way that I'd respond to your question.

I think you should learn a foreign language so that you can read at least one poetry in the original, and thus you will not become dependent on translations, most of which are bad. And I guess you have to teach yourself how to corner yourself, to teach yourself a way to feel your own resistance so as soon as possible you might learn what really concerns you and what doesn't concern you—what will be the handful of ridges or painful areas of your life that seem to have some depth and complexity, so that you can begin to cultivate these and work off these rather than writing somebody else's poems. That is really the most difficult thing to do, don't you think? To find out what your poems are to be. In a culture like this, given the amount of poetry that's been written in this century and the extent to which you can be flooded and overwhelmed with what other people have done, it's awfully easy to unconsciously just start writing like somebody else or some group of somebody elses.

What is it exactly that you do when you go to the caves you mentioned? I mean what do you do psychologically when you go; what kind of dialogue do you carry on with yourself?
Going to the caves initially means learning how to look, how to be in the caves, because the caves themselves are sometimes a couple of miles deep and labyrinthine, each having very much its own personality and creature aspect to it. This is often as powerful as the art you find inside. It has been necessary for me to go to certain caves maybe fifteen or twenty times to get to the point that I can relax enough to really look at what is on the wall.

So that's a kind of dilemma—to look once as a tourist might doesn't really serve for the kind of looking that I'd like to be able to do. I've done a lot of reading and then reflecting upon what I've seen in the caves in terms of what others have recounted. Also, I've spent much time looking at photographs; they are really very different in that they are far cleaner, brighter than what one actually sees on the wall. I've kept daybooks, jottings on various caves. I've tried to "gang up" on a particular type of interpretation of a cave, or part of a cave, like taking the "shaft" in Lascaux and reading everything that's been written on it, collating the various interpretations of the "shaft" and trying to see their limitations. The caves have to a certain extent been the prisoners of a kind of reductionist and highly conventional archeological hunting-hypothesis for seventy or eighty years.

There was no prescribed plan for me to become an archeologist; it's like any area of experience that suddenly starts to turn you on and so you want to try to master it. In a sense, you get to a point where you know at least as much as anybody else knows about it, so that when you are writing and it comes up in the poetry you are not at the mercy of somebody who tells you that you've got it all wrong. I feel a certain responsibility on that level, though I feel the same responsibility about things that are less an area of study. If I were going to write a poem on St. Valentine's Day I'd want to know who St. Valentinus was; I wouldn't want to be stuck with the cartoon image we have of Valentine's Day. It's a certain sense of having to determine how far and how responsible you feel you must be for an area even before you do imaginal thinking within the area.

I don't think you've answered my question, though maybe I didn't ask it clearly enough. It seems to me that it's pretty artificial for a man living in Los Angeles to suddenly go stick himself in a cave.
More artificial than if I lived in New Mexico?

Well, to me it's a divisive approach.
Divisive? What do you mean?

You can go to the bottom of the sea, go to the moon. These are things that are not a part of your immediate life.
My imagination is in my immediate life.

Well, Gary Snyder goes and works on the land and writes about working on the land. You go to caves and it seems to be a choice like going to the movies.

Walt Whitman rode a streetcar. What difference does it make whether you write about planting in your garden, or your dreams, or your wife, or eating shit, or looking at a bison that was painted twenty thousand years ago in a cave? On one level it's all imaginal material, and I don't really want to give greater status or lesser status to a particular set of materials that a writer is going to use. It all depends upon how seriously you use it. You are setting up a foppish grid, implying that if someone lives in Los Angeles it's divisive for him to go to France to a cave. That's ridiculous. It doesn't matter where you live. Another thing I'd like to say is that my cave poems are not, obviously, about caves. I'm not interested in writing descriptions of paleolithic caves. People never lived in the kind of caves I visit. I go to them like someone else might go to the library. For the Upper Paleolithic caves might be said to contain the "library" of Cro-Magnon consciousness.

May I ask a question in another area? Could you talk a bit about your Vallejo translations, especially how the work of translation has affected your own poetry? What is the connection between the two?

The journal *American Poetry,* which comes out of this university, has published a paper of mine called "Translation as Transformational Reading," which is probably my most articulate statement on these matters. In that paper I more or less coined a phrase because I couldn't find one to describe what I wanted—*assimilative space*—a kind of slowness in reading in working with a text like Vallejo over a period of years. Reading is so slowed down, while at the same time one is working trying to transform a text from one language to another, and constantly being in the situation, of increasing or decreasing the associational grid, hardly ever being able to come up with something one feels is an exact translation. This happens even if you are very much against "imitations" and all sorts of "interpretative" translations that lots of people think is translating. That sort of slow resolving or handling of the text, for me, allows something about Vallejo and that body of work to sink in, in a way that I have a hard time letting it sink in when I read in English. I don't think I'm a particularly fast reader, but I know that for me reading Vallejo over this vast period of time I still find myself turning phrases over in maybe two or three different versions from different strata of the translations, and these sometimes come into my own poetry. However, I'm being influenced by the process of translating Vallejo more than actually being influenced by Vallejo.

Also, you are getting it from the horse's mouth when you are translating. You are forcing yourself to think very subtly in looking for the word, finding the right word that makes the line balance and work at the same time as it's accurate. It makes you think about English in a way that is harder than when you read an American poet. The closest I've come to that in thinking about language when reading English is with Wallace Stevens. Stevens makes me think about the subtleties of the language in a way that other American poets don't.

Translating poems that have been translated before is very different from translating poems that haven't. I see no point in simply hiding one's head in the sand if there are other translations, saying that you don't want to be influenced by them. Reading other translations gives another take on the meaning. In fact, when I was editing *Caterpillar* back in the late sixties I started something based on Louis Zukofsky's *A Test of Poetry,* called "A Test of Translation." I would ask someone to find all of the versions of the Rilke panther poem; they would come up with four or five and we'd simply print them all together with the original side-by-side. Then the person editing the "test" would do a version if he wanted to, and make some brief comments. After a while the thing degenerated into essay writing, so I stopped the series. They were good essays, but the idea was to try to do what Zukofsky had done, to force the reader to do a comparison of different translations. It's astonishing at times. If you look at a Montale against a Lowell "imitation," you'll see things even if you don't read Italian. You'll see that he's added another line there, or that there's a whole piece missing. How many people just reading the Lowell translation realize that he dropped ten stanzas of Rimbaud's twenty-five stanza "Drunken Boat"? What an act of hubris that is! If you read several English versions of a poem with a dictionary at hand, you will understand certain things about the original even if you don't know the language it is written in.

So you think many contemporary translators are somehow suspect?
Well, curiously enough, it seems as if most translators of poetry feel that there is a kind of poetry involved in making their own alterations in the original, as opposed to trying to get the original across in the second language with as much integrity to its own intentions as possible. An example: Ben Belitt translating Pablo Neruda. Take a simple line in an uninteresting poem, but I happen to remember it. A bug is climbing up a vine. Neruda speaks of his "piernas metales"—*metal legs.* Not particularly interesting, but it is *metal legs;* there is just no other place to go with it. Belitt translates it as

"iron-clad trousers." So the "metal legs" become "iron-clad trousers," which makes it ridiculous. This acts then as Belitt's idea of his need to not just translate but to add something of himself. Lord knows where the "iron-clad trousers" come from. When "metal" becomes "iron-clad," "legs" no longer work, so to jazz it up he puts Disney trousers on this poor bug. He ends up with a ridiculous line. There is a certain attitude towards translating that says Belitt's phrase is more interesting than "metal legs," *but* "metal legs" is what Neruda wrote!

My sense of this is that in translating you want to show the poet in his weaknesses and strengths, in his dullness and his great moments; if you are going to take on the body of work the obligation is to reveal as much as you can of the other, and in that sense the translator is a servant. I'm not working my poetic fate out on Neruda's back, the way the message is written in the prisoner's back in Kafka's *Penal Colony*. That sort of an image comes in a certain kind of interpretational attitude toward translation. You are stuck in interpretation in the first place. When Vallejo uses the word *casco*, there are immediately four or five words that are "accurate" translations— skull, helmet, shard, hoof all come to mind. So I must pick. It is as if I had a file of density for the word facing me, and even if I'm trying to be as accurate as I can I must pick one level for that word. I must take skull, for example, or hoof, and the difference between them on a certain level is enormous. So without wanting to I have considerably reduced the density in the original Spanish and thus have performed an interpretational act on Vallejo. Now, if I were to turn "casco" into an "orange peel," I would be doing the same thing that Belitt does in the example.

So when we read your Vallejo we are not reading Eshleman, but Vallejo.
You are reading my version of a poem that comes as close to the original text as possible.

But the text, *not the spirit of the text.*
The "spirit of the text" is a nice phrase, but the spirit of the text ends you up, I'm afraid, in iron-clad trousers. One of the proofs of this is if you read Ben Belitt's poetry. . . . Well, look, I'll bet that if I took Neruda poems and Belitt poems and shuffled them you wouldn't be able to tell the difference.

How much research do you do? Do you take into consideration locality, historical period, all of the other elements that inform language?
The context helps. When Lorca walks out into the streets of New York after

being unable to sleep all night, and everyone looks as if they've returned from a "naufragio de sangre," it's a "shipwreck of blood." Now you wouldn't want to translate that as a "bloody disaster," as Belitt does, because it sounds like English—English slang, and it empties the context of meaning. When Annette Smith and I were translating Aimé Césaire, we knew that there are certain fauna and flora that occur again and again in his poetry; this helped us know what to do with a single word much better than if we had simply a single poem where such a word might be mysterious. For example, because Martinique is an island when the French word *anse* occurs and has the possibility of being translated as a "cove" or as a "handle," we knew, in the Césairean context, it is obviously a "cove." Another translator has translated that word as "handle" because he thought that because Césaire was a surrealist that he should go for the wackiest interpretation of the word. It's a very funny thing—the translator out-surrealizes Césaire and comes up with something that makes Césaire look rather foolish. Again, the context helps. That's a good reason for translating a lot of one poet's work if you are going to translate it at all, because there will be other points in the constellation that will help you at any given point.

Often it is just a matter of insisting on getting the right word; when Césaire uses "hanneton," an earlier translator translates it as "beetle," but it happens that this is a certain kind of beetle. It is a "cockchafer." If I translate that word as "beetle" and then put it back into French, which is another thing you can do, I don't get "hanneton." Sometimes the word will be hard to find, as in Césaire's case when he uses African dictionaries and he converts African words into French neologisms. In those cases we had to literally go to Césaire and ask what the word means. But in the case of "hanneton" if you go to a big enough dictionary you'll find out it's a "cockchafer" and as far as I'm concerned that's how it should be translated. Not as "beetle" or "bug."

How long did you study Spanish?
I never did. I'm self-taught.

Do you really feel like you are qualified to translate, then? The reason I ask is that my mother is fully bilingual and currently she's working on translations from an eighteenth-century journal from the Spanish. Even given her background, which includes years of formal study, she's having a tough go at it, because some words just no longer exist.
Eighteenth-century dictionaries, as well as much older lexicons, *are* avail-

able. With those, or by contacting scholars, your mother should be able to find the words.

My experience has been that the ideal is for an American poet who has at least a good reading knowledge of a foreign language—I've got a good reading knowledge of Spanish—to find his José Rubia Barcia, which was my good fortune. I had spent a long time on Vallejo and had had terrible problems with the text because of its levels of difficulty. I thought that I could do my own versions, then go to a Peruvian, for him to go over them with me, but these people didn't understand the text and made more errors in the long run than I did. It was very difficult to find Barcia. He's a man in his mid-sixties, and he's a linguist as well as a man of literature. He has been at U.C.L.A. for years, he knew Vallejo's work, he is bilingual. So finally we sat down together and the two of us presumed that we could cover sufficient ground with me on one end as the so-called English authority and with him on the other end as the Spanish authority, and at the intersection of ourselves, we could translate Vallejo. Then we set out to retranslate everything that I had translated on my own, from the eight years that I had worked by myself.

I translated Césaire with Annette Smith, who is a French person from Algeria. She has a very strong sense of colonial literature of the French language and she is a scholar. This is very important for translating Césaire because he's from Martinique and is writing in his colonizers' language. So Annette and I met and we tried a little translating together, and we realized that we could work together. One of the ironies is that I found myself at times correcting her French and she found herself at times correcting my English. Finally, the words are so intermingled in the translation we can't say whose is what. That's my solution to the problem you pose. I'm very much against the situation of the poet who doesn't know the language he's translating from going to a native speaker, getting literal versions of the poems, then "poeticizing" them. Anything can happen there.

You were talking before that about locating a few particular experiences in one's life. Do you mean by this that you think poetry has to come out of a necessarily painful personal experience?

That's a good question. I don't have an absolute answer to it. I think there is a sense in which we need a certain kind of anguish, but not necessarily much of it, to learn. Too much of it becomes suffocating. However, Artaud was able to articulate derangement and René Char was able to make entries in *The Leaves of Hypnos* after watching, from a concealed place, resistance fighters tortured. There is a sense in which contacting areas of abuse, humiliation, sadness, being terrified, enables the soul to begin to move. We all live in some great construct called the North American or the Western will and ego. We are all so involved in power structures as, for the most part, white Americans in 1983, that I've found the things that finally have moved me to more imaginal awareness have been those points in my life where I've been down and things haven't been going right.

To give you a concrete example, one of the things that made a difference in my life was having grown up as a WASP football player in Indianapolis, in the early forties, going to Indiana University, joining a fraternity, and going through a terrible year of hazing. This was the last year the university allowed fraternities to beat people with long wooden paddles. You could be beaten at any time—if you looked at an "active" the wrong way he'd tell you to bend over and maybe beat you to a point where you could no longer sit down. We had a "hell week," and as an example they made one of the pledges go down to the local slaughterhouse and get a bull penis, and other pledges had to take turns wearing it around their necks. There was this incredible year of abuse that I allowed myself to go through, and I only put a stop to it at the very end by playing sick during the last half of hell week. Something began to come up in me that I couldn't tolerate any longer. That caused me to think about myself. What was I, I wondered a few years later, that I would have allowed myself to go through this? It sparked my interest in myself for the first time. I'm a late starter and I didn't know there was anything like poetry until I was in my twenties, and when I got started writing, images from the fraternity started coming back—frightening aspects of my life that were more tangible than going back into my childhood in Indianapolis.

I wonder how this might relate to your preoccupation with the primitive past of man. When you go back into the caves you are going back into a time when man was essentially unprotected on the earth and very frightened and alone.

That is a presumption, of course, and there is little evidence in his cave art that Cro-Magnon was obsessed with fear or solitude. But one of the things your question brings up is the matter of rites of passage. At one point, when I got to Kyoto and was sitting and brooding for a couple of years in the early sixties on why I allowed this to take place, I started to decide that the fraternity episode was a failed rite of passage. I thought I had been denied something that an Australian aboriginal boy of thirteen or fourteen had not been denied. If I had gone through a penis subincision, been reborn through the bloody legs of the fathers and so on . . . there is a lot of material on this powerful transitional state from the world of the mothers to the world of the fathers. At that point I decided that it would have been better to have been in Australia than to have been in this awful, macho Phi Delta Theta mess in which nobody seemed to learn anything and you just seemed to curl up tighter within yourself and be less open to the outside. But then in continuing to think about that, by the late sixties I began to question the validity of the symbolic bloodiness of the men's societies in Australia. Incidentally, there is a note in *Sulfur* #8 by Peter Redgrove on some compelling research by Chris Knight on synchronic menstruation, the Rainbow Serpent, and the Wawilak Sisters, which constellates a pan-Australian myth. New information suggests that in past times the women synchronized their menstrual periods with lunar periods and the tides at the times when they detached themselves from the rest of the tribe. Men seem to have usurped the women's ceremonies by copying them and eradicating them. As you grow older and as you continue to turn these things over in your mind they take on different shapes, and so by now I must have written seven or eight pieces on the fraternity; they all come in at different angles and the fraternity becomes more and more consummed in other materials, less and less naturalistic.

This intrigues me because you are suggesting then that there is some connection between these experiences and the primitive.
I winced when you used the word *primitive* before, because unless you are honoring its complexity I think it's a careless term to employ. Upper Paleolithic peoples were very bright and sophisticated, and I would go so far as to say that they had a world view that worked for over twenty thousand years. One of the challenges of our culture is to try to understand what Cro-Magnon thought and to do this to bring it to bear against our extinction-cocked culture. These people knew something that worked in a way that we don't; this extreme longevity of Upper Paleolithic art, this continuum that comes in at around 35,000 . . . there appears to be a continuum from 35,000 to 8,000 B.C., based on what we can observe from what is left of their civilization, that suggests that something was set during this period that was life-giving and worked. What we've moved to in literally a couple thousand years is a point where nobody knows when the sky is going to fall. Also, the animals are going out of the world. We live in a period in which there are many disappearing species, and as the living animal fabric

begins to thin then these earliest outlines and contours become more clear. There is some sort of hinge that is at work there.

Do you have any hints on the matter of publication?

The first thing I would do, if you are pretty sure that you are going to still be writing fifteen or twenty years from now, is to go to the library or bookstore and start reading contemporary magazines without any thoughts about your writing workshop. Try to figure out what seems to be being done now that appeals to you. At a certain point, after reading several issues of *Sulfur,* or *Conjunctions,* or *Poetry,* or *Kenyon Review,* or whatever, you might say that there are certain things that I'm doing that might be of interest to this magazine, there is a certain way in which I connect. Or you read a poem in a magazine and find out that this is the first appearance of that person and he or she is probably not that much older than you; I'd write that person and say that you've read the poem, explain why it interested you, and send along some of what you've been doing. Or maybe you write to the editor. And *subscribe* to the magazine.

But in either case, you should do it meaningfully, not just send poems to magazines you haven't seen and pray that somehow somebody will print one of your poems. That's like putting all your energy in the post office; and there is a certain kind of meaninglessness in trying to get published anyway, other than maybe sharing your work with people around you. After all, unless you are one of a hundred or so people in the whole history of poetry, chances are slim that you will begin to do anything significant until you have been writing a decade. The idea of thinking about publication during this early period is a mistake in priorities. Take that time and spend it learning a foreign language or a new source idea or simply reading poetry. Remember, coming into poetry in 1983 you've got a very powerful and diverse twentieth century American and European poetry behind you. There is so much stuff you've got to assimilate—you've got to learn how to read as a writer. Even when you consider the amount of Stein, H.D., Pound, Williams, Crane, Olson, all the way up through about five generations in which certain figures indisputably have made original and powerful contributions to American literature, you have not considered their contributions in the light of Rilke, Vallejo, Breton, and Montale, say, European poets who are as relevant, if not more so, to what we are, as the Americans. You really must read all this and come to terms with it, decide what is for you and what is not. If you were to do this meaningfully, it would take up so much time over the first seven or eight years that the idea of trying to get your poems published in magazines would seem ridiculous.

Now, that said, I didn't really practice what I preach. I got involved in a magazine about a year after I started writing poetry. There was a campus magazine called *Folio* in 1958 which printed student poetry and some things by the professors. Via an association with *Folio* I started to visit poets on trips to New York City, which I had also just discovered. So that in 1958 I found myself knocking on Allen Ginsberg's door, and Louis Zukofsky's door, and Paul Blackburn's door asking for poems for *Folio*. I thought it would be much more interesting putting an Allen Ginsberg poem on one page and a student poem facing it rather than simply running two student poems. So *Folio* immediately started to become a kind of quasi-national magazine in that sense, and it was immediately censored and then stopped entirely by the English department. I wanted to print a Ginsberg poem that had "fart" and "shit" in it, and I also wanted to run about a forty page piece of Zukofsky's work on Shakespeare that Professor Battenhouse, a Christianized Shakespeare scholar, could not make head or tail of; so the department move was to stop the magazine after twenty-seven years. That was an interesting lesson, demonstrating for me how institutions feel about contemporary writing. Jack Spicer called this phenomenon the "English Department of the Spirit."

Didn't you publish your own first book?
More or less. The publication date is right at the beginning of 1962, though for years it has been listed as 1961 and I haven't bothered to change it. I had gone to Mexico after I'd started writing in the late fifties. I made several hitchhiking trips there, as a way to encapsulate my terribly limiting background. Mexico really turned me insideout. I wrote a lot of poems and I started reading Pablo Neruda with my little twenty-five-cent Spanish dictionary. Then I took a job which led me to Japan, and once I got there I had about fifty or sixty pages that I thought were pretty good. And like a typical young poet, a compulsive need to have a book.

Robert Kelly was publishing *Trobar* books at that time and he offered to publish it. George Economou, who was editing *Trobar* with Kelly, didn't like my manuscript and didn't want to do it, so he asked me to have it printed in Japan and said that *Trobar* would distribute it. So I printed it myself and some copies trickled around to a few friends. Whitman, Pound—lots of people have done this, and it's probably not a bad idea to do a small, modest edition of your best writing when you feel that you've got a body of work to present. If you'd like me, for example, to know about your writing it would be nice to send me a little collection rather than a manuscript. But the most important thing for you to do is to connect with what will be your generation, assuming such a thing exists, fairly early in your life or the cold of your inevitable solitude as a writer will be intensified.

I had the good fortune when I went to New York to meet Robert Kelly, Jerome Rothenberg, and Diane Wakoski who have been allies and companions for twenty years. These are the people who have given me a sense of a "generation." Having good correspondents makes a small but essential difference. To have good literary correspondents, you need to find people who are doing something valuable and are not that much younger or older than you. If they are older and of an earlier generation (see the Olson/Dahlberg correspondence, *Sulfurs #* 1–3), no one-on-one relationship is possible. The great task is to find your own "companions of the voyage" and begin to create a sense of group of individuals doing "X" in literature that possibly hasn't been done before. That's one of the reasons the little magazine exists; it traditionally takes chances, prints people who are unknown. The little magazine should be a kind of rootwork making connections between two or more generations.

I envy you having such good friends. I've had a few like that I've been close to for maybe five years and it's been nice. But to be so close for twenty years, that must be very nice.
Well, we've had our fights and fallings out. There have been years where I haven't had any contact with Robert Kelly, for example. It hasn't all been smooth and beautiful. But we do have a sense that we are essential to each other, I believe, even though none of the people I mentioned have compromised their own sense of the poetic by coalescing into a "movement" or a manifesto-identified "group."

You went to Japan, I assume, with a language company?
No, I went with the University of Maryland. They had a contract with the American Armed Services to provide teachers for American personnel throughout the world. I went to the Far East and taught freshman composition and survey courses to G.I.'s for a year. It was very boring and I quit after a year and went to Kyoto, where I lived teaching English to young engineers at an electric company. Kyoto was a very beautiful, nonindustrial place in 1963, and at that time Gary Snyder was living there, and Cid Corman— just a handful of Americans. We saw each other maybe once a week, and

the rest of the time we were by ourselves. It was a tough and good way to be. My inclination at that time had been to go to New York, to get involved in the poetry "scene," But somehow I knew that it would be more of a waste of time than a chance to test myself and find out just how much I *needed* to write. I felt that it would be better to isolate myself and sit and think about the decision I had been making, and to start to read *as a poet*. As I said, I was a very late starter and there was a lot I hadn't read. So I spent much time working on Vallejo translations in Kyoto, and reading William Blake.

Why do you think you made the commitment to being a poet when you did?
If I crawled back into autobiographical speculation I might conjecture that my mother triggered imagination by starting me playing the piano when I was six; I heard Bud Powell and Lennie Tristano play be-bop when I was sixteen, and their discordancy set depth charges in my psyche-to-be that did not implode until 1963. For many years I had a muffled creative curiosity and I didn't know how to move. It was stuck because of the WASP context I grew up in; there was no real artful encouragement. Then in 1958 in Bloomington I met Jack Hirschman and Mary Ellen Solt, who was writing on William Carlos Williams. They pulled a string, and it was as if all the books in the world fell on my head. I don't know why it happened right at that time, but all of a sudden I was surrounded by the keys to imagination.

My mother had given me a strong sense of self-confidence, which I think more and more had to do with my willingness to believe in the keys. I had a certain kind of nerviness because of her adhesive love. However, I came very close to ending up as a used-car salesman in Indianapolis.

Looking over a list of your books, I'm stunned at the amount that you've written in such a relatively short period.
I now publish only a small portion of what I write. Only about 10 percent since 1974. I had one period from 1966 to 1971 in which I stopped revising. I went into Reichian therapy and started to blow out repressed anger and grief; I read Robert Duncan's statement that he never revises a poem, that he simply writes a new one, and for a period of time I used that idea to break up my compulsion to polish poems into dead, perfect things. It's that time that makes me most uncomfortable at this point. But since finishing *Coils* in 1973, I've published only a very small percentage. A book like *Fracture* must have come to 2,500 pages of worksheets; the book is 140 pages

long. I rewrite, splice, and try to only present what is taut and vital. I work on this poem, then that poem, then I see suddenly that I like this part here and that part there and move them together to see if they actually work as a piece. I also discuss *everything* I write with my wife, Caryl, who is other, companion, and editor to the "middle passage" of any poem. "A Kind of Moisture on the Wall," which is three pages in print, has twenty or twenty-five pages of worksheets as well as many "notes" made during visits to the caves behind it. The way I write resembles, as a matter of fact, the exploration of a maze or labyrinth, filled with dead ends and nodal points. Anton Ehrenzweig discusses this creative approach in the first part of his book *The Hidden Order of Art*.

That doesn't seem to me that much different from the way other poets work.
Well, I know a lot of poets who write out a version in longhand and more or less type it out with corrections and that's it. They don't go to the poem until they more or less have the poem in mind. Diane Wakoski would be an example. Robert Kelly hardly ever revises. He eliminates irrelevent passages and lines, but he does very little rewriting and splicing, as far as I know. I think I do much more revision now than most people whose work habits I'm aware of.

Lately I've found that after I've finished a manuscript, and I've been doing this for about ten years, I feel that I must immediately write and finish some good new poems to fill the void. I realize that most of the time it's not a matter of not having anything to say, nothing as simple as that, but I generally am in such a state of turmoil and confusion as to what I want to do that imposing finishing things on myself is a pointless and harmful activity. So I decided to do the following: for the past year, after I write a page I turn it over and put it in a stack. I've not looked at anything I've written since last January, other than in the process of writing it. No revision, no redoing. I imagine there is a lot of repetition because writing this way there is no check on what has been written. Now I've got a stack about six inches high. I'm going to wait until this January to open it up and see what is inside.

Like getting your own Christmas present.
Yes, or your own Palm Sunday.

I often find that my own best writing seems to be those poems that I fool with very little.

That is really a hard thing to learn—revision as a way to open up material and draw more edges into the material, as opposed to sanding the material down so that you end up with something smooth, polished, and featureless.

Do you feel that it is important to save worksheets?

I do, but it may not be important for you. On one level, I'd like to have all my archive intact so that if somebody wants to study my work someday there will be all of the mistakes and dead ends and difficulties right there, so that the dirt will not have been shaken off the roots. So that the *compost* is there. Also, it is useful for me to go back at times and to see that the thing that was a second draft that I thought was shit at the time is a very interesting piece of writing. Why didn't I see that then? That the thing that I ended up with in draft fourteen is relatively uninteresting. It is only by keeping a fairly good record, chronologically and in little files, that you can do that.

Could you say a bit more about opening up a poem?

In freshman composition when I went to school, as they say, finishing something, revising it, meant polishing it. It meant that you make it more clear, more appropriate to the understanding of the instructor and his grade. So there is something that is loaded into us that suggests strongly that revision has academic "checks and balances" built into it. I would prefer to think of revision as an opening up *and* a clouding, or a making deeper and more murky—a feeding of more material into the process so that you can finally see how much material, how much traffic, this context will bear. Then you might abandon the piece at the point where you think you've reached a maximum level, which is hardly clear or hardly polished, but where the greatest amount of material is contained in focus. This is an anticonclusion attitude. I want to keep that poem from coming to a con-clusion as long as I can, to leave the poem up in the air, because that sense of conclusion. . . . Look , if I come into the poem with something that feels like a statement, a long time ago I would have said, boy that's a good line. I'd plunk it down and try to figure some interesting way to get to it. Now I find it much more interesting to take that so-called conclusion and use it as the first line. Then where do I go from there? That is the real joy of writing—discovering something in the very act of writing that you didn't know before.

Doesn't Pound warn you against knowing the difference between your notebooks and your literature?

Pound's early aesthetics seem to me to be outdated and useless. Vallejo, Artaud, and Olson, all in their own way, represent gains in the ways that information and materials are brought into the demand of the poem. Pound's distinction between "literature" and one's "worksheets" is questionable because it is often possible that "first thought *is* best thought," as Allen Ginsberg said, or that you are most free and open in a notebook context. So many of these barriers have been broken down. Pound probably made comments like that at a period when there was a fairly intact sense of what was prose and what was poetry. There was a feeling that one thing was poetry, another was dirty laundry. Now we recognize that the dirty laundry has more of the person in it than what comes out of the dry cleaners. When the worn materials are handed over to the finishing, or critical—cleaning—mind, the rote contractions of one's earlier education are quickened. One is to a certain extent, looking *over* the shoulder of one's soul, a judge, trying to straighten things out, to force the creative melee at the very best into a synthesis.

The Lich Gate

Waiting, I rest in the waiting gate.
Does it want to pass my death on,
or to let my dying pass into the poem?
Here I watch the windshield redden
the red of my mother's red Penney coat,
the eve of Wallace Berman's fiftieth birthday
drunk truck driver smashed Toyota,
a roaring red hole, a rose in whirlpool
placed on the ledge of a bell-less shrine.
My cement sits propped against the post.
To live is to block the way, and
to move over at the same time, to hang
from the bell-less hook, a tapeworm in the packed
organ air, the air resonant with fifes, with mourners
filing by the bier resting in my hands,
my memory coffer in which an acquaintance is found.
Memory is acquaintance. Memory is not a friend.
The closer I come to what happened,

the less I know it, the more occasionally I love
what I see beyond the portable
gate in which I stand—I, clapper, never free,
will bang, if the bell rope is pulled.
Pull me, Gladys and Wallace say to my bell, and you
will pass through, the you of I, your
pendulum motion, what weights
you, the hornet nest shaped
gourd of your death, your scrotal
lavendar, your red red glass crackling
with fire embedded mirror. In vermillion and black
the clergyman arrives. At last
something can be done about
this weighted box. It is the dead who come forth
to pull it on. I do nothing here.
When I think I do, it is the you-hordes
leaning over my sleep with needle-shaped
fingers without pause they pat
my still silhouette which shyly moves.
The lich gate looks like it might collapse.
Without a place to wait,
my ghoul would spread. Bier in lich,
Hades' shape, his sonnet prism reflecting
the nearby churchyard, the outer hominid limit,
a field of rippling meat. I have come here
to bleed this gate, to make my language fray
into the invisibility teeming against
The Mayan Ballcourt Of The Dead,
where I see myself struggling intently,
the flux of impact, the small hard
rubber ball bouncing against the stone hoop.

Equal Time

Somehow it seems wrong,
a minute on Vietnam refugees
at sea, starving, not allowed to
dock, followed by a minute

on a new world's record in cherry
pit spitting, wrong because
the pit record trivializes a human
plight—so, should we dwell
on an imagined deck, imagined
cries? Somehow the dwelling itself
seems wrong, not only being here
but dwelling on what thought does
not alter. Or on what thought only
raises as thought, say my presenting
suffering to you as language
instead of handing you an actual
refugee. The baby wild hare
my son and I found had
abscessed legs, so we set it back
in its tall grass. Its tremble
brings the refugees closer, its being
alone, frightened, defenseless,
might enter the champion
cherry pit spitter's mind as
he dreams in a structure that includes
an altered sense of language
that must include the desert
mountains this morning not as part
of the news but of the evolving net
writing poetry throws out,
wanting to include, hesitant to
look back, knowing violence and
the moral impossibility of balancing
the refugees, the pit champ and the hare—
or is the poem to fictionalize such
a balance, is it to hang each with a counterbalancing
weight so that, clearly unequal, they
float over to an immense ear, an Ithacan
grotto, as the magical things upon which
the homecome wanderer rests his head?
It is too easy in a world that refuses dockage
to refugees to play on the spit out pit,
to allow the Odysseus of one's imagination

to rest for more than a moment on
an archetypal pillow in which hare,
champ and refugee are bees, producing
a distinct but unified Mass, an eatable
hosea, a surge toward a drooping prophesied head
from which flows a common honey
—tu viens, chéri? This structure
must include a sweetness in bed
as well as the mascara in the coffin-
deep rue St.-Denis doorway where the empty
champ touches the abscessed refugee,
where he mounts her in the hold of
a dingy, stranded before a coyote lighthouse.

For Aimé Césaire

Spend language, then, as the nouveau riche spend money
invest the air with breath newly gained each moment
hoard only in the poem, be the reader-miser, a new kind of snake
coiled in the coin-flown beggar palm, be political, give it all away,
one's merkin, be naked to the Africa of the image mine in which
biology is in a tug-of-war with deboned language in a tug-of-war with
Auschwitz in a tug-of-war with the immense demand now to meet the
     complex
actual day across the face of which Idi Amin is raining
the poem cannot wipe off the blood
but blood cannot wipe out the poem
black caterpillar
in its mourning-leaves, in cortege through the trunk of the highway of
history in a hug-of-war with our inclusion in
the shrapnel-elite garden of Eden.

Fracture

The crutch you hand to another
is a furious indescribable beast,
tectiform of your own shape as Eve staggers

out of Eden, the vile legacy in hand,
wandering the dust, offering to whoever
passes by a rotting piece of it, one peso,

by a Mexican roadside, her palm outstretched—
an open heart ceremony announcing
that all dark, all light, is the sawing

of being on being, a circular coring,
a ceremony lit by tapers made of entire
kingdoms. Earth, pieta. And as the dark

is serrated by the light you will start to hear,
as if at Gargas, the chalky cries of
hands, mutilated negatives, clouds of mouths

rising up the walls, virgin moths
mourning over caterpillars they have gathered
into their wings, crying the oldest cry,

that earth is responsible for our deaths,
that if we die collectively
we will take the earth with us *if we can*—

who does not hear our cries
seeks to contain us in that American cottage
where a nameless stand-in coils about

the solitary fang of a Snow White dead at 27.
Please let our howls, so elastic with water,
become that still lake most men abhor,

out of which Excalibur rises in the grip
of a drowned living Harlow whose wavering
stench of generation is holocaust to

all who seek to destroy their need

for that gleaming nipple below whose face
enwound with coral snakes is a squid haze of stars.

Manticore Vortex

This will be, then, my primal scene:
the Rashomon Gate of the American poem,
a kind of panopticon in which viewpoint upon viewpoint,
shafts of late afternoon light, slant through
this ruined tower at the western edge of civilization—
and the muse upon which the self of the poem is begotten
is none other than that hair-pulling hag,
that wig-maker, fashioning the poem's destiny
out of what she can draw from the dead.

There is a cave below this gate,
the midwestern basement where Sylvia Likens is on view,
where pledge larvae are huddled
during the nights of Hell Week that is furnace and father,
a dead washing machine, the wringer
one was cranked through so as to learn octopus sleight of hand,
the various dodges of the nascent self as it tiptoes around
the terror of the dream that tells it it is religious
because it not only entwines its mother
but feeds on her underarm fat while she is dying.

The self is an active cannibalism of its own matrix
and the co-producer of its birth.
To the visitor it would appear as if there were only
a large bolted screw in this basement floor,
but there is Aztec density here.
A pubescent boil has been transformed into a crystal ball
through which the poem sees the guardian rattler
dreaming at the Amerindian stratum of the world.

In the vortex of the whirlpool below,
animals are separating and recombining with men—
the archetypal grotesque is constant,
from Lascaux to Disneyland, intersected by Rabelais,

by Belsen, by gargoyles
poised for eternity on the periphery of the holy,
that periphery is the furrow in which
the crossbreeding of the marvelous takes place
but turn it, like a prism, a few degrees in your hand
and the gargoyles are the damned of any century,
turn it back the other way and they recede into a cave,
nothing more than sockets observing us.

And who are we?
A holding pattern between heaven and hell?
Gaudi bends in a roller rink centripetally seeking God?

       O pillbox
in which I find all the space I am not taking up
is taken up by you, we
completely filling the space
yet encased

    it was into this core
we fell, two drops ceaselessly
seeking to reamoebize

three billion years of single-celled life

Such is my lust for merger
on the rubberband of pendulum flitting

nicked
periplus
of that oldest beauty:
    the slow running diaspora of burning semen
incense to the schizophrenic fissure

       ape eye to human eye

         me to you.

4. William Everson

"The claw moon talons the west"

William Everson was born in 1912 in Sacramento, California, and grew up in the San Joaquin Valley. He attended Fresno State College for a term, where he discovered the work of Robinson Jeffers. During World War II he served as a conscientious objector, then returned to the Bay Area to join the group of poets around Kenneth Rexroth. In 1949 he converted to Catholicism; two years later he entered the Dominican order, taking the name Brother Antoninus. In 1969, after eighteen years as a lay brother, he left the Dominicans to marry. Over the next decade he was poet-in-residence at the University of California at Santa Cruz.

Everson has published over forty-five books of poetry, prose, and scholarship, including *The Residual Years, The Veritable Years, Masks of Drought, Birth of a Poet,* and *In Medias Res.* He received a Guggenheim Fellowship in 1949, the Shelley Memorial Award in 1978, and a National Endowment for the Arts Fellowship in 1982. He is also a hand-press printer of distinction.

"All art," Everson has written, "seeks to express the silences before and after conceptualization. It is essentially the aesthetic element. When one speaks of art as something seen under the aspect of eternity, it is at that point that cyclical and linear time converge and find their harmony. It is that point in which even the most abstract sculpture becomes the essence of cyclical time, the point of eternal return. The poet uses words to transcend words, to get beyond speech, to register the silence that follows speech."

Do you consider yourself a religious poet, both specifically Catholic and in a more general sense?
Yes. The distinction I'd make would be between a religious poet and a nature poet, though. The religious poet would be more generic, the nature poet more specific. I'd also include I suppose the erotic poet, given the emphasis I have on the sexual.

Which of the three is the strongest?
The religious poet. At least it's the most inclusive in that it subsumes the other two.

But by religious you don't necessarily mean Catholic then?
No. I was a religious poet long before I was a Catholic.

How did that change when you entered the order?
It gained specificity when I became a Catholic. The order didn't change it

all that much—it was my conversion to Catholicism itself. The entry into the Dominicans was simply a further specification, a deepening of focus.

And from the point of conversion you began to work with Catholic subject matter?
Yes. I converted to Catholicism in 1949, and the first poem I wrote following that which didn't have a specific Catholic reference point was my elegy for Jeffers, *The Poet Is Dead,* in 1962. Everything between those years was specifically Catholic.

Why did you make the shift in 1962?
I didn't want to subsume Jeffers into the Christian hegemony, given his total witness against it all his life. He was my literary master. It was when I found him, at Fresno State College in the fall of 1934, that I discovered my own vocation as a poet. It was one of the great turning points in my life.

Which explains Fragments of an Older Fury *and the rest of your prose work on Jeffers.*
Yes. I didn't really write any prose to speak of before my conversion, but Catholicism gave me a frame of reference. Before that everything was touch and go, highly relative, and I didn't have any orientation point save through the emotional dimension of my poetry. It wasn't until I had the frame of reference which the church gave me, along with its intellectual tradition, that I could begin to work these things out in prose. Also, it was a question of maturation. I converted at age thirty-five, and my mind was just starting to wake up then.

Do you consider yourself a narrative poet?
More and more, especially now that I'm writing *Death Shall Be the Serpent's Food.* It's an autobiographical epic, and almost totally narrative. Actually, narrative elements began to creep into my poetry around 1942, when after the death of my mother, I began to ingest more content and narrative appeal in my work. But really the narrative broke through pretty completely when I began to read the Bible seriously. Poems like "The Massacre of the Holy Innocents" in *The Crooked Lines of God* are almost wholly narrative retellings of biblical episodes.

What would the death of your mother have to do with embracing the narrative?

Nothing really. There was just a liberation, a great leap forward towards the intellectual. In a sense there was a deliverance point from the bond of the maternal. That is psychologically one of the great crossover points in the evolution of both the aesthetic and the mystical psyches. In studying other poets, like Jeffers, you can often place their emergence into creative autonomy with the death of the mother. Ginsberg is another very good example of that.

Masks of Drought *seems thoroughly narrative.*

Yes, by that book I've got the narrative at my fingertips. I move towards it instantly when I feel a poem coming.

So you don't feel the approach to be worked out.

Well, the only danger is that it might get a little dry, merely narrative at the expense of the lyrical dimension. I think this is the relevance of *Masks of Drought* in my own evolution as a poet, the constant balancing between those two factors.

What is your plan for the long poem you mentioned?

Death Shall Be The Serpent's Food? I begin with the classical epic formula, *in media res,* the low point in the fortunes of the hero. The plan calls for the use of flashback to explain how he got to that point, as well as his going forward to apotheosis. The first canto begins at the end of World War II in 1945, the death of my father. It should run about ten cantos; I'm writing the second one now. *In Media Res,* the first canto, has just been published in a limited edition by Adrian Wilson in San Francisco.

So you think of this poem not simply as a long poem, but as an epic?

Yes. It comes out of my teaching a course called "Birth of a Poet" for a decade at the University of California at Santa Cruz. In that course our text was Joseph Campbell's *Hero With a Thousand Faces,* which describes in archetypal outline the journey of the hero as it has come down to us in myth. Through the program I arrived at the necessity for the artist of the classical heroic attitude in order to survive the storms of the charismatic journey. Thus in my course I began to narrate the story of my own life as an introduction to the journey. After a decade of doing that I became so accustomed to seeing my life in archetypal terms that I moved naturally towards the writing of epic.

Since you've been working on this longer poem have any shorter poems come?
They've kept coming at their own pace. I've just this last year published another book called *Renegade Christmas,* including five poems which are extensions of *The Masks of Drought.* In a sense I had published its poems too soon. A short time earlier I had collected my Catholic poetry into *The Veritable Years,* and I wanted people to know that I wasn't stuck there. But I moved too fast. The five later poems came, and I'm writing another one right now. I can't seem to let go of the theme.

You mentioned teaching. Had you done this in the order?
Not formally. I was on the reading platform constantly at universities across the country, and I participated in a lot of writing workshops at various conferences. But until Santa Cruz I was not formally connected to a university, which meant that I didn't have to do the work of evaluation, which turns out to be the difficult part. Everyone loves to teach, but evaluations are a pain in the ass.

When did you take the job at Santa Cruz?
After I left the order and married Susanna, we were almost two years at Stinson Beach, then in 1971 the job opened at U.C.S.C. I retired in 1982.

Did you teach creative writing workshops?
No, I avoided them. They are a solution to a pedagogical problem—do you teach creative writing?—but I don't cotton to them. Americans are sold on them, and the students pour into the universities demanding to be taught. But in the history of the world it's never been done this way before, and there are a lot of drawbacks. The established poets especially, even the ones who teach in the programs, are starting to take a second look at the whole process. The workshops are getting so good, and the students are all so technically proficient, that it's hard to distinguish between poems. Sometimes I'm asked to judge poetry contests, and when I see a dozen well-crafted student workshop poems before me I just can't tell the difference. A natural or sexual image may strike me, and I'll choose that poem for that reason. But it's got nothing to do with distinguishing between levels of qualities.

So do you see creative writing workshops and programs as being rather dangerous?

Not really. It's not that serious. The direction of poetry will be the direction of genius. The real poets can't be hurt by these programs, unless they become dazzled by the technique of the teachers and start drifting from one university to another. Study with Lowell for a time, then Roethke, and so on. I think that's dangerous for a young poet. The traditional way is to find your master and adhere to him until you outgrow him. You have to watch out for distractions. That's my big problem with Modernism, in fact, that it demeans influence and strives for an impossible and undesirable originality.

So young poets should stay clear of universities?

I didn't say that! I think young writers are drawn to universities, as I was myself. It was at Fresno State College where, as I said, I found Jeffers. But the important thing is to find your peer group, after you find your master. Your master gives you direction and your peer group gives you support.

If "Birth of a Poet" wasn't creative writing what was it?

A course in charismatic vocation, in the necessity to find your vocation. The structure was a series of meditations. As I said, I took Campbell's book for my outline. The notion of vocation came to me both from my own experience with Jeffers and from my years in the order where vocation was the primary factor. There, it is essential that you discover your vocation before taking final vows, and you've got seven years to do it. The emphasis is on the inner call which carries you forward to your creative destiny. It is natural for religious life, and I simply made the transition over to the aesthetic life.

How many students did you have?

It varied from quarter to quarter, year to year. I threw as broad a net as I could. I wasn't simply interested in writers, but I wanted to establish the general principle of vocation, and thus I drew people from every discipline. In fact, what made the course popular was the assignment of keeping a dream journal, which allowed considerable latitude. This also satisfied the academic requirement for written work. My intuition was to teach the basic concept of vocation during the fall quarter, the American calling in the winter, and the Western calling in the spring. Two years ago Black Sparrow Press published a year's collection of these meditations taken from the mid-seventies. I sometimes had two to three hundred students, though eventually the college made me limit it to one hundred.

Can we shift the topic a little? You were a C.O. during World War II.
Yes.

What was your argument?
It was pretty obscure, actually, the way those predominantly and profoundly attitudinal situations are. Both pacifism and revolution seem more attitudinal than intellectual, which is why both are hard to explain. There are many sources, and your articulation is always limited by your lack of experience. You often get off on idealistic ground which you don't understand until many years later. Thus you often find yourself embarrassed by your most deeply held convictions.

I now realize that there was a lot of the Oedipal complex in my early pacifism. I was simply unable to put my neck on the line for the patriarchy.

Was your father displeased with your stance?
Profoundly.

So it was a rebellion against your father?
There was a good deal of that, but on the other hand there was a deep conviction. I would never have let mere rebellion be the determining factor. I think even at that time I had too much self-knowledge for that. Actually, when I was finally drafted I was thirty years old, so I wasn't all that young.

Weren't there many other writers and artists in the camps during the war?
Yes. I was at a camp at Waldport, Oregon, and we got a number of other writers, artists, and musicians to join us there as part of the Fine Arts Program.

The painter Morris Graves?
No. He once visited Waldport, but though he was a pacifist he never went into the C.O. system. He went into the military, refused to put on the uniform, and they threw him in the brig. After a year or two they managed to get rid of him as a mental case. Of course, William Stafford was in a camp.

Did you know him?
Not at the time. He was down at Santa Barbara. I've never asked him why he didn't come up to our Waldport program, but I intend to do it before I

die. His beautiful little C.O. journal written during that period has just been reissued. The printer Adrian Wilson was at Waldport; he came as a musician, but he found his printing vocation there. Today he is one of the finest printers in the country.

Are you still a pacifist?
I consider myself one, though I can't honestly say that I retained my pacifist beliefs through my Dominican period. My abandoning of those convictions through the years was a mistake.

Did the Church require it?
No. Somehow it had to do with my identification with the institutional. In political terms it made sense, but it was an error. Reading Guerard's book, *Violence and the Sacred,* illuminated for me the whole point of Christ's "resist not evil," though it's been awhile and I don't think I can be more specific about it. Just that he gave me an insight into the contagious nature of violence. The only thing that can contain it is human specification in terms of law, application of rule. Otherwise, vengeance becomes law, and on the primitive level this is a reflexive disaster. You'd think that would be an argument for the just war, but as I say I am unable to take this any further right now.

What about the role of violence in your work, or Jeffers's?
That's the central problem in life. Look at Shakespeare, Milton, Dante, Homer especially—the work is saturated with violence. It's the obsessional part of human life that is unsolvable save through the religious dimension. I was preoccupied with Old Testament violence, the relation of violence to the sacred. I tried to get through to the heart of it by seeing some of the most violent biblical episodes from a Jungian perspective, the theory of archetypes and mythical structure.

Have you read a lot of Jung?
I don't know anyone who has read all he wrote, but I've pondered on his thought deeply for some years.

How did you come to have an interest in his work?
Through Victor White, the English Dominican priest who was a Jungian. He came to teach for a year at St. Albert's College in Oakland where I was stationed as a lay brother. My friendship with White led me to the whole

matter of the unconscious. My emergence into Jung was a way of answering certain problems I was having at the time.

There was no conflict between the Catholic and Jungian systems?
Not at all, save for a few technical points like the nature of evil. But that has nothing to do with the therapeutic aspect. In fact, Fr. White did a wonderful job of equating St. Thomas Aquinas, the great Dominican saint and master theologian of the Church, with Jung. I wrote a preface for the recent reissue of his book *God and the Unconscious,* published by the Jungians.

What about Robert Bly, who also speaks of Jung often? Do you have any points of disagreement on Jung?
Not really. We always seem to be fighting, but I'm not sure about what. We have this sense of comradeship based on the fact that we are both Christians, both Norwegians, both poets, both Jungians. That's a pretty strong bond, considering how rare Christianity and Jungianism is in American poetry. But when it comes to poetry itself, he thinks that I'm too rhetorical, while I think he's too surreal. We are like two bulls in a pasture, just butting our heads together and not giving each other his due. He is the best reader on the platform today.

So you've heard him recently?
Yes, not too long ago in Santa Cruz. In fact, the reading has become something of a local legend. I arrived after the hall was fairly full, and Robert and I embraced in front of everyone, an open declaration of brotherhood and amity. I sat down and soon after he began to read. It was a beautiful performance at first, but he had just read Elaine Pagels book on the Gnostics and soon he was into a thing about them. He is so political that soon he was breathing fire about the suppression of the Gnostics; he began to get warmed up to the subject, and I began to feel uneasy. I was waiting for the intermission so that I could slip out. But finally he declared, "Christianity must renounce the doctrine of the one God!" I just found something grabbing me by the seat of my pants and heading up for the door. He made a great mistake then. He stopped his discourse to call to me, "Are you leaving, Bill?" I had to say something, so I barely paused in my exit and flung over my shoulder: "You'd better believe it!" and kept going. The audience broke up.

   I heard many reports that at the time he took the whole thing very well. But after a few days he began to steam. I wrote him a letter the next day and sent it along with a book; I told him that I'd looked forward to his appearance and that I regretted what happened. Before he got that, though, he wrote me a savage letter saying that if I differed with him I should have stayed to fight. Further, he said that I stood for the Inquisition, that a few hundred years back I would have reported him to the priests and watched him burn at the stake on the plaza in Santa Cruz. So I immediately wrote back and told him that it wasn't my place to dispute with him at his reading, and closed by telling him that he'd left me only two options, to leave or to punch him out. And I finished by saying that maybe I made the wrong choice!

Have you corresponded since?
Naomi Clark, who runs the Poetry Center in San Jose, got us back together. She and her husband brought Bly and his wife to our house and we had a fine evening together. I have great respect for him.

Any other literary feuds in your seventy years?
Well, there was my confrontation with James Dickey back in the early sixties. He reviewed *The Crooked Lines of God* for the *Sewanee Review,* putting it down very forcefully. It came at a time when I felt that I had to reply, as the Beat Generation was running out of steam. His put-down was actually as much against the Beat Generation as it was against me personally. I can't remember exactly what kind of letter I wrote to the journal, but I left myself open somehow and he swooped in with his reply. I was put in a position where I had to wind up my long right arm and let him have it from the ecclesiastical heights in a second letter. I shouldn't have done it—I stormed with the wrath of God. There was nothing much he could say, but I was really out of order to hit him from the sacred sector.

Later I began to feel guilty, as I did after an earlier controversy with *Poetry,* which was one of the stumbling blocks of my career. I felt remorse, and began to beat my breast. I wrote him a letter and quoted Hardy's poem, saying that like the two soldiers if we had been able to sit down over a beer we'd have had a nice toast together, but as it was we shot at each other. He was in Italy at the time, and eventually he wrote a jubilant letter in reply, which I greatly appreciated. I let matters rest there because I knew there were deep aesthetic divisions between us, as well as cultural and attitudinal differences, but I should have replied. He took my silence amiss, feeling that I had been insincere in my gesture. I just didn't know how to handle the deeper issues, and that was that.

What was the problem with Poetry?

The scene in the late thirties was heavily dominated by the Proletarian movement, which might readily translate into the Communist Party. The party was riding very high then. The struggle against fascism was just starting, and the communists seemed to have the only answer to it. They had the bulwark of the Soviets, tremendous prestige, the intellectual elite, and so forth. Many of the great liberal minds who were later disillusioned in those early years were very hopeful.

Communism wasn't a problem for me, but proletarianism was. I wasn't writing proletarian poetry; I was writing nature poetry, as well as trying to find my way into the religious dimension. Before she died, Harriet Monroe accepted a couple of my poems, but it took years before they were published because of the backlog. When they finally appeared, Morton Zabel was editor; then he left. I started sending in my work, but the poems just kept coming back, as by this time *Poetry* was publishing a lot of proletarian verse. Subject matter seemed to dominate the selection. To prove my hunch was right, I concocted a hoax. I wrote a proletarian-sounding poem, then wrote a cover letter saying I was a fruit worker between Imperial Valley and Yuba City, that I'd drift into cities and see *Poetry* in libraries. I used my mother's maiden name, and scrawled the thing out on a piece of binder paper with a stub pencil. They accepted it! This didn't really prove anything, but it implied so much. I sent another in, and they accepted that also. But as I said, I felt remorse and sent a letter of apology. Needless to say, I never got into the magazine again.

Do you submit unsolicited work to other journals?

Almost never anymore. I should do it, and in fact if I'd done it from the start I'd be further ahead in terms of career. Not vocation, as that has handled itself. I've been far more attuned to vocation than to career, though because career is my weakness I've spent a lot more psychic energy, and ego energy, there than on vocation. It has been so up and down, so erratic, that it's driven me frantic. My introverted relationship to God and women has been harmonious, fruitful, and developed, and I should be content. But I've got this inferior-complex relationship to the world which is very painful; far too much time worrying about my rank in the poetic pantheon.

Why didn't you send out work early on?

I started that way just like everyone else. I just found out that for me the rejection slips kept interfering with the creative process, so I stopped. It took up far too much time, far too much psychic energy. In fact, when I had a hundred copies of my second book, *San Joaquin,* I simply gave copies to friends rather than sending any out for review. *Poetry* was the only exception. But my advice to younger poets is if you can do it, do it.

Do you read much work by younger poets?
No, not at all. I think it's typical of poets in old age that they only read their contemporaries and show little interest in what's coming from behind. I feel better about my insularity having seen people like Eliot go through the same thing, expressing a profound obliviousness to younger writers' work. It seems pretty natural.

Are there any contemporaries who you think are doing interesting work?
Robert Duncan comes immediately to mind. Also, I was happy that Carolyn Kizer received the Pulitzer Prize, as she's the second West Coast poet to receive one. We're starting to gain on them! Some of the people in the Bay Area didn't take that as well as they should have. Thomas Parkinson called me up for my signature on a letter trying to get an award for Robert. I'm just glad that a West Coast poet got it.

Though she seems very much part of the East Coast group. She's always at conferences, in American Poetry Review, *and so on.*
Well, yes. And for years she was a wheel in the NEA. Probably Duncan should have won. You know, after the Ekbert Fass biography of Duncan appeared, a lot of questions I'd had about him were answered. I think that the study ensures him a much stronger place in our literature. Somehow, when you get a man's life in front of you it makes a profound difference. My own orientation has always been substantially biographical in terms of poetry. I know that's against New Critical precepts. When New Directions published their Poet of the Month series and wanted to include photographs, Randall Jarrell balked at it, which was the Modernist position. It was a reaction against the excessive biographical interest of the Victorians, who let their judgment of the work be swayed by their view of the life. But I know that my life stands behind my work in an archetypal way I can't renounce, and so does Robert's.

Is it important for younger poets to read a lot of poetry?
Can you keep them from it? They read everything that comes out, always trying to relate themselves to it. After a while they get to know, however,

and seem to lose that point of curiosity. The attention shifts to your rank with your peers, and this you never get over. Read the biography of Stevens or Williams and watch how they jockey for position right up to the end of their lives.

Why?

I take it to be another archetypal factor, not a blemish. It's part of the creative process, writing to the sense of your time and the sense of the leading voices. The future is blank. The past, however, comes up to a burning point of consciousness, which is you, and you keep looking around to find your level. It's a little bit like a swimming race—you are swimming against both your time and your competition. You see this in the ovum and the sperm. Each sperm jockeys for position to score with big mama, and it's archetypal in that sense. We are all sperm of God swimming toward the great ovum of the future.

This is important because the way the artist goes determines the direction of consciousness. The artist isn't just in there beating his or her gums, but rather struggling for the potentiality of the whole race as a measure of the future. The artist can't afford to rest just because of the creation of a well-rounded work; the drive must keep on to the last inch of being.

So when you write, is it for a particular audience or yourself?

I write for the past. For Shakespeare and Milton, Homer and Dante. For Jeffers. The voices that shape you are the voices you listen to and work for. I don't write for Stevens or Williams. I don't write for Zukofsky or Olson. I write for Duncan, but I don't get his whole attention because he's beating out a different course.

Of all my peers, Robert is probably the closest to me. I don't have the points of contact with him that I've got with Bly—he's neither a Christian nor a Jungian. We are poets, though, and I feel close to him on that level in a way I can't feel close to Bly. I honor Bly, but there is no ring of identity. This is odd in that there are even antipathetical points in our relationship. Duncan is homosexual, and I get no insight from this. Also, there is a rivalry between us which sometimes surfaces. For instance, when my manuscript collection went to the Bancroft Library at U.C. Berkeley, there was a large public celebration and reading at Wheeler Hall on campus. Robert went and he was so jealous it was painful. He sat in the audience with a young gay poet on either side, and at the end of my reading when the audience rose to its feet, Robert didn't budge. He kept the two of them nailed down, too. Afterwards he could hardly speak to me, he was so pissed off. He has given a lot more to Berkeley than I ever have, and he was understandably angry that I should be honored that way, before him.

Duncan is published by New Directions, you were, Snyder is, and you are all more or less from the same area. How did that come about?
Through Kenneth Rexroth. He fostered the San Francisco movement which was an entering wedge. He had a strong connection with James Laughlin before we ever met him. My book was published by New Directions in the forties, and I can honestly say Rexroth discovered me. He sold Laughlin on me, and I owe him a great debt for that. Jeffers was my ideal; Rexroth was my mentor, my manager. Eventually, because of a personal problem we had a falling out which never did get straightened out properly. It has been painful for me. I was committed to his program, but I couldn't fulfill what he expected of me. I should have taken more care, but it was impossible.

Rexroth saw me as an autochthon, a nativist in the American tradition of Sandburg, Jeffers, Henry Miller. When William Stafford wrote his introduction to *The Achievement of Brother Antonius,* a kind of brief anthology of my poetry, he tried to place me more in line with the prevailing, antinativist aesthetic, and that made Rexroth very angry. It denied everything he had written about me. When I honored Stafford's introduction, he was upset. But it was more complex than that. His biographer told me that she felt that when Rexroth talked about me he talked about the best he hoped for himself. That's high praise, and in that sense I truly was his son. But like all sons and fathers our relationship was tangled.

Would you say that he was pretty much single-handedly responsible for the San Francisco Renaissance?
Sure. Duncan of course labored hard at it, but he was too young. He just didn't have Rexroth's stature. He was not a polemicist, which was one of Rexroth's greatest strengths. Ginsberg also, whereas both Kerouac and Duncan were the writers. Rexroth got the thing started in San Francisco, then Ginsberg took it back east and sold it to *Time.* Kerouac and his group wrote for ten years before the Beat Generation emerged, and it was Rexroth who made the difference.

Over the years have your work habits changed?
I don't think so.

Do you write on a typewriter?

With a pen for two or three drafts. I generally go to the typewriter when I want to see what the configuration of the poem is going to be. But first I have to get the rhythm worked out. I don't see any reason to write poetry on the typewriter; in fact, the whole idea seems ludicrous to me.

And where do you write?

Right in the family. I've got a studio, but I use it for printing or typing. I find that the hatching process is right there in the morning in front of the fireplace.

What about notebooks?

I keep a dream journal. I've been keeping it for a long time, and fairly regularly.

And do you use it in your poetry?

Often. In fact, I think I used it pretty extensively in the *Masks of Drought* poems. Often I'll go into the dream atmosphere in order to get the poem under way.

You mentioned printing. What is the relationship between your printing and your poetry?

It's part of the struggle for consummation. Going back to the analogy of the sperm and the ovum, it's another dimension that the poem goes through in order to achieve apotheosis.

Which means . . .

I'm not satisfied with a poem until I see it perfectly printed. I'm not satisfied until the idea is perfectly articulated, perfectly expressed, and perfectly printed. That's as near to beatitude as I can carry it. When I first got into printing during the war my idea was to write my books, print them, and make a life as a poet-craftsman. I hoped to leave behind me a work of coherence. But when I converted I moved into a different frame of reference and began to worry about my egocentricity. I began to take on printing projects outside my own work, and these turned out to be my "masterpieces." The only thing I do regret is that I couldn't do my own collected poems. I planned the project a few years ago, made a start, but the thing fell through. It was a great disappointment to me.

If I had my life to live over again, I'd develop my artistic capacity more fully in terms of my woodcuts. Then with the hand-press, I'd try for coherence, book by book, section by section. I would establish the folio format from the start, so at the end it could all be bound together. But after all, I didn't even know what I was going to write, let alone the rest of it. Still, maybe it gives some idea of my priorities, even if I couldn't accomplish it.

First Winter Storm

All day long the clouds formed in the peaks,
Screening the crags,
While the pines stared through the mist.

Late-afternoon the sky hung close and black,
And when the darkness settled down,
The first large drops rapped at the roof.
In the night the wind came up and drove the rain,
Pounded at the walls with doubled fists,
And clamored in the chimney
Till I felt the fear run down my back
And grip me as I lay.

But in the morning when I looked,
The sky was clear,
And all along the creeks
The cottonwoods stood somnolent and still
Beneath the sun.

A Canticle to the Waterbirds

Clack your beaks you cormorants and kittiwakes,
North on those rock-croppings finger-jutted into the rough Pacific surge;
You migratory terns and pipers who leave but the temporal clawtrack
    written on sandbars there of your presence;
Grebs and pelicans; you comber-picking scoters and you shorelong gulls;
All you keepers of the coastline north of here to the Mendocino beaches;
All you beyond upon the cliff-face thwarting the surf at Hecate Head;

Hovering the under-surge where the cold Columbia grapples at the bar;
North yet to the Sound, whose islands float like a sown flurry of chips
    upon the sea;
Break wide your harsh and salt-encrusted beaks unmade for song
And say a praise up to the Lord.

And you freshwater egrets east in the flooded marshlands skirting the sea-
    level rivers, white one-legged watchers of shallows;
Broad-headed kingfishers minnow-hunting from willow stems on
    meandering valley sloughs;
You too, you herons, blue and supple-throated, stately, taking the air
    majestical in the sunflooded San Joaquin,
Grading down on your belted wings from the upper lights of sunset,
Mating over the willow clumps or where the flatwater rice fields shimmer;
You killdeer, high night-criers, far in the moon-suffusion sky;
Bitterns, sand-waders, all shore-walkers, all roost-keepers,
Populates of the 'dobe cliffs of the Sacramento:
Open your water-dartling beaks,
And make a praise up to the Lord.

For you hold the heart of His mighty fastnesses,
And shape the life of His indeterminate realms.
You are everywhere on the lonesome shores of His wide creation.
You keep seclusion where no man may go, giving Him praise;
Nor may a woman come to lift like your cleaving flight her clear
    contralto song
To honor the spindrift gifts of His soft abundance.
You sanctify His hermitage rocks where no holy priest may kneel to
    adore, nor holy nun assist;
And where His true communion-keepers are not enabled to enter.

And well may you say His praises, birds, for your ways
Are verved with the secret skills of His inclinations,
And your habits plaited and rare with the subdued elaboration of His
    intricate craft;
Your days intent with the direct astuteness needful for His outworking,
And your nights alive with the dense repose of His infinite sleep.
You are His secretive charges and you serve His secretive ends,
In His clouded, mist-conditioned stations, in His murk,
Obscure in your matted nestings, immured in His limitless ranges.

He makes you penetrate through dark interstitial joinings of His
    thicketed kingdoms,
And keep your concourse in the deeps of His shadowed world.

Your ways are wild but earnest, your manners grave,
Your customs carefully schooled to the note of His serious mien.
You hold the prime condition of His clean creating,
And the swift compliance with which you serve His minor means
Speaks of the constancy with which you hold Him.
For what is your high flight forever going home to your first beginnings,
But such a testament to your devotion?
You hold His outstretched world beneath your wings, and mount upon
    His storms,
And keep your sheer wind-lidded sight upon the vast perspectives of His
    mazy latitudes.

But mostly it is your way you bear existence wholly within the context of
    His utter will and are untroubled.
Day upon day you do not reckon, nor scrutinize tomorrow, nor multiply
    the nightfalls with a rash concern,
But rather assume each instant as warrant sufficient of His final seal.
Wholly in Providence you spring, and when you die you look on death in
    clarity unflinched,
Go down, a clutch of feather ragged upon the brush;
Or drop on water where you briefly lived, found food,
And now yourselves made food for His deep current-keeping fish, and
    then are gone:
Is left but the pinion-feather spinning a bit on the uproil
Where lately the dorsal cut clear air.

You leave a silence. And this for you suffices, who are not of the
    ceremonials of man,
And hence are not made sad to now forgo them.
Yours is of another order of being, and wholly it compels.
But may you, birds, utterly seized in God's supremacy,
Austerely living under His austere eye—
Yet may you teach a man a necessary thing to know,
Which has to do of the strict conformity that creaturehood entails,
And constitutes the prime commitment all things share.
For God has given you the imponderable grace to *be* His verification,

Outside the mulled incertitude of our forensic choices;
That you, our lessers in the rich hegemony of Being,
May serve as testament to what a creature is,
And what creation owes.

Curlews, stilts and scissortails, beachcomber gulls,
Wave-haunters, shore-keepers, rockhead-holders, all cape-top vigilantes,
Now give God praise.
Send up the strict articulation of your throats,
And say His name.

The Way of Life and the Way of Death

I
Mexico: and a wind on the mesa
Blowing its way out of sluggish centers,
Coaxing a tropical fragrance,
The moist rains of December.

Mangoes and rum, the bright
Blades of poinsettias.

A soft call of birds in the forest,
A sound of women dipping water at wells,
The taunting of little children.

I think of poinsettias out of the earth,
Red as a rose in the teeth of a woman,
Black as the hair of the Virgin of Guadalupe,
As shaken with passion as the spilled Blood of Christ.

I split my heart on the blood of Mexico.
I have nailed myself to the Mexican cross.

II
I have nailed myself to the Mexican cross,
The flint knife of her beauty.

I hunger the solace of mango fruit,
The woman-flesh of the guava.

Desire splits on the quick of poinsettias,
Stung to the rake of Mexican nettle.

I am shambled in trees,
Thirsting the riverstone of God,
The waterwells of passion.

Her limbs! Her limbs! the witchery of her excellent legs!
The Mexican glimmer along the lips!
The clicking teeth of her laughter!

Nailed. Split. Crucified. Scourged.

Shrieked on the cross,
Flayed to the slump of the devastated heart,
My body blazes.

III
My body blazes.
In the pound of blood all meaning moves,
All movement dazes.

She flashes her eyes.
Mexico shudders under the leaves,
Shaking the branches.

In the lithe ripple of whispering feet,
In the clear spurt of laughter.

In the high peal of rivering lips,
The stunned lurch of passion.

I am agonized on the Mexican cross
In the hopeless fashion.

I cry. I cry.

Will she burn me out,
Char the body ashen?

Let the white hope live,
Make the black hope die.

I suffer the lance-thrust under the rib:
   One pierce of her eye.

IV

I suffer the lance.
I faint on the sexual cross
Of this Mexican madness.

I am fierced. My flesh is stitched
With a riddle of lips.

On the blade of the crimson poinsettia
She has gashed my side.

With one wound of her lips,
With one of the little wantonnesses
She works with her fingers.

The flesh of the mango fruit!
The ravishing meat of the guava!

Why must God deny me?

Where is my boast?
What has come of my strife?

On the Mexican cross,
Between the two thieves of her eyes,

I nail my life.

V

I nail my life.

Am laid in the tomb of immolation.

Wrapped in silence,
Packed about with aloes and spices,
Her pledge suffices.

I rest in rock.

Hidden behind a slab of stone,
Shielded and safe from the curse of soldiers.

I await her word,
The syllable of grave inflection,
Salving the sting of crimson poinsettias,
Healing the wound of the Mexican cross.

I dream the dawn of the longest night:
The one resurrection.

Blackbird Sundown

High Ridge Ranch: back of the barn
A live-oak-thicket, and redwing blackbirds
In the late afternoon. They cluster on fence posts,
Twig stems, barbed wire, telephone lines,
Any proximate perch. Their brilliant epaulets
Gleam in the fading light,
Vivid scarlet on glistening black.
Intensely alive they frolic and strut,
Chatter the twanging blackbird tongue,
Jubilant in the bird-loud evening.

A sudden hush. In the suspension of sound
Silence drops to stunned terror.
Then all explodes, every bird for itself,
Up, down, out and away.

     For over the ridge,
Her shoulders of flight massively outstretched,
Her hunched body tense with hunger, gravid with need,
The Great Horned Owl glides implacably in,
Wide staring eyes fixed on her prey.

Instantly every bird recovers. Springing back to the defense
They converge on her, a racket of protest, a squall of imprecation.

Undeterred, she spans the yard, plunges into the oak thicket.
Behind her swarm the defenders, the stiletto beaks
Stabbing and yanking, a flurry of snatched feathers
Ragging her sides.

     In a trice she emerges,
A half-dead fledgling gripped in each fist,
Her malignant face swinging right and left
As she scans the yard, glaring down her confronters.

Again the redwings close on her, railing and scolding,
Their punishing beaks a fury of reprisal.

She shrugs them aside, contemptuously,
And pauses a moment—ugly, umbrageous, triumphant.

Then she takes off, her dread profile
Humped in departure. Insolently unhurried
She clears the corral, skims the fence, and is gone.

And with her going the dusk drops. Where a moment before
Late light glimmered, now darkness
Swoops on the land.

                        The redwings
Circle and descend, seeking their roosts,
Pulling their shattered world back together,
Settling into the oak thicket, drifting toward sleep.

Out in the woods the she-owl's mate
Hoots once, hoots twice, his soft tattoo
Muffling the hush. She does not reply.
Her silence is the answer of the hearkening dead,
Listening for life, when life is no more.
Over the ridge the darkness shuts like a wing;
The earth-chill tightens; the claw moon
Talons the west.

5. Thom Gunn

"For a sign of other than love"

Thom Gunn, who has lived in northern California since 1954, was born in Gravesend, Kent, in England in 1929. He served in the British Army from 1948 to 1950, and took a B.A. degree from Trinity College, Cambridge, three years later. Gunn went to Stanford on a fellowship in 1954, where he studied under Yvor Winters, and since 1958 has taught at the University of California, Berkeley, where he now teaches part-time. His first full-length book of poetry, *Fighting Terms,* appeared in 1954, and since then he has published eight additional collections, including *My Sad Captains and Other Poems, Touch,* and most recently, *The Passages of Joy.* Gunn's *Selected Poems, 1950–75* was published in both America and England in 1979. His awards include *Poetry*'s Levinson Prize (1955), the Maugham Award (1959), a Rockefeller Award (1966), and a Guggenheim Fellowship (1971).

"I am a rather derivative poet," Thom Gunn has written. "I learn what I can from whom I can, mostly consciously. I borrow heavily from my reading because I take my reading seriously: it is part of my total experience and I base most of my poetry on my experience. I do not apologize for being derivative because I think a lot of other poets work in this way. . . . Specifically, I have found usable modes in the work of other poets, and I have tried to invent some myself. Moreover, it has not been of primary interest to develop a unique poetic personality, and I rejoice in Eliot's lovely remark that art is the escape from personality. This lack in me has troubled some readers."

I'd like to begin by pointing out the obvious about myself, which I suppose is the obvious about any poet. It's something that the poet himself doesn't realize at the time. When you start writing seriously, or when people start actually looking at what you've done—I was twenty-one before anyone took anything I'd written seriously—you think what you are doing is unique. You think that what you are doing has never been done before, never been said in that way. Actually, though you don't know it, this is the time that you are conforming most closely to the current fashions (unless, of course, you are a Blake or a Rimbaud, and there aren't many of those around). What most poets do when they start is fit in marvelously with the current fashion. But they simply do not know it.

When I started writing I began in rhyme and meter. Everyone else was doing the same thing in England at that time, as they were also on the east coast of America—James Merrill, Anthony Hecht, Donald Hall. Even Robert Bly didn't start with free verse; he started by writing like Robert Lowell.

If we are able to, we suppress our early writing, and Bly fortunately has done that. All these people are of my generation, or roughly so.

Students of literature speak misleadingly about influence. "Are you influenced by so and so?" they ask, or "Who are you influenced by?" It's as if one were willingly or consciously influenced. Most of the time when I'm writing I don't think, "Well, I'm sounding like John Donne here, or Yvor Winters, or Robert Lowell." Rather, I think that I'm sounding like nobody who has ever written on my subject before. It's only afterwards that you realize with a feeling of chagrin, if you realize it at all, that you got the intonation, the tone, the music, even the vocabulary from someone else. Of course there may be occasions where you deliberately set out to write in a tradition of some sort, or with deliberate reference to some writer, but those are special cases.

So when I started writing I wrote like all the other young poets of my generation. I didn't realize it, and it was a good thing that I didn't. I was much influenced by the people I read as an undergraduate. I mentioned John Donne already, and not fortuitously. He really opened my eyes. It was exciting to read him.

So you read a lot when you were young?
I was a fairly sophisticated reader as a teenager, but I wasn't taught all that well. I had tried to read Donne in my teens, but I just couldn't quite get through to him. But during my first year as an undergraduate his poetry suddenly took and began to influence my own, as you can see if you bother to look at my early poetry. I say "bother to" because most of it is really pretty juvenile stuff.

After my three years at university I got a creative writing fellowship to Stanford in California. I didn't know what I was in for. I'd done it for the free trip. There was somebody at the other end who was supposed to take charge of me named Yvor Winters, but I'd hardly read anything by Winters. I can be forgiven not knowing who he was because nothing by him was in print in England.

Was this a general problem, getting hold of work by American writers in England?
I couldn't get hold of the obvious American poets, let alone the less obvious ones. If I had wanted to read William Carlos Williams in 1954, I'd have had to go to some extremely well-stocked library with American editions. There were no English editions of Williams. No English editions of Hart

Crane. The first *selected* poems by Wallace Stevens came out in England in 1954. The English were very late in publishing the American poets, and so naturally I didn't know anything about Yvor Winters.

In any case, I got to Stanford and Winters was a formidable mind with a very closely worked-out theory of poetry, against which I first rebelled then began to understand. So I could say that I was considerably influenced by him for a year or two. Then I was on my own.

Why does poetry seem to hold very little interest in the United States?
Oh, but it does. If you look at other societies earlier in history you will find that poetry sells here awfully well in comparison. A lot of people come to poetry readings, which barely existed in either the nineteenth century or the earlier part of this one. We have a large public hungry for poetry both here and in Europe. It's nothing like the public for the novel or for the performing arts, but it never was. A very unusual situation—unusual in the history of poetry—obtained in Elizabethan England when plays for popular entertainment were written in poetic form. So in a sense poetry *seemed* to be a popular form, but it wasn't the poetry which was popular. It was the swordfights and the action. You go to see Macbeth and you see swordfights and ghosts. You don't see poetry.

I really do think that the poetry public is large and hungry right now. There are an extraordinary number of first books of poetry published in New York every year. For some reason I get sent a great many of them, though I do little reviewing. These are books by major publishing houses—Harpers, Random House, Farrar, Straus & Giroux—and I must say that many of these books are not very exciting. It's amazing. I just don't understand it. In my arrogance I think I know one or two poets I can name, though you probably wouldn't have heard of them, who are quite exciting but don't yet have first books out. But these large houses just aren't publishing exciting new poets. Maybe this is just a product of my time of life, however; maybe thirty years ago Robert Frost said the same thing about his juniors, and I'm just being a sour old man. But the *audience* is there, and they are looking.

Who are the two poets?
August Kleinzahler, who is from New Jersey and now lives in San Francisco, and James Powell. Very good poets. And I'd like to add Tim Steele and Ray Oliver.

What about the distinction between American poets and English poets?
Does that hold?

I'd say that even today there is a considerable difference. The English poets are still in love with meter and rhyme, and you don't get many of them writing good free verse. On the other hand, you don't get many American poets writing good meter and rhyme. There is a loss on both sides. British poetry and American poetry do seem to have grown much farther apart during the last ten or fifteen years. For a brief period, in the 1950s, they had been coming closer together and enriching each other, but they don't seem to be learning from each other at the moment, or even have much of anything in common. I don't quite know why.

You mention meter and rhyme, and thinking back over a number of the poets we've spoken with, you are by far the most interested in traditional structures and rhythms. When you write more formal verse, do you begin with a particular structure or metric and then come up with a subject?

That's an interesting question, though I don't think it usually works that way. I say "usually" because obviously if an Elizabethan were writing a sonnet sequence, once he started into the sequence in a deliberate way all the poems would necessarily be sonnets. In my own case, and I think this holds true for other poets who are interested in more formal structures today, the decision comes at a very mysterious stage near the beginning of the poem, when you are messing around with words and images in a kind of random way. I don't usually think, "Well yes, Thom, today you'll write in a particular meter." I suppose what happens is that you start trying out a line or two, and sometimes it seems to have the feel of free verse, other times the feel of metrical verse.

Feel?

Yes. One of the best things I know about the difference between free verse and meter is an essay by D. H. Lawrence, sometimes printed under the title "Poetry and the Present." It was the introduction to his collected poems published in America in 1920. That book contained about half metrical poems and half free-verse poems, and in his essay he tries to explain the difference between them. It's a piece worth reading and rereading, because at first you think Lawrence is just being Lawrence again. As usual, he's got that wonderful, enthusiastic phrasing, but on a single reading you are not quite sure what it means. If you scrutinize that essay, however, you'll see it says a great deal. His argument, to summarize it, is that free verse is poetry of the present, while metrical verse is poetry of the future and the past.

Metrical verse is poetry of the future and the past. Well, I don't know what he means by the future, though I can see it as having to do with the past, even if it's simply past of a few moments ago. There is something more settled, formed, shaped, in the way our more decided thoughts are. You think, "I'm going to go into that room and tell her off," but before you go in you consider a few good phrases. In a sense, that's more metrical. It's certainly not spontaneous. Obviously, there are many exceptions, and obviously this way of talking applies best to Lawrence's own poetry. But it does apply rather well to William Carlos Williams's poetry also.

So in other words, you "feel" your way into the poem.
Yes, exactly. I feel my way into any particular poem. I couldn't have put it any better. I feel my way into the elements of the poem.

Of course, it's not always so undecided as that. Sometimes you have a little plan in mind. There was one time in the mid-sixties, for example, that if you'd walk around Haight Street in San Francisco you'd come across a lot of dope dealers, usually very young and offering an amazing assortment of drugs. I was fascinated by this because it reminded me of how in early societies most selling was done on the street, by people carrying their wares on trays around their necks. Particularly at the end of the sixteenth century, poets seemed interested in developing rudimentary street cries into elaborate songs. Herrick's "Cherry Ripe," for example. The seller would call out "Cherry ripe!" so that you'd know that cherries were being sold in that part of the market, and Herrick developed it into a wonderful song. So I decided to write a poem for dope dealers called "Street Song." Obviously there my decision initially was to use rhyme and meter because I wanted it to be a song, and songs pretty much always involve rhyme and meter.

This is why rhyme and meter are never going to die out, by the way. Even if every poet in the whole country were to write in free verse, still those tunes would go on. Even lousy tunes, lousy songs on the juke boxes. People want to listen to songs, and song is the origin of meter. I don't suspect, with the sophistication I see in this room, that the people here are prejudiced against meter as such, but sometimes people are. Young students especially often complain that it's old-fashioned and confining. It comes too pat for them. But if you ask them to think of meter in terms of a tune, you'll find it's a way of getting around it for them. We think of tunes as being flexible, which of course meter is once you get used to it.

Do your individual volumes have structure?

Yes. A thematic structure. I think I got the idea from studying Baudelaire's *Flowers of Evil,* which is arranged thematically, when I was an undergraduate. I must have been influenced by that. If you take another kind of poet, somebody like Duncan who doesn't believe in that kind of organization at all, you get something different. Duncan arranges his work chronologically, which is its own kind of fitting together.

Looking through Selected Poems, *it seemed to me that you use military figures often. I sense it symbolizes to you a person at a certain stage in life.*

I've written about this somewhere in my prose because I was curious about the same thing. The figure has two origins. One comes from my childhood: I was of a generation which grew up during World War II, and everywhere there were figures in uniform. The other is from a few years after the war ended, I too had to do national service, and I went into the British Army acutely aware of my unsoldierliness. I think that figure, particularly in my early books, came to stand in for all role players. Wearing a uniform is much like playing a role. Is that man wearing it really a soldier acting like a soldier, or is he really a rather awkward boy of eighteen in a soldier's uniform having to march around with the rest of them but with killing the last thing on his mind?

When you began you mentioned Yvor Winters, how you were first put off by his "system," then attracted to it. Might you clarify that a bit?

I was afraid someone would catch me on that. It's such a long answer, but I'll try.

Winters was a poet who started out in his twenties with very precocious and effective free-verse poetry. In fact, he wrote most of it at places very close to here. When he was about twenty-one and recovering from tuberculosis, he came to New Mexico for the climate. He had quarreled with his father and had nothing to live on, and thus he started to work as a schoolteacher at what was then the coal-mining small town of Madrid. During that period he wrote some amazing free verse, which is still not all that well known.   Toward the end of his twenties, he became increasingly dissatisfied with his free verse, however, comparing it to the poetry of those he most admired—Shakespeare, Ben Jonson, Thomas Hardy, Valéry—people who had always written in meter, and often rhyme as well. He felt that what he had been writing was only a partial poetry, compared to the kind of completeness which they got into their work. So he trained himself—imagine the difficulty after writing verse for almost a decade—to write metrically, and wrote that way for the rest of his life. He thought of meter as being capable of holding material and emotions of greater complexity, of having greater control over them, and thus doing far more than free verse was able.

You can see the kind of thing he's talking about if you look at a poem by Gary Snyder. Snyder is a poet whose early work I greatly admire, and a poet who Winters probably never read. It's very interesting that in most of Gary Snyder's poetry you do not find the verb used in its finite form, but rather in the present participle. Thus, instead of saying "I swim in the lake," he'll say "swimming in the lake." Doesn't that somehow sound more like modern poetry now? Modern poetry doesn't say "I swim in the lake," but gives you a fragment instead. Now there are obvious advantages to this. It seems more present, not so self-enclosed. The action doesn't begin or end, but instead is in a continual present. However, there is less control of that continual present, more danger of what Winters would have called a "reverie," a perpetual kind of half-consciousness. My description is all somehow not adequate to Winters, however, and I apologize for that.

What was it then that caused you to rebel from Winters?
I wanted to do the other thing as well. I wanted to be able to write that silly reverie stuff as well. Even though I'm fifty-five now and should know better, I still want to be able to do everything.

To change the subject a bit, do you see anything much new happening in American poetry at the moment?
Well, there is always talent around. I don't really see a new movement of concentrated energy, like the Beats in the mid-fifties, for example. There was a real impulse in Snyder and Ginsberg and Corso and their friends. They really thought they had hold of something.

The Language poets?
I suppose I should tread carefully there, as you've had one or two of them speaking to you before me. But I will venture to say that they don't have much chance of appealing to an audience other than that of fellow Language poets. Or so it seems to me.

But I'm generally depressed by the stuff that comes out of the larger New York publishers, and this has no reference of course to the Language poets. There are a lot of new books that appear each year, as I said earlier. Something came to me by someone called Brad Leithauser, who has a kind of following right now, *Thousands of Fireflies*. Then there is Amy Clampitt's book *The Kingfisher*, which has done quite well indeed. But both books strike me as having no pressure behind them. I suppose what I want of new poetry is some kind of pressure.

Emotional pressure?
Not just that, not just what you get from Sylvia Plath, but also the kind of pressure that you get behind a Williams. A pressure that makes things clean and clear and startling. A lot of the best Williams still seems startling on the page, doesn't it. And this is because of some kind of pressure beyond the mere emotional. I do find that lacking in a lot of the books published by large houses. Probably our salvation will come from the small publishers, like it always has before. I really do think that the large publishers mean well, but they just don't seem to make good choices.

What kind of education should a young poet get?
That's an interesting question, and of course every poet will give you a different answer. Keats, who did not go to a university, decided that he was going to go systematically through the English poets, which he did to his benefit. Gary Snyder has said that a poet should get learned in at least one discipline that has nothing to do with poetry, a body of knowledge against which that Western knowledge he is born with can bounce against. And Eliot believed that no one preparing to be a poet should ever study English in a university. But obviously you've got to pick up that knowledge from somewhere. I studied English, and maybe that makes me overliterary a poet. Quite possibly it does. Still, everyone should read as much poetry as possible. But for education, you really know yourself what you need; your curiosity takes you in the right direction. Snyder's curiosity took him in the direction of Zen Buddhism, and that then became the material for his poetry, as well as one of its reference points.

Speaking of your reading of poetry, you seem to consistently bring reference to Homer, and especially Achilles.
I'm hardly alone in this. The same could be said of Ezra Pound, for example. I'm reminded of a wonderful anecdote someone told me about Stravinsky. He was being interviewed by some dumb interviewer in his old age, and the interviewer asked him, "Mr. Stravinsky, who have you been influenced by?" The composer paused a moment, then exploded—"I wasn't born in a

field you know!" He meant, of course, that he had inherited the whole of world culture.

I'm not alone among poets in having been influenced by the stories of Homer. You are right; they are an important reference point for me. But even a poet like Snyder who decided early on to get rid of *Western* reference points, in fact incorporated simply another body of reference points, Amer-Indian lore, into his work instead of the well-worked lore of the Greeks and Romans. If one doesn't have either, I suppose there is a real danger of being impoverished. This isn't to say that one can't write directly without literary antecedents, or literary references. William Carlos Williams did much of the time, and successfully. But even he is not entirely unliterary. The further you go into Williams the more you see how his reading comes into it. As I tried to say earlier, reading is part of your experience.

I'm struck by the two different ways you present femaleness. In your treatment of Odysseus and Circe, Circe is always converting very nice boys into animals.
She wasn't a nice woman.

Right. But in your poem "Odysseus on Hermes" you seem interested, as does Robert Duncan at times, in the contrast between the elevation of these two young men, for example, and a not nice female in the distance. Yet at other times you seem to really present a multifaceted female con-sciousness.
You have to realize that sometimes one's subject matter dictates. If you take a story like the *Odyssey*, you are stuck with certain facts. Circe was a witch-goddess, and nobody could make her terribly sympathetic. Actually, Odys-seus had a very good year with her, which they spent almost all in bed, or on whatever kind of ferns she had in her cave. But I've never thought of "Moly," for example, as being a misogynistic poem.

Maybe I'm thinking more of Homer himself in that context.
Well, there is Penelope, who is no pushover, and Nausikaa. (Did you know Samuel Butler had a theory that Nausikaa was the real authoress of the *Odyssey?*) Again, though, you have to remember that when you are speaking about sympathy toward the sexes, you have to be aware of the historical situation. Some things in Shakespeare are quite embarrassing now. Both Hotspur in *Henry IV* and Brutus in *Julius Caesar* have plans afoot; their wives ask what is occupying them and both husbands reply that women can't be

trusted with such knowledge, that they are too flighty. But you can't blame Shakespeare for not rising above *all* his age's assumptions. He rose above quite a few of them, after all. And he had some pretty strong women in other plays.

On this men/women question, I heard a talk by Tennessee Williams to a conference of all gay women, and he asked why he shouldn't have a perfect right to an access to what women feel?
He made the correct statement. An imaginative writer is supposed to have some imagination, after all. That is just the kind of sympathetic imagination that we expect from our writers.

Would you be willing to reveal who, in your poem "My Sad Captains," are the "men who, I thought, lived . . ."?
I have been asked this before, and there is no real answer. These are people I've admired: teachers, friends, relatives, other writers, people from history. Substitute your own.

Well, what struck me is the word men. *Why men and not women? But then I thought I shouldn't be thinking that way.*
But you should. That's the way language has changed since then. In 1959, when I wrote it, *men* indicated both sexes. The language is now in a very difficult state because one has to, if one is going to be fair and aware of one's audience's sensitivities, say things like "his or her," "men or women." But that is very clumsy. I think we are going to have to agree on something soon. There was a childhood writer I used to like a lot, and she'd get around this very well by saying "its." I don't see anything wrong in that! It might seem silly at first, but once we got used to it things would go along fine.

That does seem to be a real concern of the Language poets.
Yes. And, also, sometimes it just doesn't matter. Sometimes we are just being unduly polite when we say "his or her." If my line were, "They were men or women who I thought . . ." that wouldn't work.

You mentioned "Moly" earlier on. Can you talk about what you had in mind there?
Sure. I wanted the poem to be grotesque. It is a grotesque situation to find yourself coming out of sleep finding yourself becoming an animal. But what kind of animal is it? Is this leathery hide? Or feathery? Or scales? What

have I become? I know I'm not a man any longer. Bringing in sharks and parrots and crocodiles I wanted to emphasize the grotesque predicament of someone who has been given a magic potion.

When you teach workshops, do you make assignments in forms?
I teach two different kinds of writing classes at Berkeley. One is very elaborate and for beginners, for people who have never had a workshop and want to see if they can write poetry, short fiction, or short drama. I do give them some exercises, though not in forms, at least the way we've been using the term. I got a wonderful assignment from a novel by Richard Price, *The Breaks*. There a teacher tells his students to describe a transaction in a Greyhound bus station, and I've used that to good purpose to teach them dramatic writing. Then, fairly early in the term I tell them that they've got to give in three bodies of work to me—short stories, short plays, or groups of poems. Or they can give in a mixture of genres. My object in doing this is not simply to get work so I can give a grade, but to push the students. At that stage in one's life one simply needs to be pushed, to get out a lot of work and get through one's mistakes, to see how one can grow. It's an exciting and arduous course.

The other course I teach, and I must confess I'm less interested in it, is called "Advanced Poetry Writing." Graduates can be in it, though it's mainly juniors and seniors, and they've taken often up to three previous advanced workshops from other teachers at Berkeley. These students know what they want to do and don't need any of us to tell them, but understandably as they are students they'd like to get university credit for their writing. They might be imitating Robert Bly or John Ashbery, but who am I to tell them they'd be better off imitating me? If they are any good, they'll get through Ashbery or me and end up doing something of their own.

So creative writing courses have a value.
Yes, though of course ultimately the writing has to be done on your own. What I like is the elementary course, where I kick them out into the water. That's exciting, getting someone from nowhere to somewhere else. But they've got to find out for themselves whether or not they really are writers. You've got to feel the pressure of a certain kind of subject matter within your own life. It might be your everyday experience or your imagination, though more likely it's a combination of the two. But to be a writer you've got to feel that pressure working on your language and your rhythms, and you've got to work this out yourself.

One problem with advanced courses is that they can get too pleasant. I'm not a bad-tempered person and like things to be easy. It's very easy to have fifteen or twenty young people sitting around you, all very nice, and have them pick up a poem and say, "Oh, she's so good on that subject. This is such a nice poem. And Rob writes about eagles so well. Let's have another eagle poem, Rob!" Well, you can see how everything goes wrong here. Everyone gets so comfortable. Let's say they do have some talent—it should be more difficult for them, not just another eagle poem. Maybe they should tell Rob to try something different, extend himself a little. Ultimately you have to please yourself, not your friends. And for a writer, pleasing yourself is in the end more difficult as you are far less kind to yourself than your friends.

It seems to me that your poems have become increasingly erotic over time, and the eroticism, while certainly generalized to human affection, has become more overtly gay.
Well, I am gay. I suppose that the early nonappearance of overtly gay subject matter in my poetry had to do with the taboos, or even the laws of the time. It was very difficult being gay in the 1950s and 1960s; you didn't get jobs, for one thing. If you think things are hard now, just look back into the newspaper files to see what things people had to go through. So I think probably in my first few books I was just being discreet.

I never actually changed genders in the way some writers have. Once, in a Canadian gay newspaper, somebody accused me of having done this, and I wrote an indignant letter to him saying I hadn't. There are some dishonesties to which one does not stoop. In my own writing, I think the greater openness had something to do with gay liberation, maybe with the influence of San Francisco itself. I think more than anything else it had to do with my maturing in some way or other. And I have written an article about Robert Duncan in which I said that his example was of some help to me in this respect.

Do you think of your Hamm's Beer sign poem as erotic?
Oh no, I don't see that as erotic at all. It was a fascinating thing, however. It had to do with drugs, one of those extraordinary trips where you really don't set out to meet God, maybe don't even believe in him, but there he was anyway. What the LSD trip focused on at one point was this wonderful beer sign on top of the Hamm's brewery. In fact, almost as soon as I wrote about it, it got broken, then torn down. I seem to write about things and

then they vanish—I almost feel like a killer. There is a wonderful line in the film "Liquid Sky": "I've got a killer cunt," a woman says, because everyone she has sex with immediately vanishes. So maybe I've got a killer pen.

Anyway, this beer sign was a wonderful model of a huge beer glass, and you'd see it fill up as the lights went on, then empty. Unfortunately, it got stuck after a time and they could only blink it on and off. But it was for me, that day, a most extraordinary image of the whole created world, filling up with good things then draining out again. It was actually a rather pompous poem, though; one can get awfully pompous about one's acid trips. I got into implications of Heraclitus and all that.

Do you feel that your more recent work, say of the last ten or fifteen years, is somehow more personal than the earlier poetry?
When I was an undergraduate at Cambridge, I was the contemporary of a lot of people who would get very famous in the British theater: Peter Hall, Peter Wood, John Barton, and others. Almost as soon as they graduated they started to become very influential, particularly in Stratford in the production of Shakespeare's heroic theatre. At Cambridge as undergraduates these people were doing really astonishing performances of Shakespeare, and I'm sure it was an important influence on me. There I was in the 1950s thinking about heroic action, which is what I was trying to get to in my first book, *Fighting Terms.* Then I read Sartre, and I found a way of speaking about heroic action in terms of Sartrean choice. So I think the two things in combination have a lot to do with the subject matter of my first two books. After that, I began to get more interested in personal experience, though you have to remember that when you are young you just don't have so much personal experience to think about. At that time you madly want to fall in love so that you'll have some love poetry to write.

Another obvious question, why did you stay in America, and why the West Coast?
I love northern California, and almost as soon as I got there I knew it would be my home. I can't think of any good literary reasons.

Well, to put it a different way, which reviews do you pay more attention to, the American or the English?
Somebody called me a few years ago an "Anglo-American poet," and I'm in some ways a very unsatisfactory hybrid. I really don't think that I find many reviews on either side of the Atlantic very useful. It sounds unlikely, but

actually it's just as annoying to be liked for things you know aren't there as to be disliked for things you know are there. And then the gay press always gives me extraordinarily good reviews, but that's just because they like the fact that I'm gay. When I do get a really bright review, I deeply appreciate it. It sounds lofty to say all this, because when you are starting out you desperately want any kind of review. But as the years go by and you realize that almost any book published by a large press gets reviewed, you begin to get a lot more choosy.

On the Move

The blue jay scuffling in the bushes follows
Some hidden purpose, and the gust of birds
That spurts across the field, the wheeling swallows,
Have nested in the trees and undergrowth.
Seeking their instinct, or their poise, or both,
One moves with an uncertain violence
Under the dust thrown by a baffled sense
Or the dull thunder of approximate words.

On motorcycles, up the road, they come:
Small, black, as flies hanging in heat, the Boys,
Until the distance throws them forth, their hum
Bulges to thunder held by calf and thigh.
In goggles, donned impersonality,
In gleaming jackets trophied with the dust,
They strap in doubt—by hiding it, robust—
And almost hear a meaning in their noise.

Exact conclusion of their hardiness
Has no shape yet, but from known whereabouts
They ride, direction where the tires press.
They scare a flight of birds across the field:
Much that is natural, to the will must yield.
Men manufacture both machine and soul,
And use what they imperfectly control
To dare a future from the taken routes.

It is a part solution, after all.
One is not necessarily discord
On earth; or damned because, half animal,
One lacks direct instinct, because one wakes
Afloat on movement that divides and breaks.
One joins the movement in a valueless world,
Choosing it, till, both hurler and the hurled,
One moves as well, always toward, toward.

A minute holds them, who have come to go:
The self-defined, astride the created will
They burst away; the towns they travel through
Are home for neither bird nor holiness,
For birds and saints complete their purposes.
At worst, one is in motion; and at best,
Reaching no absolute, in which to rest,
One is always nearer by not keeping still.

Touch

You are already
asleep. I lower
myself in next to
you, my skin slightly
numb with the restraint
of habits, the patina of
self, the black frost
of outsideness, so that even
unclothed it is
a resilient chilly
hardness, a superficially
malleable, dead
rubbery texture.

You are a mound
of bedclothes, where the cat
in sleep braces

its paws against your
calf through the blankets,
and kneads each paw in turn.

Meanwhile and slowly
I feel a is it
my own warmth surfacing or
the ferment of your whole
body that in darkness beneath
the cover is stealing
bit by bit to break
down that chill.

   You turn and
hold me tightly, do
you know who
I am or am I
your mother or
the nearest human being to
hold on to in a
dreamed pogrom.

What I, now loosened,
sink into is an old
big place, it is
there already, for
you are already
there, and the cat
got there before you, yet
it is hard to locate.
What is more, the place is
not found but seeps
from our touch in
continuous creation, dark
enclosing cocoon round
ourselves alone, dark
wide realm where we
walk with everyone.

Rites of Passage

Something is taking place.
Horns bud bright in my hair.
My feet are turning hoof.
And Father, see my face
—Skin that was damp and fair
Is barklike and, feel, rough.

See Greytop how I shine.
I rear, break loose, I neigh
Snuffling the air, and harden
Towards a completion, mine.
And next I make my way
Adventuring through your garden.

My play is earnest now.
I canter to and fro.
My blood, it is like light.
Behind an almond bough,
Horns gaudy with its snow,
I wait live, out of sight.

All planned before my birth
For you, Old Man, no other,
Whom your groin's trembling warns.
I stamp upon the earth
A message to my mother.
And then I lower my horns.

Moly

Nightmare of beasthood, snorting, how to wake.
I woke. What beasthood skin she made me take?

Leathery toad that ruts for days on end,
Or cringing dribbling dog, man's servile friend,

Or cat that prettily pounces on its meat,
Tortures it hours, then does not care to eat:

Parrot, moth, shark, wolf, crocodile, ass, flea.
What germs, what jostling mobs there were in me.

These seem like bristles, and the hide is tough.
No claw or web here: each foot ends in hoof.

Into what bulk has method disappeared?
Like ham, streaked. I am gross—grey, gross, flap-eared.

The pale-lashed eyes my only human feature.
My teeth tear, tear. I am the snouted creature

That bites through anything, root, wire, or can.
If I was not afraid I'd eat a man.

Oh a man's flesh already is in mine.
Hand and foot poised for risk. Buried in swine.

I root and root, you think that it is greed,
It is, but I seek out a plant I need.

Direct me gods, whose changes are all holy,
To where it flickers deep in grass, the moly:

Cool flesh of magic in each leaf and shoot,
From milky flower to the black forked root.

From this fat dungeon I could rise to skin
And human title, putting pig within.

I push my big grey wet snout through the green,
Dreaming the flower I have never seen.

Bally *Power Play*

Everybody looks at him playing
the machine hour after hour,
but he hardly raises his gold lashes.
Two fingers move, his hips
lean in almost imperceptibly.
He seldom takes his eyes
from the abstract drama of the ball,
the descent and the reverses

of its brief fortunes. He is
the cool source of all that hurry
and desperate activity, in control,
legs apart, braced arms apart,
seeming alive only at the ends.
His haunches are up against the wood now,
the hard edge which he presses
or which presses him
just where the pelvis begins,
above what in the skeleton
would be no more than a hole.
Bally's drama absorbs him:
amongst the variety and surprise
of the lights, the silver ball
appears, rolls shyly towards him,
meets a wheel of red plastic,
at once bounces away from it,
franticly dashes from side to side
and up and down, it is
trapped, it is released,
it springs to the top again
back to where it entered,
but in the end it must disappear
down the hole at the bottom
—and the fifth act is over
leaving behind it only
the continued inane flickering
of coloured light. Between games
he recognizes me, we chat,
he tells me about broken promises
with a comic-rueful smile
at his need for reassurance,
which is as great as anybody's.
He once told me he never starts
to look for the night's partner
until half an hour before closing time.
The rest is foreplay.

6. Kenneth Irby

Photo by Edward F. Grier.

"The breath on the edge of the lip"

Born in Bowie, Texas, in 1936, Kenneth Irby was educated at the University of Kansas at Lawrence and Harvard; he has a M.L.S. degree from the University of California at Berkeley. Between 1960 and 1962 he served in the United States Army and was a regular reviewer for *Kulchur* magazine. Irby's books include *The Roadrunner, Relation, To Max Douglas, Catalpa,* and *Some Etudes,* and *Set.* His *Poems 1973–1979* is forthcoming.

"My concern *seems* to have been muchly with *pastoral* verse—that is, poetry that *feeds* us," Irby has written of his work, "drawing on a common Great Plains Mysticism in the face of the landscape, that the landscape, *especially,* demands of us. But the concern of *poetry* is not finally at all limited."

In your work geography plays an important role, and you've spoken before of Carl Sauer's influence. What role does Sauer play in helping you define your sense of geography or place?

He was a remarkably intelligent man. If you've read any of his books or articles you'll get the idea right away that you are dealing with someone with a broad and incisive intelligence. Admittedly, he is demanding—not an easy person to read. His thought is not convoluted or oblique, but he is concentrated. Like a lot of people, I heard about Sauer by Charles Olson simply mentioning him. Mentionings are important—names that people give you at a certain time in your life when you are ready to really hear it. Somebody that you may have known about for years, but that wasn't the time to read him, and suddenly there it is.

Let me give you a little personal history that may answer this in a rather roundabout way. When I first came here to Albuquerque I was in the army. I had been a graduate student of Chinese history, regional studies to be precise, and I had finished my masters degree. The government wanted to draft me, and I was not at that point ready to go on for a Ph.D. If I could have gotten out of the army, I would have, but this was before Vietnam and the development of techniques for getting out. You couldn't, or didn't think to, say anything odd on your exam. Do you hear voices? You wouldn't say yes, because obviously you didn't. So they sent me in their enlightenment, since I had studied Chinese, to Albuquerque. I was thus a typist out here at Sandia Base, first in the publications department, then in the weapons test division; that sent me eventually out to Nevada, then on to the Pacific on a little island.

During that time I met some people here. I had met Olson already in Cambridge when I was a graduate student at Harvard. I'd been writing for a long time and had read a lot of Latin American writers because my brother, who now teaches at Princeton and is the translator of the New Directions Borge's *Labyrinth,* led me to them. But I hadn't really found anything in contemporary American poetry at that juncture that turned me on very much, except Robert Lowell, and I didn't like his politics. I was much more interested in English writers, the Neo-Romantics. When I got to Cambridge there was a good bookstore run by an old man named Gordon Cairnie who knew all sorts of people. Allen Ginsberg came to town that spring with *Howl,* and read it to an overflow crowd; it was an exciting event. Charles Olson had come down from Gloucester. They were reading for the benefit of a magazine called *Big Table,* which as you probably know had been started in Chicago by Irving Rosenthal, the graduate student editor of the *Chicago Review;* he had wanted to publish parts of *Naked Lunch* by William Burroughs, and the university said they'd have none of it. So he started another magazine and published the first excerpts of Burroughs anyone had ever seen except friends.

So there they were, trying to sell the magazine in Gordon Cairnie's bookstore one afternoon and Olson was sitting there. I had already read some of his books so I was curious to meet him. And later when I was in the army I got hold of Don Allen's *New American Poetry* anthology, and there was this interesting poet in there named Ed Dorn, whom I imagined to be short, fat, and in his mid-forties. The book said he lived in Santa Fe. I came out to New Mexico with friends I had met in the typist school, and one of them had a car; so that's all we did for weekends—just buy a case of beer or two and get in the car and drive. We went up to Santa Fe one weekend, New Year's Eve as a matter of fact, and we looked Dorn up. Then through Dorn came Bob Creeley, eventually, who came back from Guatemala the next year where he had been teaching on a coffee plantation. This will all come back to your question, don't worry.

Creeley asked me if I'd ever read Carl Sauer, via Olson. I said no, not really, I know the name but I haven't read him. And that set me off on him. It sort of paralleled a man that I had known of as an undergraduate at the University of Kansas. There I was a history major, though I had avoided American history along with the English department. I took only one course in the English department, figuring why should I take courses in something that I'm reading all the time anyway? When I did take a course, it was a survey of American literature from the Civil War to the moderns, and there I found a book I hadn't read—Henry Adams's *Education,* which was a major book for me and I do owe the discovery to that course. In any case, there was a man in the history department named James Malin, whom I knew of because he was a kind of kooky man who published, finally, his own books. We thought it was because nobody else would touch them, which might have been the case, but actually I think it was because he had had bad experiences with editors and didn't like to be rewritten. He was interested in what we would call ecological history, and his collected books would come to an immense number. He is still a vastly neglected major historian of the Great Plains. Malin and Sauer were kind of antagonists, always sparring. When I finally met Sauer and mentioned Mailand he said, "Oh yes, that *prairie* historian."

Well, I got hold of Malin's books about the same time, finally, as I was reading Sauer. His *Grasslands of North America* is a survey of early explorations, soil microbiology, all the ecological information, plus a vast bibliography. It is filled with quotations poets would enjoy, and which I instantly started stealing. So there is my poem in *Catalpa* called "The Grasslands of North America." In a way, these two men gave me permission to deal with where I had grown up. Here were these men of immense learning and seriousness who offered ways to approach the geography which weren't just driving around or tourist-attraction oriented. Though Malin tended to be a recluse for the most part, at least in his later life, Sauer wasn't and he knew just about everybody. Later, a good friend named Bob Callahan became Sauer's literary executor, and through talking to Bob about this I became aware of just how many diverse intelligences Sauer was into. He really was, and this is why Olson liked him, a man of synthetic intelligence—not made up out of plastic, but capable of bringing things together. His notion of a geography department was certainly interdisciplinary, and he kept running into trouble.

And this freed you up to use such material?
Yes, sure. It opened it all up for me. Sauer did the same for Dorn.

I'm curious about your use of place names. In "To Max Douglas," for example, you use a great number of specific place names. How can you justify using such a local vocabulary?
They are real places. Anybody who wants to can find out about them.

Well, I know these areas because I have relatives in Kansas. But I was thinking that if I hadn't been there before I'd want a map.
Sure, that would be the first thing I'd want also. I don't find anything wrong with that at all. How else can you talk about places if you don't use their

names? It is, after all, a poem about moving around a lot so you are going past a lot of places.

I guess what I'm wondering is this—does a place-name have a totemic value?
It certainly may. There is a whole romance structured around that idea. Stephen Vincent Benét, for example, writing poems about the fact that he's writing poems about the names, calling them out in a litany. Woodie Guthrie songs. We've always enjoyed the oddity of place names in the U.S. For me, however, it goes beyond that usually. I have picked out strange names, as we are all inclined to; in *Relation* I have a poem for Bill Dodd, the second part of which is simply a list of towns chosen in a circle around Lubbock, Texas, because of the resonances of their names. It ends with towns called Dawn and Good Night. It's like a mantra, perhaps. But that is what I was writing then, and it wouldn't be the same today. I'm living back in Kansas now and I write about it differently.

Did you ever think of yourself as a "midwestern poet"—like Thomas McGrath, Dave Edder, people like that?
No, honestly not, though that's been a label people have used. I guess when I first went to Harvard there was this built-in sense of wanting to outrage people, of pushing, in reaction to that milieu, where one came from. What I didn't realize was that so many of the people who I was trying to push this on came from the same places. But I never thought of myself as being a "Kansas poet." Years ago I saw a review by Keith Waldrop of an anthology like that, it may even have been of Kansas poets. He was complaining about it. If they are going to do it properly, he said, they should have included Michael McClure, who is from Marysville, Kansas, though this is something McClure never used to admit. That was another thing—there are simply a lot of people who never wanted to admit to it. McClure went to high school in Wichita, and when he went to the West Coast he told everybody he was from Arizona. Charles Plymell always said he was from Wichita, but he actually came from a little town called Holcomb, that then became notorious because that's where the *In Cold Blood* murders took place. *Then* he would say he was from Holcomb.

But look, that makes sense. My first experience of a really big international city was Mexico City. My brother did a graduate degree at the National University there when he returned from Korea, so I spent two or three summers with him. I remember going to a party where I met this couple from Canada; they asked me where I was from and when I told them they asked me if that was anywhere near Joplin, Missouri. Why they knew Joplin is anybody's guess, but there you are. But since I've written a lot of other things that aren't really tied down to a geographical connection in that fashion, I wouldn't think of myself as promoting some kind of mystique of the plains.

So you don't think of yourself as regional?
Well, that's a different matter. That's not a matter of mystique, but there you are, your connections. We all live in regions. We're all locals in some regard.

Another book that Dorn turned me on to and which I like, though it has many shortcomings, is by Haniel Long. He was born in Rangoon, as his parents were missionaries, but he grew up in Pittsburgh and taught there. Because he was not well, he came to Santa Fe and lived out his life there. He wrote poems, as well as one book about New Mexico called *Piñon Country* that has some interesting sections, though much of it is kooky now. One chapter is an appreciation of peyote; another has every cliché about marijuana that you can imagine, how it drives people mad. But it is very good at the start about the nature of the climate here, what defines the region in that sense.

Place is very central to you then.
Yes. Some people have accused me of writing about a place in a poem only when I'm not there, which is something we've all experienced. Thomas Wolfe can only get impassioned about the United States when he's in Europe. In a way I guess that's true. I was in California when I wrote "To Max Douglas," but then that poem is really about going back and forth more than the "there." And I had driven the route a lot. It's like when I lived in New Mexico, we'd get off work and just drive. Only in the United States can you do this. You come out of a party in Berkeley and say let's go to Los Angeles. So you go, see some people, then turn around and drive back.

Do you ever think of your poetry as musical, as being scored?
To a certain degree. It's not that I hold my breath as long as I can, but there is a sense at times of the extended unit. Duncan was saying about Olson that if you think about him talking about the breath as a unit you have to realize that Olson had no breath at all—he was always panting. You

hear him read and these gasps keep coming. He smoked like a chimney. So of course breath was important to him, and you make important in your aesthetic things that are central to your life.

Do the ends of your lines have anything to do with breath pauses?
I've always tended to write pretty long lines, simply because I do hear them that way; I do have a felt sense of their muscularity which is precise to that moment. I can't in all honesty, however, say that they are *counted* precisely. Now Duncan has a set called "The Regulators," which has appeared in pieces in magazines, running the long axis of the page. He swears that he knows precisely how many letters—because he counts by letters and spaces—that are in each line, that they are calculated. I wonder about this, but in any case they certainly are not measured by traditional meters, which are not at all sufficient to account for what is going on in American and British poetry. I don't think of these long lines as being like Whitman's lines either, which are long and meant to be beyond measure, having a movement of the sea to them. I've always felt that they are like casting flies in the sense that they are aimed somehow and cast forth to a particular area. Though aimed at the same area, they will not light in the same place each time. I don't know if there are baits or not. Some of my lines are conceptual, in the sense of units of topic and comment. A sense of a center axis in some of the poems. The axis of the body, as a matter of fact.

I have noticed in my collection *Set,* especially in the first section, I've tended to end the lines with two stresses. Someone pointed out to me that this is also true of Eliot's "Gerontion," which is perhaps why I like it. But I don't know. A lot of this is happening as your writing is beyond the immediate—you want to know exactly what you are doing, but at the same time you want to work past it. It is after all working through a complex of the ear.

Do you think you can divide down the middle poets who revise and those who don't.
Maybe. But even those who say they don't, do. Duncan certainly revises his work, though he has made a lot out of the fact that he doesn't. It might be more interesting to think about what kinds of revisions are done, how they are done. Everybody changes his mind. Ginsberg says "First thought, best thought," but is that necessarily true? It can be a discipline that is valuable.

What about you?

In my own case, it is very common as I'm writing I am hearing alternatives at the same time. And it is difficult. I'm not always capable of resolving my own discriminations. I started using brackets years back to indicate to myself that the thing was tentative, a possibility, something else I heard at the same time. I sometimes feel that maybe the poems should be left just that way, with the alternatives right there. So in that sense I'm always trying to solve this, and maybe these brackets count as a re-vision, a re-seeing.

You don't publish these bracketed words.

No. They are of use in the writing of the poem. I find two rather distinct stages here. Both are primary, but one comes first—when you start with a piece of writing, or a line or two or a fragment, the "inspired" stage. Then comes another which could be called a revising stage, which I always call a recombinatory stage because it involves not only going through the piece saying this word will work better there, but of shuffling things around. I don't write everything in notebooks, but I do keep one, and often there is a continuity of material that I'm dealing with at any one time, and I flip through and start looking; suddenly I'll see that something I wrote months before fits with what I'm doing now. So the time frame becomes juggled completely. Or again, while I think my handwriting is perfectly legible, most people find it extremely difficult. Actually, I do have trouble reading what I wrote sometimes, and thereby it suggests other things. I misread myself and get new ideas that way.

This isn't so rare; people do it with foreign languages all the time. At the moment, Robert Kelly and Dick Higgins are proposing an anthology that will be entirely made up of translations that try to work, as Zukofsky did with his Catullus, to recreate the sound of the original in English. David Bromige worked on a farm as a kid in Sweden, and so he knows a little Swedish, and he misreads Swedish texts to suggest other possibilities all the time. This is like being given an exercise to do that is quite beyond your intentions, the cathexis of emotions you are involved in at the time. All these things have to be set aside for a time because your head has to be focused on operational activities. It might be writing to a particular scansion or rhyme scheme; it might be vowel patterns. A friend used to give his writing class the basic English vocabulary of about 500 words and they'd have to write poems just using these words. Not that anything at all had to come out of it—certainly not any great poems—but just the experience of working that way so that your habits are shifted for a moment.

You mentioned that you studied history. Do you work sometimes in larger forms where you make use of found material, historical material?

Well, I've got one longer poem that's about the explorer Jed Smith that I wrote because I had driven with a friend from Berkeley to see some people in Oregon, about a 500-mile drive. On the way back we stopped at one of those roadside historical markers for a reason I don't remember—probably to piss—and there was Smith's party having been ambushed on or near this spot in the 1820s. I don't know why at that juncture that excited me, but it excited me a great deal. When I got home I started digging around in the books I had to find out something about it; somehow I had never really realized that Smith was even in California. One thing led to another. I discovered that Josiah Gregg, who wrote a book called *The Commerce of the Prairies,* had been in the next wagon behind Smith crossing the Santa Fe Trail coming to Santa Fe when Smith got killed by Commanches. In turn, then, Gregg led the first party of Anglos to Eureka Bay in northern California. Suddenly, you see, there was all this exciting material.

The poem, then, resulted from dealing with that, as I discovered it—making this line of movement from California to Oregon, back through the circle which ended in death. It was essentially the movement we made driving up there, so that I had something to hang it on. Instead of just writing a poem about Jed Smith I had my own parallel line. Otherwise it wouldn't have worked. My only regret about the whole episode is that a man named Dale Morgan who wrote a book about Smith that I referred to a lot was living at that time in Berkeley and working at the Bancroft Library. I was there through the whole period, but I didn't discover his whereabouts until after he died.

Was your poem meant to be biographical?

Accurate, but certainly not biographical. There are vast amounts left out that I didn't even try to deal with. I just tried to get those two lines into parallel movement and explore just what that meant.

Do you know Ronald Johnson's work?

Yes, very elegant. A Kansas boy who became more European than the Europeans.

He has a Southwest cookbook.

And a new one coming out. I think he ran a bar in San Francisco for a while.

You've said that you consider yourself a pastoral poet . . .
I was playing with the root. My interest in pastoral came about reading
Bruno Snell's book *The Discovery of the Mind.* The last chapter discusses how
Latin poets, particularly Virgil, created Arcadia from reading Greek poets
and taking seriously things that the Greeks themselves wouldn't have. I
discovered that the term *pastoral* comes from the Latin, meaning "to feed,"
because that's what the sheep do. And I thought then that we "feed" on
pastoral poetry. I liked the pun.

So it's more in a sense of the language than the subject matter?
Well, no. Again, I'm interested in micro-relation, that we all must deal
with the local. Malin's proposal that it all has to happen some *place,* that
there has to be a particular place where things are going on—and thus all
history really is local. Of course there is more to it than that; what we make
of all this needs to have input from other sources. But the experience of the
local is crucial, and thus one's yard is a potent local.

Like Robert Duncan's "Meadow."
Yes. There is a Cuban poet of considerable interest that my brother has been
working on—Jose Lazama Lina, now deceased, the same age as Charles Olson.
He has a poem that is strikingly similar to Duncan's. So I'd say that I'm
pastoral in that sense, but I'm not out tending sheep or anything like that.

What about an epic?
I've never tried my hand at that, but maybe that's the next move. On this
trip I bought Robert Fitzgerald's new translation of the *Aeneid,* thinking
that I never have truly read the poem. I've owned more than one translation,
but it's always more or less bored me. Maybe though I'm old enough now,
and in my decline I'll be able to appreciate it. And with Fitzgerald's translations you can just sit down and read these poems—he's done both the *Iliad*
and the *Odyssey* as well—like stories. So maybe it's getting to be my time
for the epic, though I don't know what my great vision, the connecting and
informing myth, would be.

You mentioned your brother's translation work. What about you?
I've done some, though I've stayed away from publishing it. I used to translate
a Russian poem—usually Pasternak—every Christmas and put it on a card
for friends. My brother and I have talked about collaborating on some sort
of project, though we just haven't gotten to it. Translation is a great and

wonderful exercise for poets, obviously. Kenneth Rexroth used to talk about it as a finding of kinship.

One of the questions we've been pursuing is the "fiction" of translation versus the idea of the literal.
Sure. I don't, of course, accept the idea of a "literal" translation. Walter Benjamin proposes that the syntax in a translation should remain literal, but that the rest need not. That gets into peculiarities, of course. Have you read Benjamin? *Illuminations* has in it the piece I'm thinking about, the essay on Baudelaire. Benjamin doesn't cite Frost, but Frost is a perfect example here. Frost claimed that poetry is what doesn't get translated; but Benjamin would argue that on the contrary poetry is what *demands* to get translated. There is a yearning—and I don't know whether or not Benjamin would uphold this idealistic notion in his later work—but there is a yearning for a language of languages, and poetry comes closest to this. Thus it does ask that we translate, that we overcome the limitations between languages.

You studied Russian?
Yes, some, though really not enough to do adequate translations of a writer like Pasternak. He is a difficult and ambiguous poet. But maybe in his case you need a certain ignorance. The occasion was Christmas and the cards would all be done in hand, English facing Russian. I really do feel that the desire to translate is the desire to get closer to someone you respond to. Clayton Eshleman was here. What did he have to say about it?

Plenty.
Well, as a professional translator he's gone through many stages on this question.

He believes very much in the literal.
Yeah, sure. Nabokov argues that too. With the people Clayton is working with especially, in the great richness and denseness, the phanopoeia, of the poetry, literal translation is demanded. But I don't know what would happen if he were trying to translate someone for which that doesn't work. Stephen George is an example. A wonderful writer, but when he gets translated literally it just is not there.

Or how could you translate Gertrude Stein literally into Russian?
Or the hardest poems of Vallejo, which Clayton did not deal with, and

reasonably enough. The poems in *Trilce,* which are full of weird things even native speakers who have studied Vallejo can't fathom—the intricate word-play, the deformations. But then there's the challenge.

Your brother is working on—
Lezama Lima. He is certainly of immense difficulty. In fact, in my experience Lezama Lima is as difficult a poet as I've ever encountered, Mallarmé, ninth-century Scandinavian poetry, and others included. He's fiendish and entrancing. Knowing my brother, he wouldn't be attracted to it otherwise. Lezama Lima wrote a couple of novels, including *Paradiso,* which were translated and published about a decade ago. *Paradiso* never went into paperback, but it did gain a certain notoriety. Lezama Lima was gay, and there are some explicit homosexual scenes; it was enough to get him into trouble in Cuba. Interestingly, the copy in the public library in Lawrence, Kansas, where I live, has been read to pieces—it's falling apart.

Jim did a wonderful set of his prose poems which appeared in *Sulfur,* which were written at the start of World War II. I like those a lot. A while back when he was working on the translations, I used to open my readings with one or two. They are just so good.

And what is your project at the moment?
Well, along this line, I've been editing the poetry of Mary Butts. She was mainly a fiction writer, deeply involved in hermetic philosophies. Some of the poems I'll read tonight will be hers as at the moment I feel a great kinship there. She too had a particular sense of place that is not so common in English poetry of her generation. Robert Kelly proposes that my work, like hers, really is being on the threshold of the "inside-outside."

So you do have an interest in the hermetic?
In hermetic thought, yes. Do you mean it that way, or as an adjective?

The hermetic tradition.
Yes, as above, so below. That's what draws me to Mary Butts.

So do you see your work as having value beyond the purely aesthetic?
One would hope so. What, exactly, I'm not always sure. It all comes back to the here and now, to the actual world—the world of acts. The essential world. There is an imaginal world—as opposed to the imaginary—of the mind's imaging. There is a universe of this which we can all hope to know

better. Everybody has had the experience where you are lying to go to sleep, and your eyes are closed but you are not asleep, and a series of vivid images comes. These are neither dreamed nor willed images.

In the old *Encyclopedia Britannica,* eleventh edition, there is an article on crystal gazing by Andrew Lang, the folklorist. He did the "fairy book" series. Lang proposes there between that experience and what might be going on in crystal gazing if you are not a fake. I got into a terrible argument with a guy once about this. He said that it was just telling the future, but I argued that it wasn't really that at all, that you don't do it in a *predictive* fashion. You might, I suppose, just as one use of Tarot cards comes down to that. But that's not all that's going on with crystals, or cards, or even dreams. The message isn't there just to be interpreted. It's part of its own world.

It seems that from the Imagists and Objectivists on, American poets have been interested more in the concrete world, while the French seem maybe a more prophetic and visionary tradition. Do you think the two interests are mutually exclusive?
No, I don't at all. There are certain poems of Williams's that are as strange as any you'll ever run across.

Rexroth describes Objectivism as an hallucination of fact. He traces Objectivism from the Surrealists.
He was interested greatly in Reverdy. Reverdy works by collages of little, discreet units of sensual perception. They don't seem so odd to us now, but they were at the time. Rexroth himself, of course, was a Cubist painter as well as a writer. I've never seen any of his work, but the paintings are well thought of. He once wanted to get a whole set of Toynbee's *Study of History,* and James Laughlin of New Directions exchanged a set for a painting.

What about Hart Crane?
Yes, certainly Crane is in the high prophetic tradition. Whitman of "Passage to India." Any number of others. I see no reason why the two traditions should be seen as separate. I never cease to be excited by Hart Crane every time I read him. I reread him in some fashion as if I were fourteen, which is the age at which I first got on to him. Ever more *exalte!*

Strawberry Canyon Poem

We followed the fire road up into the hills
for night time's sake, for smells of jasmine and of amaryllis
the faintest light register on the side bush growth
ceanothus? I said to Lowell would cover
most of any guesses what
not for the unaccounted registers of recollection, not
of tabulation *whose*
                         Lowell for the
distance from those lights of the Rad Lab and chicken farm
still lit our way
                 and I was off for
any, stripping off my shirt
till the mosquitoes
                sensuality
of unintended impingements
                      trying
incorrectly as we argued and I lost
to place *this*
pace along *this*
fire road
with all the other times
a *here* that is the mappist's
fixed by what should be the necessary
lineaments of growing things
that nonetheless follow no
and will not be described by a
                     Sheer memory
the greatest adjunct only if
more important attentions
are incessantly at work
                The path
back by the quickest
weight of the rut in the dark
only the feet to the contour worn
by the same
suspended searching blind
and certain as the vine

But it's clear our
                    (two, for Lowell
went first down the path
the last stretch)
                    way is polysemous
remembered and at
the fingers and the words
renerved

The Grasslands of North America

(for Bob Grenier)

Only a succession of far-reaching green prairies
the grass that is in
my backyard

As we moved down the hill in the grass
looking past the highway toward Hammond
our pants and legs caught thick in it
the same winds blowing

Where Pike entered Kansas
and drunk after drunk in highschool
we ended, the piss in the clover
the smell of clover so strong for miles
we stopped the car and got out
drunk in the roadway

That same country as entered
the first time it was ever seen

is entered again and again
each time I come to it
as I came here at three
out of Texas

was the New World

    •

There must be in the juice
and flesh a same plain

as these, the same moving
wave as this grass

the body comes back to
only having heard as they
only heard, by hearsay
and believed it

Three Geographical Variations

(for Ed Dorn)

   North out of Lawrence we turned
east before we had to a back
track to Valley Falls and Ozawkie back
roads north into Hiawatha
Old trips of the past will not save us
Noon meals in or out of a calendar
picture quiet and readdress the east
turn into White Cloud and Iowa Point
to reach toward the river and where
the river's urge in us eased us a little
That is the flow the urge toward
each other links hand in hand as
word in word driving drinking beer all Sunday afternoon
I have come west and at the far ocean remember
It does not matter loose specifics of whose
the linkage matters the flow
the closeness possible the intimations of divinity
as intimations of the dreamed spread land
spread before the eyes of those White Cloud diddled sooners
even the willful wily promoters
looking west at the land's run
out from under them

*

I will not let blood and I do not know
if there is any turning back upon the land
to traverse, how much

traversing now will reopen
what spaces seem nowhere
ease us together—it is not different to go past
the endless misuse of landscape
here in Berkeley or there in New Mexico, what space
is open beyond is open across the whole world
Looks past whatever salvations of individuals
realizing salvation is only to pass
into the space all people live in

*

There is no need to substitute any world for this one
in order to come into any wonder or more
enter the open imagination. Good and evil
seem kindness and indifference   at each footstep
At the other edge of each tree   another pasture
the shade fallen on each face into the sun
Into each lit house dark street we walk home
The stories where we are all changed
beyond the wardrobe's back wall   pass through
The eye is blue wonder brown opener the horizon
shines through upon the toss and fling the ring glints
head up in the air   grass goes by   like starlings
iridescent in the sky

[equinox variations—"by the sills of the exquisite flexible doors"]

petunia midnight purple throat
a life to share, more than, lit by, ever
crushed tomato vines ahead, burr of stramonium, hands unburying
    potatoes
kisses of capsicum, nic fits conquered, come and gone
the way out past what isn't ever guessed for
like
dependence
eggplant star eyes
Solanaceae heart glow

grass · well · piano keyes : not glass or mirror scryed
but yoke · yoga : shouldered dark and light

leaning over, staring into the grass, into the piano player bending over
the keys playing into the Limbus

not to see anything but squarely take the yoke of light and dark

chrysanthemum, petunia, cottonwood hold out and in, such yoga the
clear voice tells is numbering

adding up your breathing in the dark against my back, the blades of
grass, the shadows of the blades of grass

from [exercitato/praecipere]

the night flight is to the chestnut square

I think my mother and myself approach death by air backwards to the
flare of the plain and the work of the day

long anima, there is a coil of dark hair about the nacelles of the moment,
and that smile, of course, that does not rest or satisfy

launching and calling back the same small ships of the engines, this ship,
this offering of her food, my mother and I do not take

but stare below us to the square of commerce that has been made with
our desire, coming and going and the tickets being taken, and the low
wicker gate at the back way in, ours

7. Michael Palmer

"The man by contrast is fixed symmetrically"

Born in New York City in 1943, Michael Palmer took his degrees in comparative literature from Harvard. While there, he edited *Joglars* magazine with Clark Coolidge and since 1969 has lived in San Francisco. Often mentioned as one of America's most exciting and influential younger experimental writers, his volumes include *Blake's Newton, The Circular Gates, Without Music, Notes for Echo Lake,* and *First Figure.* His translations appear in *The Selected Poetry of Vincent Huidobro* and *The Random House Book of Twentieth-Century French Poetry.* Palmer is a contributing editor to *Sulfur* and is also on the faculty of the poetics program at New College in San Francisco. Since 1974, the poet has collaborated on over a dozen works with the Margaret Jenkins Dance Company, as well as with a number of performance artists and composers. Additionally, his radio play, *Idem I–IV,* was produced for public radio in 1980. In 1975, Palmer was awarded a National Endowment for the Arts Fellowship.

"I have an interest," Michael Palmer has written, "in the generative semantic function of the poem and the polysemous, often veiled nature of poetic meaning. The poem as an act of signification then, a complex (or radically simple?) gesture of disclosure and withholding which derives from yet exists somewhere apposite to our everyday discourse. As should be evident my work does not 'frame experience' according to any traditional mimetic model, nor does it follow a linear path. Its heuristic impulse often seems to bring into question the character of the first-person (the so-called speaker) as well as the linguistic sign itself."

May we begin with a quote from an advance review of your new book, First Figure, *from* Publisher's Weekly? *"Unconventional in the extreme, Palmer's works resemble poems only because of the ragged right-hand margins. . . . He is excruciating to follow, lacking as he does even the slightest pretense to logic and reality. . . . The audience for this kind of poetry is small." This is stupid for a variety of reasons, but specifically, why do mainstream reviewers and readers seem to consider difficult work almost to be fraudulent work?*

There is an Anglo-American empirical tradition that takes as a model a kind of simple version of reference, where a poem is a place in which you tell a little story, the conclusion of which is at the bottom of the poem just where it is supposed to be. It easily mirrors a shared emotional experience, a sort of consumer verse that you'd see in the pages of the *New Yorker* or the *Hudson Review,* where the function of the work and the mechanisms of the poem do not admit a certain level of mystery. This is the kind of thing that's taught in most creative writing workshops. If you go to such a workshop with the intention of learning one or another circumscribed formula in order to publish the results in the *American Poetry Review,* usually you'll produce this well-wrought verse which effectively denies the mysteries of reference embedded in the poem. Further, it denies the level of profound human risk that goes into being a poet, in the way Baudelaire or Dickinson or Rilke understood being a poet. It doesn't admit that the question of how language means is continually an open one.

Is this peculiar to Americans?

Well, I was struck once on a visit to France by a certain generosity towards what must have been the obvious difficulties in work of mine. I realized that, among certain people anyway, there was a curious difference in attitude towards complexity and consequently towards the bewilderment that can come in the face of work that is not talking about shared experience in a superficial way—not talking about, that is, how sad you are because grandma died and the leaves just turned brown. Not using symbols in a one-to-one relationship to a referent. The French had a curious generosity, which is to say in the proposition of poetry they would trust to an initial experience of the words. If it did interest them, they would then take for granted that they could come into a living relationship with the poem. Over here in poetry-business land, the place where critics and reviewers make the canons of literature which then dissolve after a few years, I think there is a desperate fear that they are going to be made fools of by these people who get up and talk crazy talk, who don't follow the Frost-Auden-Eliot lineage that has been set up over the last seventy years. In their eyes you are an unprincipled person, and they are not going to allow themselves to be fooled by that.

There is also another problem with a poetry that is not in some simple sense a consumer item. It takes an effort of attention that is as active as that which goes into the writing. It will not stand as a kind of decor in one's life, not the kind of thing for hammock and lemonade, where at the end everything is in resolution and we all feel better or worse, depending upon the poem. We feel something, in any case, that is utterly definable and closed. When you begin to open up those terms, to examine the sign itself— the mystery of how words refer and how they can empty out of conventional meanings and acquire meanings that threaten the very way that we talk to each other in a certain respect—in the larger sense when that structural rigidity of a closed form begins to tremble and we begin to feel the anxiety of losing structure, it can be a terrifying experience. To be resolved, it calls for a dwelling in the poem. You have to decide what your relationship to the poem is. It is a kind of poetry that insists that the reader is an active part of the meaning, that the reader completes the circuit.

This is very different from a New Critical model, which to some degree is still dominant in the byways of American critical literature, where the poem has an absolute meaning. There the reader's job is to get in there and find his or her way into that absolute meaning. Of course, no reader can do it as well as the professor. It's a hideous job and you are glad when it's over. That proposition of a reader who has to penetrate some perfectly enclosed thing pretends to put a responsibility on the reader, but actually it is a very trivial responsibility. If the thing is already in place, why bother? If you have a more open discourse, where the reader brings a range of experience to a text that you could conceive of as having multiple levels of meaning, so the readings of the poem as you go along will have great differences according to the ideolect, the language that each of us speaks. Thus the act of translation which a reader undergoes is itself profoundly significant to the ultimate form of the poem. A lot of people don't want that responsibility, but others do. They take it as a gesture of generosity rather than as a closing off.

So you'd say that the community of good readers would be much smaller in this country than in Europe?
I don't know. It's not so much that, but simply that there is a rigid conservatism among those who put the canon in place here. It seems singularly ignorant and immovable. After all, poets just barely survive in Europe too. But there is one level of understanding there which I see, possibly from a longer tradition of work that is more open. Actually, I'm surprised to have as many readers as I do. I never sought to have an Allen Ginsberg level of readership, but there is a very active and intelligent reading community.

There has been a radical disjuncture between what is proper behavior and improper behavior in American poetry, and in this age of Reagan it seems solidified. There is a psychology of reaction in the arts, or at least in literature, which reaffirms the old values which were never really values in the first place. The eighties remind me in that respect of the fifties. Whereas in the sixties and seventies you did have a kind of opening out, and the poetic field had a broadness of address that was quite extraordinary.

What is, do you suppose, your "community of readers"? Who is "understanding"? Do you identify with the so-called Language poets?

Well, certainly it's a lifelong proposition for me to understand my own work. There is the famous remark by Robert Browning about "Sordello": "When I wrote it only God and I knew what it meant; now only God knows."

My relationship to the Language poets is this: First, there is a certain disservice that's been performed, partly by themselves, in grouping a fairly diverse community of writers under that rubric for the sake of self-presentation. They came along at a certain point and were generous toward work such as mine and Clark Coolidge's. Part of that had to do with a degree of common interest, an attempt to bring into question surfaces of language, normative syntax, and so on. For me, though, this was less a conscious attempt than an insistence by the poem itself. In that respect, I was happy to see them as people to discuss the poem with.

On the other hand, a poet like Barrett Watten, let's say, works much more rigorously from an aesthetic program than I do. There are many directives and proscriptions in Barry's world, and for him that's a fruitful mode of procedure. It's a little bit like André Breton setting up a world of surrealism in which aesthetic priorities become operative. I don't work from that proposition at all; in fact, I don't even believe in an "avant-garde." That's just a military term which has lost its meaning. Nor do I believe in progress in the arts in any way. The arts obviously move along in certain directions, but to consider this a progress is an illusion. And there is certainly no necessary direction.

Likewise, I would say that the way I inhabit language, or language inhabits me, is in a sense more traditional than the way through procedural models that many of the so-called Language poets work. In that respect, I'm a little bit outside, just as a Matisse or a Rilke would be outside the ongoing schools, would be working with things that have their own demands yet remain in some doubt as to what those demands are until the poem itself is in place. It's a thoroughly Romantic sense, though I don't have a romance of the text; I don't care about it at all, per se. Nor do I have a romance of the code, of language itself. In recent years I've been very much interested in an attempt to return to a physicality of word as gesture, as an embodiment of the variety of selves and nonselves which propose themselves as language on the page. Now that is both like what may happen in Language poetry and unlike it. In my work degrees of emotional texture come through which at least some of those poets might find problematic.

But this is hard to generalize. It's like Impressionism. If you start trying to apply it to all those different people who were included as Impressionists it would be nonsense. At one point in America, even Cézanne was called an

Impressionist; do you put Van Gogh and Monet beside each other, or Monet and Seurat? Those categories are obviously ultimately reductive, and it's perhaps a disservice to writers to use them. Still, one of the good things is like any movement it tends to challenge orthodoxies. The Language poets challenge the workshop poem, challenge the procedural methodologies that make poetry a kind of unquestioned medium in which we merrily go along producing work like everybody else, and the more it's like everybody else the more everyone is relieved. I admire that "effort in resistance," that stirring of the pot practiced by Bernstein, Hejinian, Silliman, Steve Benson, Carla Harryman, and several others. Without it I'm sure we would not currently have such a significant debate about poetics, at least in San Francisco. Certainly there have been times when that debate could have been conducted in more informed terms, with less unreflective polemic, but that could probably be said regarding any issues or movements which arouse strong feelings for and against.

Roman Jakobson was a wonderful linguist who was, of course, of the generation of the Russian Formalists of the twenties, then part of the Prague Linguistic Circle in the thirties. He was in constant dialogue with poets in his early work in semiotics, and was one of those seminal figures who crosses all boundaries, doing work of real significance. Among his friends were the Russian poets Krucenik, Khlebnikov and Mayakovsky. Khlebnikov was a sound-poet who wrote in nonwords, morphemic and submorphemic fragments, that built up into a curiously resonant and interesting body of writing that had never been seen before. He was one of the most radical poets of his time. Not a greater writer, certainly, than Pasternak, Akhmatova, or Mandelstamm, but of real interest in terms of his methodology. During an interview with David Shapiro, Jakobson paraphrases Krucenik's remark on *zaum* or sound poetry, "that this . . . poetry is a very important thing, but that it is mustard and that you cannot eat only mustard." So there is that consideration also of alternative models, alternative relationships to subject, voicings, text—the telling.

Do you feel your responsibility as a writer to be more to yourself or to that anonymous individual you're trying to challenge? Or even, in a romantic sense, to the body politic?
I don't think I'd separate them out in that way. For me they are all part of a dialectic that comes to be enclosed in any poem that has a fullness of address. I'm not interested in *myself*—that's just this guy who sits here drinking coffee and making a fool of himself. If only a *self* got posited in a

poem we might as well be having lunch somewhere and not bothering with poems. A self that is transformed through language, however, interests me, though that already includes the reader as we are all part of a shared language. So for me it's one point in that respect. It seems to me to become reductive exactly at that point where you focus on the self alone and thus end up with a poetry of personality, and that exhausts itself as soon as the personality exhausts itself. If it's only the language, on the other hand, then it moves into an idealization of language per se, endless semiotic activity. If it only concentrates on reader response, then invariably you'll have a cheapening of the address. You get some laughs and some bucks, but that's it.

I'd like to talk specifically about Notes for Echo Lake. *I seemed to notice a narrative line throughout a number of the poems, yet often there is inclusion of materials which seem to be almost extraneous accretions. What kind of filtering device is at work there?*

I hope this isn't too vague . . . I think at a certain point a lot of this involves the myth of technique—that is, technique as something you can have or not have. Across a lifetime of working as I now understand it, one learns to listen to the poem as it unfolds. This might be outside a proposition that a given Language poet, Ron Silliman for example, might admit. Ron would have more prior insistences (or at least more conscious prior insistences), and he would want to take greater command of the poem as it unfolds. He would not so much allow a vertical expansion of resonance, but would want to control the form in some very rigorous way in order to implement its extension. For me it is to some degree at least a tuning to that which becomes appropriate as the thing itself comes into being. As Robert Duncan has noted, there is the term Dante uses, *intendo*—not what *you* intend as a writer but what the *poem* intends as it comes to be, what it is moving toward meaning. That for me is very much the informing principle (or perhaps "myth") of the work, and so I begin to hear it as it begins to unfold.

In this way things acquire the particular decorum of the particular poem in the process of the making. If you worry too much about what is right or wrong with the thing under hand, you end up thinking too much about something called Literature, rather than the poem. I think a lot of stultified work comes from thinking about Great Literature. If you look at the poetry of Robert Lowell in that respect, a certain amount of it is stultified by having to exist under the sign of Literature. Am I making Great Literature? Is Delmore Schwartz going to be angry with this poem? Is Allen Tate going to scold me?

So I like to shift the question of the making of the poem from any prior critical proposition that would, say, censor any one thing. Obviously, it is very easy to make a mess in that regard and thus to lose it. Still, I'd rather risk losing the poem than having no risk, then end up with a poetry of intellectual discretion that is more appropriate to Richard Wilbur than to myself.

What about, specifically, your sense of the narrative in Echo Lake?
I think the question is a complicated one. There are threads of an evanescent order of narration that do appear in that work. But remember that unless it posits itself as a narrative, a poem doesn't have to attend to narrative as a primary effect. It can have much more of a verticality in time. Story is, of course, not primary in modern poems, though wonderful stories have been and can be told there.

We are left with a mystery of what the narrative is, something that often shimmers at the edge of the page. We get only scraps. A narrative, after all, is something that in a sense is built up to mirror our own being-in-time; it becomes a picture of time, that strange experience of time which we go through, and we order it to give our various pictures of being-in-time. There are also untold stories in the world, our own for example, which we find out about only after we are dead. I don't necessarily mean a Freudian notion, though Freud investigates this in a very interesting way. There is a great body of poetry that examines the texture of the untellable which surrounds us in the world, and that is a fundamental part of our experience—the lived experience of our language, the layers of word beneath the surface, where are we going, how did I end up as a poet speaking in Albuquerque, New Mexico, at age forty-one, and so forth. These are all extraordinary mysteries which have behind them layers of chance and unforeseen conjunctions. A lot of what the poem unfolds as invisible narrative is exactly that level of experience. But this is all *very* difficult territory to talk about.

You spoke of "listening to the unfolding of the poem." Are there any ways that you cultivate your own psyche to enhance your receptivity to this unfolding?
Schiller, in a letter to Goethe, talks about the condition of receptivity necessary to the poem coming, how one must "be" for the poem to come. I've thought a lot about this recently. The material of the poem is always there, the world is always there, the language is always there. Why the hell can't we always make poems the way we want to? It is necessary for me to

reach some level of openness to language, which closes down and opens continually, for poetry to happen. I realized a few years ago that I'd have to go much further into an interior discipline of attention to get beyond a certain level in which I would simply write more Michael Palmer poems of a particular order. I wouldn't say there is any one "technique" for that, except for a kind of heightened attention to that possibility, so that when the time comes you won't blow it.

For me, a lot of this has been learning that I have to be quite private in my life, that I have to read and think in a certain degree of solitariness a lot of the time—unlike, say, a Frank O'Hara who gets on the bus and suddenly there's a bus poem, or who sits eating lunch with Mike Goldberg and soon you've got a poem on Abstract Expressionism. And yet I hope that doesn't mean I write a poetry which is closed off from the world. It is that condition, in fact, that opens me to it.

Are you implying that you make yourself open to some kind of "voice" which is declaring itself to you?
I'm not sure about that exactly, though what I'm talking about may amount to the same thing. If you are speaking through language, it is after all not only your voice. It's going to be partly recognizable: my poems are recognizable, have a distinct shape to them because I have a particular sensibility and body and so on. But at the same time if they are limited by that then you have not arrived at the poem.

It's like the question of Blake. When he says a fairy sat down on his desk and whispered "Europe" to him, you wonder did it *really* happen, or is this simply a metaphor for the poem which arrives from "outside," a case of pure inspiration, breathing in? Jack Spicer represented that notion of dictation by talking about Martians and spooks arriving and giving him his words. For Yeats there are the famous other-world figures who gave him his metaphors. For me this represents virtually a linguistic model—an abolition of pure subjectivity. You become receptive to a whole variety of language that is more expansive than your own, that can see more than you can see. When you do enter into the poem in that respect and trust to it, in looking at it afterwards you wonder, did I do that? Well, the answer is, of course, that you didn't. Various *selves,* aspects of a heightened attention, did it in a certain way, but not your *self.* You are that paradox, both sender and receiver, and as such you modify the sound, transmit the highs and the lows effectively or not, and thus alter the signal in a dramatic fashion.

Are you trying to communicate, if not an idea, at least a feeling?
I don't think about it in exactly those terms. When a poem is working, I come over time to a consciousness of the form it's going to take, as well as its thematic threads. But in terms of a particular resolution that one could codify, I don't think so. After the fact, often, the nature of the subject matter becomes clearer to me. But I find that when I attend too schematically before the fact to what the poem is "about," if I try to force the figure to emerge, I come into a trouble of contrivance. I then am working in an area that is somehow alien to my sensibility. For some people this is the equivalent of saying the poems can't be "about" anything, but actually it is simply that the notions of subject and content seem to locate themselves differently.

Maybe in the sense of recurrence?
I've thought a lot about this in working with dance, for example, which I've done extensively over time. There you can be polythematic and nonlinear, but if elements recur a number of times through a piece, people can actually become as "familiar" with them as they would in a story in which events are located where you expect them. So to a certain degree, forms of recurrence do have the function of clarifying or helping readers to locate.

But I don't think I was coming to it that way. There is a mystery, once again, of unfolding which sometimes just seems to embody itself in that way. So that from a phrase comes an expanded phrase, then a further expanded phrase, the syntax flowering over time. You end up in a structure of variations, as you do in music, an open-ended series of variations on a theme that are meant to explore the richness of a particular melodic line. The lines thus acquire an incantatory character, a returning and returning to a first place. For me this is simply a mode of thought.

May we be specific for a moment here? I've noticed in Echo Lake *that the color blue seems to appear again and again.*
There are some things which function quasi-referentially for me. For example, a very important book for me is Wittgenstein's *Remarks on Colour.* Starting back a bit, color has always fascinated me for a variety of reasons, but singularly because it is the place where meaning and language seem to be most in question. When we name a color it brings up something central. Within our own American language, red is necessarily the color associated with the word *red,* but of course it's a different name in German, a different name in French, and so on. It is necessary in each case, but arbitrary in terms of the thing itself. All the questions about perception in language

which are fun to explore—if we didn't have a word for red, would we perceive red?—are certainly not simple to answer.

When we think of Eskimos who have myriad terms for white in its various gradations in order to help them exist in the landscape, we are at a loss. By the fact of having those gradations encoded in the language as necessary to survival, Eskimos are constantly perceiving degrees of whiteness in the snow which we do not perceive. We simply don't have them as categories of thought, nor do we need them. We have, likewise, our own distinctions which Eskimos would never dream of having. So there is that phrase of Wittgenstein's, "If red is the name of a color, what is the name of the word red?" It regresses the question *ad infinitum,* which for me is always potentially behind the sign. In a poem this is an experience of meaning which is very much foregrounded.

What about number, which seems also important in the book?
It's part of the same thing. We count necessarily "one, two, three, four," and it seems a kind of measure. We can switch, however, into a Fibonacci system of counting where we have "one, one, two, three, five, eight," and we can build an entire mathematical culture with that series, an entire experience of measure. So each of these things brings into question our assumptions about temporality, the succession of events in time, and so on.

Not to get too specific about individual uses of number or color because it is a cumulative thing, a lot of my use has to do with the building up of a nonsystematic relationship to color and number that begins with the fact of their own linguistic categories. It is almost like building a vocabulary, one whose meanings accrue over time.

Because of what you associate with a particular color?
Well, to some degree, sure. There is a certain synesthetic character to all this, so that these elements come to stand for areas of emotion and areas of association.

My problem in my reading, I think then, was that I was trying to associate particular colors with specific objects, and it just wasn't working out. But you are saying that you are simply at this point exploring.
To some degree exploring the fascination of what it is when Jasper Johns paints a yellow field and writes the word *red* on top of it. What is it when Johns simply writes the word *red* in yellow on a canvas? A bringing into question of what reference is. For me this has to do with the larger area of

exploration, ultimately, of what poetic meaning is. I'm not interested in making poetry if I cannot explore the areas of signification that are less available in other areas of discourse. I want language to signify and be functional, and in that respect I have to investigate all aspects of the non-logical and the discontinuous as they happen, for example, in a children's song, magical areas of language. "Step on a crack / break your mother's back." There you have a curious intuitive sound patterning that makes an extraordinarily direct emotional appeal, yet if you try to do "a + b =" you are not going to get it. It exists outside a tautological system.

Poetic logic?
Yes. When we let go the modes of logical procedure, what then is poetic logic? It includes illogicality, even glossolalia, a speech that occasionally even transcends words. All sorts of odd language functions that we tend to ignore in order to survive in the world. If I were to ask you if a particular chair were "free," and you started wondering about the meaning of the term *free,* does the chair somehow have a will, we'd never get anywhere. But in the poem, when one has the possibility of a polysemousness, multiple levels of meaning, that is actually when you have something that will open up unique areas of function. If we want to look at a political function of the poem, even if it's not a "political" poem, it can be a constant challenging, say, of the discourse of power that at this moment Reagan and Mondale are involved with. The poem in that regard gives the lie to political rhetoric by exposing the deeper nature of language, even when it is not thematically a " Workers, throw off your chains" poem.

So poems should be able to cross language barriers?
In the sense that some of these things are universals, yes. In another respect, though, they are so embedded in a particular language that it would call for an extraordinary act of translation. *Notes for Echo Lake* is being translated reasonably well into French and German now, but it takes a lot of work. The translators have to work much more toward equivalent events, but there *are* those events if the person is a skilled translator.

You mentioned Wittgenstein, and it seems to me that in Echo Lake *you have much in common with him.*
Certainly we share certain areas of interest, in the way that poetry and philosophy often do. But even when you have a philosophical poetry you have poetry primarily; when you have poetic philosophy, such as Wittgen-

stein, Spinoza, or Nietzsche, you are in a different territory from poetic understanding.

I went to philosophy at one point looking for textures which had not been admitted into poetry. In particular, that curious rigor and beauty of Wittgenstein's sensibility gave me textures that I wanted very much to have in the poem. I was experiencing a profound reaction against the given textures of the poem, even among the Modernist generation whom I very much respect. There was just something else I wanted. I had forgotten about this in a way—it was simply subsumed into my work—until suddenly Stanley Cavell, the Wittgenstein scholar and philosopher, got a copy of *Notes for Echo Lake* and pointed out that some of the individual fragments read almost as propositions. Of course, what happens is that we're different; it is not procedural in any way. But I think you are quite right in saying there is a resemblance in texture. Further, I'm interested in investigating language, as Wittgenstein is; I'm interested in investigating consciousness, as Wittgenstein is; and I'm interested in inhabiting language at a fairly deep level, as Wittgenstein is. But I'm certainly not as rigorous as he is.

What about a couple of specific words in Echo Lake? *What is* Alogon?
It's from the Greek, by way of Robert Smithson's work of that name. There are all kinds of resonant meanings. It means the irrational, though it also means something that stands aside from the *Logos,* from logical speech, outside the Word. It also means an irrational number (our "surd"). A variety of meanings, all of which I meant to touch. Also, it means horse, because horses were "crazy," as was pointed out to me by the poet and Greek scholar Duncan McNaughton when I was working on the poem. That's why when Lyn Hejinian in her series of Tuumba Press chapbooks printed "Alogon" she had an image of an archaic horse, drawn from one of the prehistoric French cave paintings, on the cover.

Another is Abragrammatica.
That has to do with the fact that at that point I was working in an area of language that for me had almost the quality of a visionary state. The book was rapidly coming together. Things were virtually appearing to me in what seemed like a magical language procedure. So I was thinking of *abracadabra,* the plays on magic that we have, and it transformed itself into *Abragrammatica* as initiatory to this experience of the grammar of the language which was being transformed in that poem. What are you doing when you perform transformations on the normative grammar of a language? I don't really use

many neologisms or odd words. When I do it is almost like when a painter wants to make us attend to the fact that the thing is made out of paint, after all. Or can something entirely strange to your personal dialect be used in the poem without sounding forced or false? It's again a question of texture.

Somewhat related, you keep notebooks. What are their function?
The notebooks are a place for me to record. I came across an interesting take by Perry Miller, which I promptly entered in my notebook, about how notebooks functioned for American Puritans. It's quoted by Sewall in his biography of Emily Dickinson: "Almost every Puritan kept a diary, not so much because he was infatuated with himself, but because he needed a strict account of God's dealings with him, so at any moment, and above all at the moment of death, he could review the long transaction." What an engaging explanation of those Puritan diaries, and of a tradition which extended well into this century, where you would notate meticulously what happened to you on a given day, what you ate, what the weather was like. Trying to get at the untellable story, in a way.

For me they became a place for a kind of receptivity. By having a place to record things in between writings, things about my reading, or thinking about poetry, or whatever, they became a way to find my way back into the poem. Also, they are a practical way of recording things I might use later. They are full of conversations I've had. A recording of a kind of practical order, things I can refer back to. They are part of the ongoing thinking about poetics that I do, simply for the pleasure of it, though to know what I'm doing as well. A notebook as a place to think about these things has been very useful to me.

How do they contribute to the poem?
That's pretty haphazard. Sometimes I find my way back to certain recordings and the material becomes present in the poem, as if it were waiting for that.

What about the sense of quotation there?
I like the possibility of intertextuality. I am a reader, perhaps too much of one, and I live to some degree in the book. I like the possibility of bringing in other people's words to reflect the fact that for me experience flows at all levels, whether it's hearing a car out the window or reading something that is affecting me profoundly. Reading becomes co-extensive with the other experiences in my life, and it enters the poem like any other object or experience. It becomes a kind of layering of the text. Maybe it is also a

directive to people to go out there and look at that in the way that a lot of the stuff Pound threw into *The Cantos* was to get people to read a wonderful Chinese or Provencal poet. So the poem becomes then a shared place among a variety of texts, without, I hope, ever becoming simply a collage.

And is your sense of the text, then, a process rather than an artifact? Are the individual poems in Echo Lake, *for example, simply part of a larger poem, and* Echo Lake *itself part of an ongoing work?*
When I was writing *Notes for Echo Lake,* as the poems came along it became clear to me that each had a place if I could just find it. The book as a unit was primary for me. I tend to like very much the idea of a book which has a particular shape, just as a sentence has, and a poem within that has a particular shape. All these units of enclosure are levels of identity. So when a book fails to have a level of identity, when it's simply a gathering, it's the loss of one possible area of resonance. I think a lot of my earlier work in series, for example, proceeded from that same idea of defining things beyond their particular events as poems. But I think you can also lose the particular shape of a particular poem if it simply functions as a unit among other units in this larger program.

My newest book, *First Figure,* perhaps has an architecture, though it's really too early for me to tell. However, it was thought about less than *Notes for Echo Lake.* The pieces, as they came along, had much less necessary place; I didn't know where they went in the book. It was only after I had finished all the poems that I could begin to recompose them into a book. After a certain point in *Echo Lake* I knew to an extent where things had to go, what was missing, almost as if you were in the process of making a building and knew you'd better put a door there or no one would be able to get in or out.

You use in Echo Lake *a technique not unlike Robert Duncan's in* Bending the Bow. *That is, he has a number of sections from a long work, "Passages," interspersed with seemingly shorter poems outside the sequence. You do the same thing with "Notes 1," "Notes 2," and so on. Is the book really two different collections—"Notes for Echo Lake" and various shorter pieces?*
For me there are two sides to that. One is that when you have a poem which is an open series, like "Passages" or my "Symmetrical Poems," that is for me making possible that a voice has its place. When I started writing, say, the "Symmetrical Poems," which appear far back in my work, it was because a

very curious voice that was uncomfortable for me was coming forward consistently and across time. I realized that it was a little bit involved with the perversity of symmetry, which is both compelling and nauseating. It's also hallucinatory—you move into a symmetrical space and suddenly right and left are in question because they are identical. If you put a mirror in a symmetrical space you are very easily lost, as there aren't the conventional markers. It thus becomes both a static experience and a dynamic one, as it stands still but is without differentiation.

In *Echo Lake* specifically, over time as the book evolved I realized that there were going to be twelve sections, and in a certain way they could be taken as twelve months of a metaphorical year. For me this was a reference to the way we keep time, which in a way is what poetry is. Twelve is embedded in our psyches, going back to Babylonian numerology. There are the twelve apostles, a day of "two twelves," and so on. We are filled with twelves in our measure. Numbers then come to have a symbolic resonance which actually frames our experience.

I found in the interstices of the sections of "Echo Lake" a breathing space, days between the months, that created a balance that felt right to the book as I was making it. If those single shorter poems seemed to have their place, I let them stay there. There were numbers of things that just got written as I went along that never appeared in the book. But there were some that definitely thematically filled out the months of the book to make a balance.

Might you speak for a moment about your sense of revision?

That is one of those questions that I've had to learn to articulate over time yet don't like to dwell on too consciously. It comes down to whatever is necessary to the work at hand. I remember when I was first writing and was very much interested, for example, in poets like Charles Olson and Robert Creeley. Bob has almost a superstition against the possibility of re-vision, of seeing the poem again. It can't be done. So for him, at least the shorter poems have to come in a wholeness that allows you to keep it if it's good or throw it out if it's not. It's a hit-or-miss thing. I realized that at the level of layering at which I was working, at the level of extension, that that poetic simply wasn't going to work out for me, that I had to work by scraping away and adding on.

I remember at some point reading about de Kooning discussing a method of working over time. He was a painter I respected very much because he combined a quality of complexity with immediacy, and I learned a great deal from Abstract Expressionists in that sense. De Kooning would work over time, erasing, adding on, until the figure had emerged and the work seemed complete. I realized that was the way I would have to work, an ongoing immediacy. There wouldn't be a point at which I would arrive at some critical distance, and say, well, the metaphor of quatrain three is not quite realized, or some such nonsense. But in fact I would have to work at a level much closer to the page over time until whatever necessary figures had emerged to some degree of articulateness.

Obviously this varies. Some work comes extraordinarily slowly. The parts of *Echo Lake* which seem the easiest were by far the most agonizing, the individual lines which are seemingly unhooked from each other, because you are so much in danger of an entirely arbitrary structure. Sometimes after a day of what seemed like very good and steady work, I'd realize I had maybe only four words. Then there is a poem like the one for David Bromige, "False Portrait of D.B. as Niccolo Paganini," which is all in octosyllabics, save for the last two lines, and people have assumed that because the form is unusual for me it must have been very difficult. But on the contrary, it was one of the easiest. Once the eights were in my head, I had a structure and the poem just unfolded itself. It is precisely when you *don't* have the eights present, when you are in a mystery of what the measure of the thing is, that it becomes much more profoundly problematic. A deeper level of formal necessity has to arise if the thing isn't going to be simply, as *Publisher's Weekly* said, "lacking even the slightest pretense to logic or reality."

Why in that particular poem are the last two lines not in eights?
Certain music will conclude with a denser structure of the drums, so that the weight of it draws the piece to an end. Suddenly I was out of eights and only at that point, and it felt terminal. It was also a surprise that the poem came to me in the eights, but then I realized that I was talking about Paganini, the octave, the magic of numbers, and so on, and of course it makes sense that it would come in that structure.

What about your titles? Notes for Echo Lake. *Why* Notes? *What is* Echo Lake?
At some point in the making of the book, a title comes into place, and if it has enough resonance it stays in place. In the case of *Echo Lake,* I was thinking in a certain way of taking notes in the book. Some of the references in "Notes 1," for example, are to being at the Vancouver Poetry Conference. The Charles there is Charles Bernstein (a letter to him), as well as Charles Olson, and it's a poem of the coming first into the actual circumstance of

poetry, being around various poets at that time. I had this feeling of taking notes on a life, in a certain way. Although it doesn't come across as auto-biographical, it is profoundly so. Further, in the back of my mind was the question of musical notes, which are never far from the feeling of my work. As for *Echo Lake,* the book in its own way, without I hope becoming dependent upon mythological references, is involved with the Narcissus and Echo legend as one of the models of discourse. I don't want to go into this too fully, but there is that occasion of the Narcissus figure, which has generally simply been analyzed in a stupid way as just "vanity." But it also has to do with looking into the magic mirror, which is the lake, out of which voices emerge. Remember, the mirror is the mirror on the wall out of which the voice of the Other, which is also the Self that you see in the mirror, comes. So that for me has always been a very resonant picture of one aspect of discourse as it happens in poetry. Echo is, of course, the other figure who is almost a reader, one who takes the words as they sound through a landscape, and who defines in a sense that landscape through the sound-waves. In that defining the landscape becomes distorted across time, which is exactly what happens as we transmit speech over time. That is the life of discourse, of any natural language as opposed to an artificial one. Natural language would die without misinterpretation. Anyway, this is all ration-alization that came afterwards. The main point is that the title came into place with a certain degree of suddenness, and began to make sense in ways which helped me to finish the book.

Likewise, *First Figure* has a range of references to figures in a dance, first figures in a book of mathematics, *figurae* in language, and so on. Then I started coming across wonderful quotes like Roland Barthes's "There are no first figures." When I saw that I realized that *First Figure* was exactly the title I wanted because the first figure, then, is an area of mystery, yet you are always trying to disclose things through language which have a quality of primacy. We want to peel away layers of language to arrive at a word which is entirely absent—once you've found your way to it it isn't there.

How did your relationship with North Point Press come about?

To give a rough context, *Notes for Echo Lake* appeared in 1981. Before that I had been publishing with Black Sparrow Press. The editor of North Point, which was then a new press, Jack Shoemaker, was a friend of mine and a reader of my work. He offered to publish the book. It's an interesting and creative experiment. North Point is a press of modest size, the idea being that it would be subsidized by work of authors who fall in the crack of the computer read-outs from the big presses in New York, but who otherwise sell a very reasonable number of copies. Poets and novelists who in terms of the bottom line in New York just don't work out, though they sell ten or fifteen thousand copies. With low overhead and good distribution, these sales would also help to support work of younger and less well-known writers. It was started by a man named Bill Turnbull, who wanted to be a writer. In the fifties he had hung out on the Left Bank in Paris, and later in North Beach in San Francisco. At some point he realized that he wasn't going to be a writer, so he went out and made substantial money in construction. Then he decided to pay back his debt to literature, and taking presses like New Directions as a model he founded North Point Press.

The nice thing is that North Point pays attention to what the author's image of a book is. I remember when Clark Coolidge was doing a book for Harper & Row in the sixties; he proposed that Jasper Johns do the cover. Johns agreed and did a beautiful drawing that went from the back to the front, all the way across. They got into the Harper design offices, where all these flunky graphics people were turning out throw-away covers, and they said to Coolidge that he couldn't use Johns's work. Why not? Because we don't *do it* that way. They wanted to chop it in half and surround it with letters, so that it turned into a nondescript work. For Clark that became the image of the kind of relationship that a poet would have with a big press, one that was not doing the work because of any real belief in it, but out of some notion of possible prestige or whatever. So at the moment, I consider my relationship with North Point a very privileged one.

To Robert E. Symmes 1933
for a gift of resemblances

His arm slept. Dream-wounded and a former
figure he wept beside the stream
to see himself becoming it.
Who would write him as a target
burned by the sun
who heard a name he would become
or once was, red
as a second following dawn? The city
is full of ones called us
who endlessly greet each other by a name
that changes each time.
It's a wonder to return, head aching,
to witness the bear to its rest
and it's odd to wake and rewrite it
as a kind of resemblance.
I am tired and would like to leave.
I have never been here. The book
wears a lion's mane. For a moment
they were visitors resembling themselves.
Laughing he had said, I am tired of this waiting to be born.
The ones called figures crowd the street.
Each is a missing part of his name
and each longs to be drawn a face.

Seven Forbidden Words

"Mon chat sur le carreau cherchant une litière"
        Baudelaire, 'Spleen'

Who peered from the invisible world
toward a perfectly level field. Terms
will be broken here (have been broken here).
Should a city of blue tile appear
no one will be listening there.
He stood up, walked across the room

and broke his nose against the door.
A was the face of a letter
reflected in the water below.
He watched cross-eyed
learning a few words at a time.
The sun rose behind your shoulder
and told me to act casual
while striking an attitude of studied repose.
You grew these flowers yourself
so how could you forget their names.
The yellow one is said to be uncommon
and the heart tastes as expected, tender
and bitter like an olive
but less violent. It has been summer for a day
or part of a day
with shades drawn. The fires were deliberately set
and the inhabitants welcomed them.

The Flower of Capital

(*sermon faux—vraie histoire*)

"Not as a gesture of contempt for the scattered nature of reality."
    Spicer, *The Heads of the Town Up to the Aether*

The flower of capital is small and white large and grey-green in a storm its petals sing. (This refers to capital with the capital *L*.) Yesterday I borrowed Picabia's Lagonda for a drive through the Bois. A heavy mist enveloped the park so that we could barely discern the outline of a few silent figures making their way among the sycamores and elms. Emerging at Porte de Neuilly the air grew suddenly clear and ahead to my right I noticed M pushing a perambulator before her with a distracted mien. Her hair fell disheveled about her face, her clothes were threadbare, and every few steps she would pause briefly and look about as if uncertain where she was. I tried repeatedly to draw her attention with the horn, even slowing down at one point and crying her name out the car window, all to no apparent effect. Passing I saw once more (and as it developed, for the last time) the lenticular mark on her forehead and explained its curious origin to my companion, the Princess von K, who in return favored me with her wan smile. We drove on directly to the Château de Verre where the Princess lived with her younger sister and a few aged servants. The château itself was encircled by the vestiges of a moat now indicated only by a slight depression in the grass at the base of the walls. Or: we drove for hours through the small towns surrounding Paris, unable to decide among various courses of action. Or: they have unearthed another child's body bringing the current total to twenty-eight. Or: nine days from now will occur the vernal equinox. Yesterday in the artificial light of a large hall Ron spoke to me of character hovering unacceptably at several removes above the page. The image of the Princess and of M who were of course one and the same returned to mind as I congratulated him on the accuracy of his observation. L knitted this shirt I told him, and carved the sign on my brow, and only yesterday they removed the tree that for so long had interfered with the ordered flow of language down our street. Capital is a fever at play and in the world (silent *l*) each thing is real or must pretend to be. Her tongue swells until it fills my mouth. I have lived here for a day or part of a day, eyes closed, arms hanging casually at my sides. Can such a book be read by you or me? Now he lowers the bamboo shade to alter the angle of the light, and now she breaks a fingernail against the railing of the bridge. Can such a text invent its own beginning, as for example one—two—three? And can it curve into closure from there to here?

Dearest Reader

He painted the mountain over and over again
from his place in the cave, agape
at the light, its absence, the mantled
skull with blue-tinted hollows, wren-
like bird plucking berries from the fire
her hair alight and so on
lemon grass in cafe in clear glass.
Dearest reader there were trees
formed of wire, broad entryways
beneath balconies beneath spires
youthful head come to rest in meadow
beside bend in gravel road, still
body of milky liquid
her hair alight and so on

successive halls, flowered carpets and doors
or the photograph of nothing but pigeons
and grackles by the shadow of a fountain.

Book of the Yellow Castle

This can be seen as placing a mirror against the page.
The mountain is where we live, a circus there, a triangle
of unequal sides the days no sun appears.

This is life in the square inch field of the square foot house,
a September particle, biochip, or liquid in a jar,
and here is snow for the month to follow, light easy to move

but difficult to fix. The cat on the book has fleas.
It's a real cat with real fleas at least,
while the book is neither fixed nor field.

As soon as you had gone an image formed in order to be erased.
First an entryway then a left and right which seemed to be the same.
This letter explains everything and must never be sent.

This other arranges figures along an endless colonnade
imperceptibly darkening toward red. One pretends to be the case
the other is. Mornings the hands tremble, evidence of a missing thought.

Arrows will tell you where the words are meant to lead,
from hall to hall apparently. The hair is thinner
and the veins stand out a bit more.

Who could have known he'd be dead within the week,
victim of a loosening thread, the system by which we perceive.
Thus the castle above valley and plain, the logical circuitry and other
    such tricks,

the constant scanning, all kinds of features built in.
And thus the difference between sign and sigh, and the bells which signal
    a return.
The dog instructs the goats, the man instructs the dog.

Should we count the remaining trees to decide what they mean as well,
traces of a conversation possibly, or a larger plan. You enter the stories as
    a surd
and sleep through them, ignoring successive warnings,

shards of cloisonné, broken table legs, a canopied bed.
They are there because the rest have left.
These are scalings of a sentence.

8. Tom Raworth

"A curious hand touches the snow raising pigeons"

Tom Raworth was born in Bexleyheath, Kent, England, in 1938. Educated at the University of Essex, he took an M.A. degree in 1971. Between 1959 and 1964, he was the publisher of Matrix Press and the editor of *Outburst* in London, and in 1965 he founded with Barry Hall the Goliard Press. Raworth's various volumes of poetry include *The Relation Ship, Ace, Writing,* and *Tottering State: Selected Poems;* other books include *A Serial Biography* and *Logbook.* He has taught, or been poet in residence, at the University of Essex; Bowling Green State University; the University of Texas at Austin, and King's College, Cambridge. His awards include the Alice Hunt Bartlett Prize and the Cholmondeley Award. Currently, the poet lives in Cambridge.

Of his work, Raworth writes, "when do brainwaves start? / do animals have the right to kill? / flaws in equipment / play their part."

Could you begin by talking about your influences?
Oh, I suppose I've been influenced by everyone, but no one in a specific sense.

By "everyone" you mean people other than poets?
Sure. How could you write poetry if you read only poetry?

What about music?
I love it. And I hear my poetry as a sort of music, though I don't think of it as music. I think of it as language.

Is there a particular writing process you go through?
Well, sometimes I start with a title, sometimes I just write the poem, then think of a title. But it varies. No particular writing process.

Do you ask yourself any kinds of questions like am I exploring language as I'm writing this poem?
No. Sometimes I worry about where the next line is coming from. But no questions.

And how does the next line come?
It comes.

Do you hear a voice?
Who doesn't?

But sometimes in your work I get the feeling that you are observing rather than hearing.

Sure, sometimes. I'm not trying to be difficult here, but writing is not a process I think that much about. It's just something I enjoy doing. So yes, sometimes I look out the window and describe what I see because that language interests me for a moment. Sometimes I overhear a fragment of conversation, or something on the radio; or sometimes the arrangement of words in a newspaper will attract me.

Do you keep a journal of these observations?

I do now. For a long time I didn't, but now I do as it seems to be a useful way of making the poem.

Why didn't you do this earlier?

I'd just keep the poem in my head and type it out.

Do you feel isolated from the community of writers living in England, given the rather nontraditional nature of your work?

I don't feel isolated because belonging to a community of writers is the very last thing I want. I've come to realize that with my oldest friends who are writers, when we get together we absolutely never talk about writing. Why would you want to talk shop when you are away from work? Of course, that's distinct from someone saying have you read so and so, or seen this by so and so. That's just information. But why would you want to talk about the actual process?

What about your contemporaries in England? Do you find much of interest?

Not really. Maybe two or three people. Jeremy Prynne. John James's last book, *Berlin Afternoon,* interested me. A younger poet named John Mead from Devon.

What is there in Prynne's work that interests you?

That I can read it. That's the test for me. My mind doesn't get bored as it wanders through the poem.

Roy Fisher?

I liked his work, but I haven't seen anything new for a great while. Because of my economic situation in England I'm limited to the books people give me. Roy Fisher doesn't send me books because we've never really been in contact. Sometimes I see things in the bookshop, but that doesn't really work.

What is your economic situation?
I don't have any money. I don't have a job.

You don't teach?
I tried it for a couple of years. I was at Bowling Green in Ohio for a year, then Chicago for a year. Texas for six months. But it just didn't work for me. I liked certain things, and certain students became friends who've stayed in touch. But I like to write and teaching was doing something that I didn't like. It is a constant drain of energy. Plus I don't have a very factual memory as you'll see as we continue.

What about American poets?
I can still read Ed Dorn. Of the younger poets I can read Charles Bernstein, Kit Robinson. John Godfrey and Ted Greenwald in New York interest me. And I remember liking Lyn Hejinian's last two long poems. The 'prose' of Dale Herd and Stephen Emerson attracts me. But that's too specific in the sense that one poem by someone may give as much pleasure as two or three books by someone else.

What do you mean by "still read"?
Well, there is a lot of writing generally that just doesn't interest me. You read two or three words and you see through that particular construction into the mind of the writer, and you sense that it's not a very interesting mind. Why would you want to go further into an uninteresting mind? I never had the feeling that I had to somehow read all the "great" poetry in the world in order to be a poet.

But doesn't a young writer have to read a lot to know what's already been done?
I don't think so. I see your point, but I don't think so. Anyway, it becomes a question of the banality of thought after a certain point, a peculiar sentimentality. It is always enough just to write the poem, and to be able to defend it. I'm not advocating illiteracy; I'm only saying that that is the way I work. I've got friends who read every book of poetry that comes out. I

just can't read anything that bores me. I'd much rather stare at a wall and think.

And how do you know the poem you write is a poem?
All I can say is I *know*. It is quite open to someone else to disagree.

Do you find yourself having to defend poems like "Ace"?
In what sense? I know it's a poem. I'm sure that there are plenty of people who looking at my whole body of work would find little there in the way of poetry. But that's the way it is.

What made you decide to write poetry as a primary occupation?
The short answer would be that I got to like reading my work.

Did you have a group of people who helped keep you going?
Yes. Meeting Anselm Hollo in London in the early sixties was important for me, as was corresponding with Ed Dorn, David Ball, and Piero Heliczer. Later in the decade contact with John Barrell. But my wife's is the only critical intelligence I accept as useful; if she likes something, that's good.

You've written a screenplay?
Yes, though it was pretty ephemeral. Somebody was doing a short film and he asked for a text. I wrote short paragraph blocks so that the voice-over could be blended with the images rather than having to be synced to somebody's lips. But it was just an afternoon's work. I saw the film once, but never again. I've no idea what happened to it.

So that really isn't a major interest.
Well, if I thought of a good screenplay I'd write it. The same is true for traditional, closed verse. If something came in that way, why wouldn't I write it? But nothing has.

So in that sense, for you writing is writing.
Yes.

And Serial Biography?
Well, yes, I do detect a slight difference between poetry and prose. Poetry is cleaner and tighter.

In the reading or the writing of it?
In the writing of it. There is a certain room in prose that you can play with. If I were writing *Serial Biography* as a poem I'd cut a lot of it. I do see a clear distinction.

You mentioned a journal earlier on. Is it for drafts of poems or observation?
It's filled with all kinds of things. Sometimes poems, sometimes notes about what I've seen or done, whatever. Graphics these days, too.

Do you write your poems longhand or type them?
I write them now. I like the feel of pen to paper. When I started out I'd often write the poem, but I'd never really see it until I typed it out. Or sometimes I'd work straight on to the typewriter. That's a habit that's changed over the years. The rhythm of typing really is different from the rhythm of writing.

What about line breaks? Are you interested in metrics?
Not as such. I usually break a line where I would if I were reading the poem aloud. So I suppose it's determined by the breath.

May I ask a question on a slightly different subject? You went through a period where your poetry got very minimal . . .
Yes, it almost disappeared completely.

Well, this was the time also where artists like Jim Dine were providing illustrations for your texts. How do you feel about the possibility of integrating poetry and visual art?
I really like those books still. As a child I used to like the frontispiece, and I suppose it's a hangover from that. It is very important to me, the way it's done I mean. I like to work with people whose art I have an interest in. I just wouldn't turn poems over to someone and say please illustrate these. A person whose work I knew would, of course, have a free hand.

How do you work, in the sense of pacing yourself?
Well, when there is something to write I never seem to get tired, but I don't write everyday either. Sometimes when I'm writing, only two or three lines come, sometimes six or seven pages. I can't see why you'd stop while you can still go. It's bad enough when there's nothing there to write.

Do you have dry spells?
Sure.

And do you get worried?
Yes, of course. With age it gets a little less because I've been through it so often, and things finally do come again. There is also a time when I'm coming to the end of a long poem and I begin to hear a kind of repetition and think it's finished and something new is starting. But it's really just an echo of the same thoughts I've been working with. Then there is nothing for a while.

Going back to something you said earlier, you hear your poems?
Yes, and I suppose I hear the graphics as well, though that sounds impossible, doesn't it? I'm talking about my own graphics now.

So you mean when you have a black square, as in "West Wind," you hear it?
Yes.

So the sounds create a graphic pattern in your mind?
Well, that seems a shorter way of getting to a certain effect, like blackness. But actually, some of these things, like black squares, just seem to be good ideas at the time.

But you are an auditory thinker rather than a visual one?
Perhaps. As far as I can see poems I need to hear them. But then I do think of my poetry as being very visual also.

Are you concerned with the reader?
In the sense that I'm reading at the same time as I'm writing. I'm not writing for another reader outside, though. I find it impossible to distinguish between writing and reading. How can you write if you've never read before? After all, I have to satisfy a reader who is bored with a lot of poetry.

When you go back to your poems as a reader do you find them of value?
Usually, though often I see something completely different from what I originally intended. Other things come floating through.

And do you sense a growth in your work over the years?
That's difficult to answer. It seems to me that I write in exactly the same
way as I did when I started writing, though clearly that can't be so. But it
does seem to me that my way of looking at things hasn't changed much.
On the other hand, I don't write a lot. Robert Kelly, for instance, writes
an enormous amount, but I simply don't.

*But over the years it seems as if you've gotten more interested in the long
poem.*
Yes, that's true, though I think that's simply because I discovered that doing
a long poem was a way of combining a lot of shorter poems within a single
context.

How long did you work on Writing?
It must have taken two years, on and off.

*Was it meant to be read in some experimental way? I'm thinking of the
way it is set on the page.*
No. It's just one long poem. The typography is simply the way the designer
decided to do it, but it is not a key to reading it. I do quite like to be able
to skim across lines from one section to another, however.

What about Ace?
It took about six months at the most. I started it in Chicago and finished
it in Texas. *Writing* was also written mainly in the U.S.

Is there something about America that moves you to write long poems?
No. I've written long poems in England as well.

I've got a question about your selected poems, Tottering State. *You left
the selection up to the four people you mention at the start entirely?*
Yes. How could I select my own poems? After all, I selected them when I
chose to write them down. Further, the four who selected them are people
whose taste I trust. After all, the operation is like asking who is your favorite
child? For a moment you may like one over another, but that changes again
and again.

Were you pleased with the selections?
Yes, very much so.

Is there anything not included that makes you a little sad?
Sure. All the other poems. I think I should have another one called "unselected poems" or something like that. *Writing* couldn't be included because it was simply too long.

Do you think of yourself as being political?
In the sense of seeing things that way, yes; in the sense of being active, no.

What about as a poet?
It must inform my work, but I don't think I've got consciously political poems because I was always suspicious of the political poem. But politics must permeate what one does, along with everything else.

Are you a member of a particular party?
I voted Labour because I couldn't possibly vote for that ridiculous woman . . . I suppose I'm a High Tory Anarchist with Socialist reactions.

All right. How did your first book come about?
Barry Hall and I had a press; he suggested we do a book, so we printed it with his illustrations: different from those in the later Cape Goliard edition. Actually we did a number of books.

Goliard Press?
First *Matrix Press,* by myself. The magazine *Outburst,* and small books by Anselm Hollo, David Ball, Ed Dorn, and Piero Heliczer. Then *Goliard,* with Barry. We did books by Elaine Feinstein and Aram Saroyan; Olson's *West;* a play by Tom Clark and a prose-poem by Ron Padgett. Books we'd planned to do, like Prynne's *Kitchen Poems* and Paul Blackburn's *In, On or About the Premises* were done by Barry under the Cape Goliard imprint after I left.

These are all fairly experimental writers.
Yes, it's work that I can read for a moment.

Are you interested in their theory, the essays and so on?
No. I'm not opposed to theory. If I'm sitting down with someone and we test something as an idea, fine. But I'm not interested in constructing some sort of theoretical scaffolding.

What about L=A=N=G=U=A=G=E *magazine?*
I used to get copies and look at them. Occasionally I'd find something interesting, but I'd never read it from start to finish.

What about as a child? What were your favorite books?
Kim was my favorite, as I remember. I grew up with *A Child's Garden of Verses*. Also an anthology of poems that my father wrote out by hand which he left with us when he went to war. The Sherlock Holmes books, to a certain point. Anything I could get my hands on, really.

Looking through Tottering State, *it seems to me that early on you were interested in "readability," then moved to a kind of hermetic work, and recently have moved back again into a concern that the reader understands.*
So you don't see it as an escalation of withdrawal, but rather a kind of arc.

Yes.
I wouldn't say that was conscious. The first part of what you say seems true enough to me when I look back over those early poems. They are very much descriptions of events. But on the other hand I've always objected to "writing down to": that is the idea that I must simplify because no one can appreciate the way I see something. To me that doesn't make anything more accessible; rather it demonstrates a contempt for the reader. But then maybe I'm just liking simpler things as I get older.

Well, I guess what I'm trying to say is I sensed in reading the more recent poems a turning outward again.
Yes, I think that's true, even in the sense of the material used. Still, I remain fascinated that other people can read my work at all. It's not the most important thing in the world to me, but it's very pleasing.

Why does it surprise you?
Because I think that most people who like "poetry" have become used to think that only a certain area of writing is poetry, and that they can't, or shouldn't, read anything that doesn't proceed from that point of view.

Why is this?
Well, I just don't think there are many people who like to think while they read. They like to see, they like to feel, but they don't like to think.

Do you read criticism of your own work?
I don't go out of my way to look for it. If somebody sends me something I'll read it. I'm vain enough to do that, to want to see whether or not I agree with the critic.

Can you mention any critics you've agreed with?
Well, there aren't that many, and yet I can't remember anyone in particular at the moment. I try to forget that material.

Why so few?
I don't know exactly. Maybe people are nervous in approaching my work. Maybe people just don't think it's worth approaching. Maybe it doesn't fit in with any theory at the moment.

Does this bother you?
Not really. I'm more interested in what ordinary people who read books think, that they can read it. I'm not really all that interested in what someone says as part of their career pattern.

Has a review ever helped you get a fix on what you are doing?
Not that I can think of.

I sense that it's been difficult for you to hang in and keep writing all these years.
Well, there's nothing else I can do. The more I did of this the less and less there was of anything else available to me.

When did you become aware of this?
Quite early on, though it wasn't until the early sixties that I began to think of it seriously.

Were the first things you wrote, before the sixties, in more traditional forms?
No, not really. Actually I was trying to write prose then. I played around with a little rhyme, but basically it was Beckett pastiches and so forth. The only poet who meant anything to me at one point was Dylan Thomas. I liked the resonance in his voice, and I liked it on the page. I wrote a couple things vaguely in that vein. But I can remember my first real poem.

Which was?
"You Were Wearing Blue." It's the first thing I can remember being interested in when I reread it. I felt that it could actually stand by itself.

How was it that you first came to the United States?
In 1970 Kenneth Koch set up a reading for me in New York. Then I took a Greyhound around the country reading. I went to Bowling Green, where Ray DiPalma was teaching. Later, after I returned to England, DiPalma wrote and invited me to teach there for a year. Since that time, I've in essence not had a job. We lived in San Francisco for a time on just odd jobs, and that's how it's been back in England.

And you obviously find that life-style conducive to your writing.
Yes, though I've no objection to working. It's just that I seem now to be considered unemployable. Three years ago I applied to be 'retrained' as a carpenter. After almost a year I was told they couldn't retrain me because "we couldn't retrain a carpenter as a poet." At any job . . . etc.

Have you taken hallucinogenic drugs?
Sure.

And have they influenced your writing?
I've not experimented like that. Actually, the only drug I've ever taken that's given me an hallucinogenic experience was psilocybin in 1963. Otherwise, for me hallucinogens never really worked. The world continued exactly the same for me, save I sweated a lot. So what was the point?

In one of your poems you say that the game is to make rules that the next generation can break.
I think to a point that's the way things work. In a sense today that's the way the Language poets work, for example. One day somebody else will shatter that body of work and go on to writing another type of poetry. Their work will seem passé. Theory leads to rules.

What are your rules?
Well, the great charm of poetry for me was always that there really aren't any rules, that there is no one who can determine for anyone else how or what to write. That's why poetry is a test of the person. Anyone can write

something and insist it's a poem. If they hold to it strongly enough as a poem, and other people begin to see it as a poem, then it's a poem.

So you see yourself extending tradition?
I don't care about tradition. But then I don't even really understand what people mean by tradition; it's like something is somehow finished. How can that be?

What about creative writing programs in England?
They don't exist, actually. I think the University of East Anglia has a prose workshop with Malcolm Bradbury, but that's it. Creation is not the role, so people feel, of the university.

Did you ever participate in any kind of writing group?
No I didn't, and I can't say what would have happened had I done so. I was always fairly solitary. In a sense, though, the people I knew in 1958 and 1959 were a form of workshop—two or three friends who had similar interests. We didn't really talk too much about writing, but if someone had read a good book he'd pass it on. But it can be useful, don't you think? After all, in a workshop it's not really necessary to talk about poems. It's more of an atmosphere, the atmosphere of a certain way of looking at the world and living in the world.

Is there the same sense of making a "career" in poetry in England as here?
The American Poetry Review, Poets & Writers, *the Iowa School* . . .
No, I don't think so. People in Europe generally still look upon that whole scene as a strange North American phenomenon.

What is the publishing situation for a young writer?
I imagine that it's difficult. I don't have much to do with it, so I'm just making an assumption here. It's difficult for established writers also, except for that group of people who still dominate through Faber & Faber. Their books appear regularly, of course. Poetry publishing is always difficult because so many things influence it. Ted Hughes, Seamus Heaney, and others are well published because they are the people whom sixth-form English teachers like to teach because they can explain the poem. Therefore, students have to buy the books. There is a market continually created as the students become teachers themselves and reassign the books. It's a poetry that can be explained on the level of a sixteen-year-old in a classroom examination.

Is there a thriving small-press scene in England currently?
Not so much any more. I'm not sure why.

What about literary magazines?
The ones that I find of interest seem to be ephemeral, maybe only lasting
for two or three issues. I don't see the long running ones too much. *London
Magazine* was all right for a while, but then it went back to being rather
boring. There was a time when Hugo Williams was the poetry editor that
it seemed to be opening up a little bit more, but then Alan Ross got rid of
him and took it over again himself. But I don't feel that I have a duty to
follow every magazine that comes along, though when you first start writing
you do. I'm interested in other things now, which is fine. After all, there
has to be room for another generation.

You Were Wearing Blue

the explosions are nearer this evening
the last train leaves for the south
at six   tomorrow
the announcements will be in a different language

i chew the end of a match
the tips of my finger and thumb are sticky

i will wait at the station and you
will send a note, i
will read it
        it will be raining
        our shadows in the electric light

when i was eight they taught me *real*
writing
        to join up the letters

listen you said i
preferred to look

        at the sea. everything stops there at strange angles

only the boats spoil it
making you focus further

South America

he is trying to write down a book he wrote years ago in his head
an empty candlestick on the windowsill   each day
of his life he wakes in paris to the sound of vivaldi in summer
and finds the space programme fascinating since he still doesn't know
how radio works   as in the progress of art the aim is finally
to make rules the next generation can break more cleverly
        this
morning he has a letter from his father saying "i have set my face
as a flint against a washbasin in the lavatory. it seems to me
almost too absurd and sybaritic" how they still don't know
where power lies or how to effect a change
he clings to a child's book called 'all my things' which says:
ball (a picture of a ball) drum (a picture of a drum) book (a picture of a
        book)

all one evening he draws on his left arm with felt-tipped pens
an intricate pattern   feels how the pain does give protection
and in the morning finds faint repetitions on the sheets, the inside
of his thigh, his forehead   reaching this point
he sees that he has written pain for paint   and it works better

Logbook page 372

caps. I have been from one to another of my friends and I feel uneasy. I
understand now that I have been dead ever since I can remember, and that
in my wife I met another corpse. This is the way salt is made. We, the salt,
get put on and in things. But we are our different taste. I am in Maine.
Did your salt taste different today? What did you expect this to be? I am
sodium—I realize now my fear and love of water. Chlorine. We have combined to save you from our separate dangers and become the sea. Sodium
rode in the bus taking care not to sweat. In front of him the strange tracery
ASHTRAY. To his left SAFETY EXIT—LIFT BAR—PULL RED CORD
BELOW—PUSH WINDOW OPEN. He copied this tracery as the bus sped
along the dotted line. Across a pale green metal bridge. To the left, grassy
hillocks then pines. In the distance a black horse cropping. He counted four
blue cars, one after another. The green tinted windows of the bus announced

a storm. TS 306, another blue car, overtook the bus. This is MAINE, he told himself. And the selectors threw up 'an island off the rocky coast of Maine.' An exit road curved down. A truck called 'HEMINGWAY' passed. What strange mutations will come from that grassy strip between the lanes— never walked on, fed by fumes, cans, paper, tobacco and typesetters who

The Moon Upoon the Waters

the green of days : the chimneys
alone : the green of days : the feel of my nails
the whistle of me entering the poem through the chimneys
plural : i flow from the (each) fireplaces
the green of days : i barely reach the sill
the women's flecked nails : the definite article
i remove i and a colon from two lines above
the green of days barely reache the sill
i remove es from ices keep another i put the c here
the green of days barely reaches the sill
the beachball : dreaming 'the' dream
the dreamball we dance on the beach

gentlemen i am not doing my best
cold fingers pass over my eye (salt)
i flow under the beachball as green waves
which if it were vaves would contain
the picture (v) and the name (aves)
of knots : the beachball : the green sea
through the fireplaces spurting through the chimneys
the waves : the whales : the beachball on a seal
still : the green of days : the exit

Magnetic Water

glare burns of nothing very near in time
surfaces split and go their own ways
in the breeze of light   so too this image
lengthens nothing   i praise your light

against the night whose skin
glistens with moving cloudy white

those burns were of themselves the image
as was the breeze   one surface was of film
the character half drawn   one coloured
the night air bright with nothing but reflection

then from my death i felt that all must die
that holding in our time was black
and cold   that rocks glowed red
that trees which formerly i climbed
swayed from their roots
in one direction   i heard
me fumbling through the scores
of ancient scripts
as forces struggled for my arm
while thought as muscle lifted from the pool
a silent waterspout whose touch
sucked out one convolution of my brain

the letters danced with changing shape
one two three four   all sound poured in
those several openings of the tube
flexed   doors on the air   no floors

empty we think we know what comes
lip readers of the slowed heart's valve
don't hear the music of those crystals set
in joints of syntax cry
love is our salve
believe us or we die

9. Ishmael Reed

"And that history is subject to the will"

Ishmael Reed was born in Chattanooga, Tennessee, in 1938. He was educated at the University of Buffalo, New York, and in 1965 co-founded the *East Village Other,* Since 1973 he has been director of Reed and Cannon Communications, and on the board of the Before Columbus Foundation. His awards have included a National Endowment for the Arts Grant, the Rosenthal Foundation Award, and a Guggenheim Fellowship; he has been a visiting senior lecturer at the University of California at Berkeley for seventeen years. He is the author of six novels and two books of essays. Reed's books of poetry include *Conjure, Chattanooga,* and *Secretary to the Spirits;* his anthology, *19 Necromancers from Now,* appeared in 1970, and *Calafia: The California Poetry* in 1979.

I've read through your early work and I wonder if you can comment on your nontraditional punctuation?
Well, I was living in New York when my early poems were written, and the thing then was to be experimental. We thought that using slashes and "wd" instead of "would" was experimental writing. I finally asked Joel Oppenheimer, who was well known for this, why he used slashes instead of apostrophes and he told me that it was because he was a typesetter and the typesetting machine had no apostrophes. So I guess it wasn't all that avant garde after all.

And with Chattanooga *you return to traditional punctuation.*
Yes. I feel that the primary problem in American poetry today is the great chasm between the poet and the reader. Poets seem to be writing for themselves, or other poets, or tenure, or whatever. But their reasons have little to do with communicating. I just don't have patience for that anymore, to try to explicate a poem by a writer who thinks he's Plato. With my work I try to communicate very directly.

Haven't you recently written songs?
Yes. The first album of my songs was released just a few weeks ago in New York. Taj Mahal sings the songs, and composers like David Murray, Steve Swallow, Allain Tousant, Lester Bowie, and so forth composed the music. So with that project I'm really trying to reach people more directly.

But you didn't always approach writing this way.
No. When I was at the university I would have said that the best poets were the Modernists, though now I'm thinking that they are probably the country-

western and blues writers. You put yourself out on a limb saying something like that, but I really don't read anything that's as good as what I hear on the radio.

What is the title of your album?
Conjure.

But your early poems do communicate.
Well, maybe. It seems to me that their major features are irony or under-statement. Paradox. But there is a little "secret" material there, some hidden culture.

Like . . .
The struggle between Christianity and Vodoun. Look, I think the best thing that happened to my poetry was that I won a contest called "Poetry in Public Places," so that my poetry appeared all over the New York subways. I thought that was great, communicating with lots of people. After all, when I was at the university I was taught that communication was bad, that poetry has to be as inaccessible as possible. I spent too many years of my life reading inaccessible poetry and not understanding much of it.

Isn't that still going on?
Sure. The bourgeoisie is being hustled by this avant-garde stuff. They feel so intimidated that they don't question anything. They go see "Einstein on the Beach" in New York, leave in the middle to go have dinner, then come back to say that they stayed till the end. At least in Mark Twain's time, artists like these were tarred and feathered. There is a hype here—"selling the unknown" is the way David White put it. He runs a dance theater in New York and has a lot of avant-garde people passing through. "Sell the unknown"—that's the hustle.

I like to have people understand my work. I'm pleased when I can stand before an audience in places as removed from each other as Harlem and Colorado Springs and see people responding to the lines.

So what changes are you making in your writing to make it more com-municative?
Dealing with ordinary language. Since at least 1912 poets have been making the point that simile, metaphor, irony, and so forth are all contained in everyday speech. Yet most of the celebrated writers in this country are

European in their diction and style. That's part of the assimilative baggage they carry, to write and think like Europeans. A prime example, of course, is Henry James, his convoluted sentences. I just found out recently that he was Irish, which makes a lot of sense. He tries to be more English than the English.

I used to hate Carl Sandburg, but now I'm getting to think that he's superior to the Modernists. He had a good ear. He could hear the speech of ordinary people in the Midwest and convert that into poetry. He's an amazing poet, though ten years ago I wouldn't have said that.

Frost?
I never understood all the fuss about Frost. Maybe I missed something. I always felt that his material was pretty trite. There are a lot of people like Frost who can write competent poetry, but the wild and eccentric genius is pretty rare. Gary Hongo, from the Iowa School, made an interesting remark. He said at Iowa workshops they teach you how to write a poem so that you can't lose, though you can't win either. You write a competent poem. That doesn't apply to him, of course. He's a superb poet.

More people know your fiction than your poetry, wouldn't you say?
Probably.

What's the distinction?
Well, there's a thin line between fiction and poetry. After all, they're both fictional. A lot of poetry I read appears to be short stories to me, it's just that the compression of language has led to a kind of hybrid. There's plot, character, and so forth.

Actually, I don't find that distinction very useful. I'm more interested in the poetry of different cultures in this country, poetry influenced by the Mexican-American culture, for example, or Native American. I don't forget the European—we grew up with it—but a lot of people I knew are really bicultural poets. Our Before Columbus Foundation includes not only black and Chicano writers, but also Irish-American and Jewish writers. When I was growing up I never thought about Irish-American writers, John O'Hara and people like that. He is not the best example as he's actually assimilationist, but you begin to discover as you read that none of the contemporary Jewish writers like Roth or Bellow are really as good as the early immigrants. When you assimilate you become very bland. None of them is as good as Mike Gold, say, or Isaac Babel. We want to get away from the first generation—from a brogue, from Yiddish—but this is powerful material drawing on the oral tradition. I'm reading one of Mike Gold's novels now, and he talks about his father, who was first generation out of Russia. He was a storyteller, and that's how the family would entertain itself. In the south when I was a kid, it was the same kind of thing—the older people would tell stories to entertain us, hundreds of stories. The second and third generations move away from this, try to be like everyone else. So you end up with a bland novel or a poem without any spirit.

Besides song writing, what else is interesting you now, in terms of your poetry?
Well, maybe because I'm writing songs, rhyme. Rhyme is considered corny. But when the Imagists began their revolution against traditional meters and rhymes, they set up their own tyranny. One tyranny replaces another. So while it's now considered corny to rhyme, that's really just another rule.

So you think that oral poetry, which almost by definition uses those devices, is an important force in America today?
Yes. I hear it everywhere. Again, song lyrics are so much better today than when I was going to high school—Prince, Bob Dylan, Jim Morrison. These people have changed the whole conception of song writing. But I'm exaggerating a bit. In my poetry class at Berkeley I start off with Cole Porter's "You're the Top" as an exercise in metaphor; it's an amusing catalogue of cultures and disciplines. Even Brooks and Warren's *Understanding Poetry* includes those lyrics. It's a poetry that communicates to millions of people.

You mentioned "assimilationist" as a danger.
Well, I'm actually not that intolerant. I read assimilationist writing all the time. I probably read more of that than anything else. One chooses what one is comfortable with.

Do you perceive something new coming out of the consciousness of this problem?
I think it's already happened. The trend I see around the world is that American ethnicity has broad appeal, everybody wants it. I was in Martinique recently, and they were selling Michael Jackson records in supermarkets. It's still a French colony, but they are Americanized. When there is a western on television the whole country stops.

We don't see this because we are inside it. If you look at the *London Times,* though, they'll tell you that American poetry is multicultural. You won't get that from the *New York Times,* will you? Europeans, because they are at a distance, can see things more clearly about our culture than we can. There are poets in the Southwest, for example, who are very well known in Europe. Simon Ortiz is one. The novelist Leslie Silko is another. But if our major critics in the East are acquainted with them they don't let on.

Why is this?
Well, I don't really know. I think that the elitists, the upper classes always think you have to import art. I understand that the upper-class Greeks neglected Homer while importing Egyptian art.

Do you consider your work political?
Sure, I think a lot of it is. Many authors who have been dismissed as art-for-art's-sake writers were in fact very political—Blake, obviously. I don't know how this opinion that art can be divorced from politics came about. I just saw Diego Rivera's work at the Detroit Museum—it's his mural on the Ford assembly plant. It is a very powerful political painting, but at the same time the guy has tremendous imagination and can really paint. Look at *Moll Flanders*. Defoe tells us that if there had been orphanages around she wouldn't have turned out that way. That's a political statement, isn't it? The only problem comes when the critical establishment becomes uncomfortable, then labels something a polemic. They are now saying the same thing about women writers as they used to say about black writers. If there is a difficult female character, they'll say she's not "well rounded." It seems like there are the elitist critics, then the rest of us: blacks, women, homosexuals, all kinds of categories.

So I'd say that I think some of my work is political, some very personal. I write in different styles and about various issues.

Reading your earlier poems I got the feeling that somehow no matter what the subject or style you had a running theme—freedom.
Well, our tradition in this country is that we want our freedom. Freedom has become almost a deity, especially in the modern civil rights speech. Martin Luther King probably mentions freedom more than he mentions God. That's my tradition. I think that in the sixties a lot of people forgot that and attempted to import totalitarian ideas from Cuba or China into this country which just simply failed to take into account our need for

personal freedom, eccentricity. Artists here just can't operate in that situation. Stalin sent a poet to prison because he thought he had laid a curse on him.

You use curses.
Of course. Look at any standard textbook of poetry and it'll include curses. Writing is the only art I know of where people are criticized for using the traditional forms of that profession. I write satire sometimes, and people point out to me that it has been long worked out. They tell me not to write invective, or curses. But these are all part of the world's poetry.

Why?
I think it's really whim. Literary critics just don't seem to be as bright as critics of painting and dance. I see them get away with a lot of generalizations which painting or dance critics would never get away with. In dance and the other fine arts you really have to know your stuff. Writing is not considered a fine art in this country. It's seen as a medium of entertainment.

Can we go back to women for a moment?
Yes, they seem to be on the hot seat right now, except of course for those who are very traditional. The critics like Joyce Carol Oates a lot. She got up before the National Book Award crowd and said she believed in "tradition." That sent a message loud and clear. But some of the crazies like Adrienne Rich get bad reviews for all the wrong reasons.

You mentioned earlier the Iowa writers poem. What's the alternative?
For every writer to find his or her own style. Everybody's got a different voice. There's a machine that measures voice prints, and they all turn out to be different. But look, if people all want to write the same way it's okay with me. I'm very tolerant when I teach poetry workshops. But the best poets I know are those whose work you can identify, they have a trademark like musicians. I can identify John Coltrane.

You have to start off imitating. I began by imitating poets I'd read in school. Yeats, Pound, the Modernists, because that was the education at the time. Now of course Freud and a nickle can't get you a cup of coffee. Existentialism is out of date. Before Sartre died he was listening to Handel's "Messiah." You get up into your seventies and you realize that you can't fool around with that cafe stuff any more. But Modernism is still the establishment. Their gods are dead but they manage to hold on to the money and the prizes.

Have you tried writing plays?

I started in 1977. A play I wrote called "Mother Hubbard" was staged at the Actor's Studio in New York in 1980. Clarence Williams of the TV show "The Mod Squad" played the lead. I've also written a soap opera, or a parody of soap operas. It was premiered in Paris, and has won a couple prizes. I've tried a couple TV scripts because they reach people right away. I'd like to see MTV format include poetry on television. If people aren't going to read, then maybe the modern poet has to use these other media. Of course the intellectuals don't like that idea, but they said the same thing about film in the thirties. They said that movie houses were where the derelicts hung out. Now we've got something called The Cinema. The same thing will happen to television. In fact, in the Museum of Modern Art they run episodes of "I Love Lucy."

You mentioned imitation. Who were your black influences?

I didn't start reading much Afro-American fiction until I started teaching it. I was drafted into the teaching profession in 1967, and I went out and read a lot of these people. In black writing there is a tremendous difference between what was written in the twenties, say, and the sixties. The earlier stuff was written in very elitist verse forms, wherein in the latter you've got real grass-roots poetry. In some ways, that later work is probably the most important thing going on in American poetry since Imagism.

The odd thing there is that Imagism began as a women's movement, but in the end the men got the credit for it. But that's the way it works. I heard John Denver say on the Grammy awards that Bill Haley and the Comets invented rock & roll. I guess Chuck Berry doesn't count.

Well, that brings me to your 19 Necromancers *anthology. You included no women poets.*

I know. It was a mistake.

Did you get criticized for that?

Sure, but I've changed. Our Before Columbus Foundation used to be called the Boys' Club by various women. Now even our president is female. But in the sixties we had a different attitude. Our workshop in New York always subjected women writers to ridicule. We told them to go make coffee. But look, I grew up with John Wayne. It was dumb, but that was the way it was. We were oppressing other people while we were talking about our own oppression. It's like a circus act where you've got people standing on each other's shoulders. But now my publishing company, I. Reed Books, and our magazine, *Quilt,* publishes mostly women writers.

What avenues of publication do you recommend for younger poets?

Small presses. Big publishers don't really care about poetry much; they'll publish it as a favor, but grudgingly. A young poet has a much better chance of getting and keeping work in print with a small press. There are plenty of good ones. I'd just take ten poems and send them out to ten good magazines—*Ploughshares, Mississippi Review, New Letters, Antaeus, Obsidian.* I think that the young poet probably has a better chance of getting published today than when I was starting out. I moved to New York because I couldn't get published with a Buffalo address. When you are twenty-two, you'll do anything.

Did it work?

Of course. The first week I was there I went to a place called White Horse Inn and I saw Edward Albee and Tennessee Williams. This country boy almost had a fit. But you'd be amazed. People are very accessible there. You meet the writers who are doing the work. There weren't too many literary magazines around then, though, and now there are thousands. They come from places you'd never expect, like Tulsa, Oklahoma.

How did you get your first book of poems published?

Well, my chapbook was published by a Dutch publisher. The second book was published by the University of Massachusetts Press. They asked me for a manuscript and so I went through my files and started trying to put a book together.

They asked for a manuscript?

Yes. I've been fortunate that way, not really having to send out much unsolicited material.

Can you give us some sense of what you feel is the current avant-garde?

Well, there was an article in the *New York Times* a few weeks ago by Michael Davidson in which he mentions some people connected with the avant-garde, the Language poets. Their influences seem to be French structuralism, though when I went to France the intellectuals told me that structuralism had been out of fashion for years.

If you read through German writers working in Berlin before the war, a lot of that poetry sounds remarkably like what these people are doing. Also, the Dadaists tried everything Burroughs does, and writers like Kathy Acker, in the thirties. Something I find missing in the American avant-garde is that the Europeans were political, antifascist, antiestablishment. The American avant-garde gets along very well with the establishment and fascism.

Personally, I feel that the real avant-garde is made up of writers working out of more than one tradition. This includes a great number of women writers. Young blacks writing in the sixties out of a grass roots language— that was avant-garde.

Isn't there a difference between an avant-garde style and an avant-garde consciousness?
I have no idea. All I can say is that the European avant-garde has always been more interesting to me than the American because they were so generally political. Here it seems so academic and so intolerant of criticism. I remember that there was a big debate in the *San Francisco Chronicle* a while back where Tom Clark wrote something mainly critical of the Language poets, and the response was very fierce. It was like a bunch of cranks who call talk shows. Some of these guys are professional linguists, and once the linguistic labs get hold of poetry it won't be long before computers are writing it. I was a little frightened by the self-righteous tone of the response. It seemed so organized and humorless.

How do you know whether or not something is nonsense?
Well, you've just got to make your own judgment. If I get the poet alone I interrogate him. Most of the time if you try to pin them down they've got no real response beyond "some voice was talking to me." It's like the Son of Sam, I guess. Or Hamlet. I think the Language poets are being adopted by the critics and the universities, or at least I hear their names a lot. But I think there is probably more theory to it than poetry. When you've got more theory than art, things are pretty decadent.

What is the responsibility of the poet?
It's hard enough to write, without considering one's responsibility.

How do you distinguish between a poet like Charles Bukowski, say, or Gary Snyder, and somebody like Rod McKuen?
Rod McKuen has a lot of trite lines. A poet is required to be more inventive than a prose writer. A poet has to come up with fresher ideas, images,

language. Prose writers can get away with clichés and trite writing; if you've got to fill up three hundred pages, not every line is going to be great. There is a lot of housekeeping there. But poets must have a fresher way of looking at things. Babette Deutsch said that a prose writer would say "babbling brook," while a poet would say "the brook engaged in small talk," or something like that. And that seems to me to be the problem with McKuen.

What about Bukowski?
I think his work is interesting, though there is a lot of misogyny in it. *Women* is a fine novel. Certainly he's a far better writer than Rod McKuen. He's very well known in France. Jack Micheline, a San Francisco poet who is not too well known here, is also very popular in France. He is one of the best poets to come out of the Beat group, which has more or less come to resemble a twenty-year-long party.

Maybe it's their subject matter.
Yeah, maybe they fulfill the stereotypes Europeans have of Americans. Bukowski's got that macho, good ol' boy, can-of-beer-in-front-of-the-television-set tone. But there is just something arresting there. Maybe it's the sense of antagonism. Also, I think people like his performance a lot. After people go to a reading and I ask them what he read, about all they say is, "He was really drunk."

What do you think of Sonia Sanchez?
I like her work. She's got a lot of integrity. She could write conventional work, but she's been writing in a tone of the "black female working class." Unlike some of the others, she's successful with it. She received an award from our foundation this year.

She's an amazing reader of her own work.
She really knows that territory. My problem, though, with at least some of the black feminist writers is that they do poor imitations of the real thing. For example, in *The Color Purple* Alice Walker has this poor, illiterate share-cropper woman using images like "her face gleamed like good furniture" and words like "ruddy." You only have to spend a couple minutes with a Mississippi sharecropper to know they don't speak like that. Also, I'm always wondering why these female characters get themselves involved with these brutish men. What I suspect is that eventually these proletariat women will begin writing poetry and fiction themselves, and then the middle-class writ-

ers will move on to writing about their own world. They are sort of tourists. The real stuff is hard to take. Maybe some welfare mother is writing something right now that will run these people out of business.

Can you talk a little bit about your foundation?

The Before Columbus Foundation has been going since 1976. We've got writers with many different backgrounds on our board. We started as a distribution cooperative representing about 125 small presses. We still perform that function. We began the American Book Awards in 1976, also. Soon as the Association of American Publishers started theirs we sent them a telegram asking them to drop the name; we had it first. They got upset and threatened to sue, arguing that they had the right to the name because they spent four million dollars on publicity.

We've conducted programs in New York and San Francisco, giving awards to writers, while promoting their books and their publishers. At first they were strictly small press awards, though now the large presses are sending in their books for nomination. This year we even gave an award to someone who had a book published by Farrar Straus.

We've started putting classes together in an attempt to organize the world's first multicultural university. We present all the instruction at one time, symposium style. It's interesting to hear the parallels of experience coming out of the various cultures. At the moment we occupy space on the Berkeley campus, and we are running an eight-week course in prose. It's amazing, the kind of materials we get—Asian, African, feminist, Latin American, political. Next year we hope to add courses in multicultural drama and dance.

Have you been to Naropa Institute?

I was there a while back and I did a story on the place.

Not very positive.

I thought it was. I said they were good poets. I said they were important writers. I just pointed out that some people were upset by the religious element there. I gave them a chance to express their point of view. I interviewed Dick Gallup and Michael Brownstein. When the essay was reviewed in the *New York Times,* in fact, the reviewer thought that I was far too polite.

But look, what promoted my piece was a remark printed in *Time* which said that Naropa was "the center of American poetry." That wasn't the way

I saw it. A Filipino-American poet told me that the "center" of American poetry is in every poet's heart. The Naropa people got very upset at my essay, but I just really don't understand why.

Anne Waldman was here about a month ago and wasn't exactly pleased about it.

I discussed this with her, and in fact I said positive things about her in the article and I have even published her work. I just feel that those poets are just one part of the whole picture. There is a multicultural renaissance going on in poetry today, and for the media to say there is one center is wrong. They call themselves the Jack Kerouac School of Disembodied Poetics, yet late in his life when he became very right wing Kerouac made a number of criticisms of Ginsberg and the rest which make mine seem very mild.

What's your opinion of "literary intellectuals"?

The New York intellectuals seem to control the literary trends. Actually, I don't know if they are intellectuals any more. They make remarks about things they don't even read. I'm trying to acquaint them with what has gone on in the last twenty years. Some of these people literally don't walk above 14th Street. They've never been to 42nd. It's enemy territory. Yet they'll come out in the *Partisan Review* with a statement about national culture. How can they know what's happening in Kentucky, or New Mexico, or California? They still think that California is a place where gurus live, that we all hang out at the beach all day. They are simply out of touch with the movement of the last twenty years. They call our writing "Third World." I don't pay any taxes in Libya. Or they call our stuff "social work." It's foolishness. So we are trying to get them to recognize that talent is common.

I am a Cowboy in the Boat of Ra

'The devil must be forced to reveal any such physical evil (potions, charms, fetishes, etc.) still outside the body and these must be burned.' (Rituale Romanum, *published 1947, endorsed by the coat-of-arms and introductory letter from Francis Cardinal Spellman*)

I am a cowboy in the boat of Ra,
sidewinders in the saloons of fools
bit my forehead   like   O

the untrustworthiness of Egyptologists
who do not know their trips. Who was that
dog-faced man? they asked, the day I rode
from town.

School marms with halitosis cannot see
the Nefertiti fake chipped on the run by slick
germans, the hawk behind Sonny Rollins' head or
the ritual beard of his axe; a longhorn winding
its bells thru the Field of Reeds.

I am a cowboy in the boat of Ra. I bedded
down with Isis, Lady of the Boogaloo, dove
down deep in her horny, stuck up her Wells-Far-ago
in daring midday getaway. 'Start grabbing the
blue,' I said from top of my double crown.

I am a cowboy in the boat of Ra. Ezzard Charles
of the Chisholm Trail. Took up the bass but they
blew off my thumb. Alchemist in ringmanship but a
sucker for the right cross.

I am a cowboy in the boat of Ra. Vamoosed from
the temple I bide my time. The price on the wanted
poster was a-going down, outlaw alias copped my stance
and moody greenhorns were making me dance; while my mouth's
shooting iron got its chambers jammed.

I am a cowboy in the boat of Ra. Boning-up in
the ol West i bide my time. You should see
me pick off these tin cans whippersnappers. I
write the motown long plays for the comeback of
Osiris. Make them up when stars stare at sleeping
steer out here near the campfire. Women arrive
on the backs of goats and throw themselves on
my Bowie.

I am a cowboy in the boat of Ra. Lord of the lash,
the Loup Garou Kid. Half breed son of Pisces and
Aquarius. I hold the souls of men in my pot. I do
the dirty boogie with scorpions. I make the bulls
keep still and was the first swinger to grape the taste.

I am a cowboy in his boat.; Pope Joan of the
Ptah Ra. C/mere a minute willya doll?
Be a good girl and
bring me my Buffalo horn of black powder
bring me my headdress of black feathers
bring me my bones of Ju-Ju snake
go get my eyelids of red paint.
Hand me my shadow

I'm going into town after Set

I am a cowboy in the boat of Ra

look out Set   here I come Set
to get Set   to sunset Set
to unseat Set   to Set down Set

                        usurper of the Royal couch
                        imposter RAdio of Moses' bush
                        party pooper O hater of dance
                        vampire outlaw of the milky way

The Conjurer

This woman in the russet dress holds a ball in her hand.
She will place it under a cup
and you,
bending over in your professional dress
will watch and say, "that one."

But, of course, the ball will appear in another cup
entirely.

I, in the background,
have performed this same trick,
know the secret of the balls. But you
would not gasp if I performed
would not think less of the lady dressed in red if I should
unmask
the trick.

The willing believer takes his lady's hand,
not because of her tricks,
but because of her.
He likes to say, "I take this lady for her tricks,"
but only because
the record looks better that way.

The Katskills Kiss Romance Goodbye

1
After twenty years of nods
He enters the new regime
The machine guns have been
Removed from the block
The women don't wear anything
You can see everything

2
Hendrick Hudson's Tavern
Has slipped beneath the
Freeway where holiday drivers
Rush as if they've seen the
Hessian Trooper seeking his
Head

3
They get their goosebumps at
The drive-in nowadays, where
The Lady in White at Raven
Rock is Bette Davis and
Burton apes Major Andre
Hanging before the Haunted
Bridge

4
A New England historian has
Proof that King George wasn't
So bad.

Gave in to every demand
Donated tea to the American needy
Yankees are just naturally jumpy

5
Where once stood madmen
Buttonholing you
Gentlemen think of Martinis
On the train to Mount Vernon

6
R.I.P. old Rip
Cuddle up in your Romance
Your dog Wolf is dead
Your crazy galigaskins out
Of style
Your cabbages have been canned
Your firelock isn't registered
Your nagging wife became a
Scientist, you were keeping
Her down

7
Go back to the Boarded Up
Alley and catch some more winks
Dreaming is still on the house

Loup Garou Means Change Into

If Loup Garou means change into
When will I banish mine ?
I say, if Loup Garou means change
Into when will I shed mine ?
This eager Beast inside of me
Seems never satisfied

I was driving on the Nimitz wasn't
Paying it no mind
I was driving on the Nimitz wasn't
Paying it no mind

Before you could say "Mr. 5 by 5"
I was doin 99

My Cherokee is crazy
Can't drink no more than 4
My Cherokee is crazy
Can't stand no more than 4
By the time I had my 15th one
I was whooping across the floor
I was talking whiskey talking
I was whooping across the floor

Well, I whistled at a Gypsy who was reading at my cards
She was looking at my glad hand when something came
Across the yard started wafting across the kitchen
Started drifting in the room, the black went out her
Eyeballs a cat sprung cross her tomb
I couldn't know what happened til I looked behind the door
Where I saw her cold pale husband
WHO'S BEEN DEAD SINCE 44

They say if you get your 30
You can get your 35
Folks say if you get to 30
You can make it to 35
The only stipulation is you
Leave your Beast outside

Loup Garou the violent one
When will you lay off me
Loup Garou the Evil one
Release my heart my seed
Your storm has come too many times
And yanked me to your sea

I said please Mr. Loup Garou
When will you drop my goat
I said mercy Mr. Loup Garou
Please give me victory
I put out the beans that evening
Next morning I was free

10. Stephen Rodefer

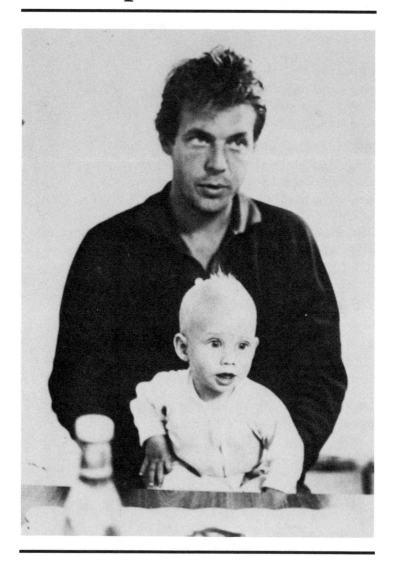

"I inhabit the language the world heaps upon me"

Stephen Rodefer was born in Bellaire, Ohio, in 1940. He attended Rossall School in England, studied art history at Amherst College, and took his graduate degree in language and literature at the State University of New York at Buffalo, where he was part of the group which published the *Magazine of Further Studies* out of Charles Olson's classes there in the sixties. Rodefer has taught at SUNY Buffalo, the University of New Mexico, San Francisco State University, and currently teaches at the University of California, San Diego, where he is curator of the Archive for New Poetry. His books include *The Knife, One or Two Love Poems from the White World, Plane Debris,* and *Four Lectures* (co-winner of the American Poetry Center's 1982 Annual Book Award). In addition to his own work, he has published book-length translations of Villon and selections from Sappho and the Greek anthology. Rodefer is a contributing editor of the West Coast magazine *Zyzzyva.*

"Writing is a graphic art," Stephen Rodefer writes, "and a word projects either stroke or color. As it is born, a poem is drawn. It can begin with a figure or a line. It can begin to clothe a cartoon or be *about* the idea of anything. It begins to paint itself. It can be made with a pencil or with a knife, with a pen or a recorder, or with a keyboard contraption that strikes the paper. It requires patience, approach, observation, technique, impulse, intent, alternation, energy, and obsession. It can be attacked by history, as well as attack history. It can be unknown and done only for itself and nothing other. Its meaning can change in time, and *always* does."

Did you grow up in the Midwest?
I grew up in Bellaire, Ohio, from 1940 to 1956—hardly anywhere else, except on the radio.

What was on the radio and what happened in 1956?
What was on the radio was rhythm and blues. We used to come home from school, seventh grade, eighth, and as it got dark you could tune in Nash-ville—they played the hits at least a month before you could get them from Pittsburgh. From Wheeling all you got was the WWVA Jamboree, and in a funny but I guess obvious kind of youthful intolerance we disdained that. Later you found out you could have heard Hank Williams on your doorstep, but you just didn't know. Ignorant of what is next to you—sounds something like the "modern condition," doesn't it. Later, going away to school—which was what happened in 1956—I remember a new friend, Jon Wagner, who was a jazz fanatic, took me into Cleveland to hear Miles Davis and his band. I learn many years later, Clark Coolidge assures me, that John Coltrane

would have been in Miles Davis's quartet in 1957, but I had never then heard of Miles Davis. The question is, if you heard Coltrane play in Cleveland in 1957 but didn't really *listen* to him intently till five years later, is it true that you heard Coltrane as a teenager—I mean literally at the same time you were first waking up to poetry you heard that elevated elegaic tone? Well part of me wants to say no, you were ignorant of it. But also I think, well yes, obviously you did. Because you couldn't miss, no matter what, what that must have been.

The world is more than itself and has being, apart from your knowing what it is. This is true for any "world." And I mean this question, odd as it may sound, quite seriously. It is almost *the* question of poetry. The poem makes this thing. Now you hear it. Then you don't. But you do. Because thought does. At first, knowing precedes naming. Then they become identical.

Let's get back to the radio.
The radio is on now. We are listening to the radio.

No, I mean what did you listen to in seventh grade?
Well, we listened as I said to R & B, everything retrospected now as doo-wop—all the records Opal Nations had to replace his floor for, to keep his room from falling through his house. All those 45's recorded in your head from 1950 to 1960. *In the Still of the Night* by the Five Satins was my favorite song. I still have a weakness for ending that way—falsetto. Repeat high up the entire meaning. Throw the voice somewhere else, but still be you, yet greater, more intense.

Did you like Elvis Presley early on?
I loved Elvis. But we thought he wasn't real. I mean literally. You know, not I mean unreal, but literally not real. We thought he was Carl Perkins. And of course that idea could be peddled. We'd go to one house after school and shoot pool, on a table two feet by three, kneeling down, the little cues over our shoulders, stroking the Eight smaller than a golf ball but larger than your best shooter (I was really into marbles). And dancing around that table it would all be perfect if Bo Didley came on. Bo Didley was our secret favorite. It felt like contraband to have his records. They were not easy to come by. Later, meeting him in New Mexico was like a dream come true, you thought, but a funny one, almost a joke.

Did you listen to jazz or classical music?

Jazz no. Not as a teenager. Although there were singers I liked who now seem almost to have been jazz singers. But crooners really. The first record I ever bought was Jo Stafford, *See the Pyramids Along the Nile.* How I was intrigued by that song. But that taste also could degenerate into Kay Starr later, or into something like *Cool Clear Water*—Frankie Lane. Vaughn Monroe, we liked Vaughn Monroe a lot. Like Bo Didley, he had a voice unlike any other, a strange voice, almost crippled sounding, but great. *Racing with the Moon.* We tried to imitate it, *rrraaacing withe mooon*—but we couldn't do it. We wanted to and kept trying. In a way, although I didn't connect the two at the time (at twelve or fourteen years old) I think some poetry was coming out of that music, or something like poetry, without your realizing. I did love some of those words. "If the sun should tumble from the sky. . . ." A strange idea for beauty. And Little Richard, another favorite, a perfect example of expression almost completely reflexive, the way he sang it.

It sounds like music was central in your early years—I mean, more than books.

Well, it was the era of the record. Books came later. My father quizzed us at Sunday dinner—always roast beef and mashed potatoes, well done. He would ask my brother, sister, and me (I was the youngest) to identify the record playing, whether it was Mozart or Beethoven and Brahms, usually. Very little Bach. He favored the nineteenth century. I still like Schubert and Berlioz because it was laid on early. It helps to get it that way. If you don't hear classical music when you're young, it's hard to get it later. In a way it's a class thing. If you think better of Rossini at ten because of the Lone Ranger, isn't that terrific, both for you *and* for Rossini. It sure beats the *Peter and the Wolf* entry which has since taken over. Even if Prokofiev is a more interesting composer, which is arguable. The tale destroys the take. But with Rossini in fact it had nothing to do with it.

Did you watch other TV shows?

TV?

I mean, the Lone Ranger . . .

That was all radio. *Tennessee Jed, Straight Arrow, The Shadow, Jack Armstrong*—there was a lot of radio to feed one's imagination.

STEPHEN RODEFER   187

You read Comics?
Well, of course, as every kid does. But I remember liking particularly Classic Comics. All that mediaeval stuff. Howard Pyle. *The Master of Ballantrae.* And what was that other one? It was my favorite book. About training to be a knight.

Fourth grade was my best year. I invented a way to subtract fractions without all that refiguring and shorthand notation rigamarole they taught you and insisted you "show." The teacher was a good one or she wouldn't have tolerated it. Miss Biehl. It was a contest at the board between me and the smartest kid in the class, as to who could do it faster, he with the book's way and me with my new short-cut method. And I won, much to everyone's astonishment but mine. And Miss Biehl had to admit that it was an interesting alternative, but she still made everyone else do it the long way. I didn't understand. It was a victory but my way didn't win. But for me it did. But I didn't feel victorious because the others didn't get it.

You sound like you're talking about something else.
No, it's just that. It was taking away a larger fraction from a smaller one, whose whole was larger. Obviously you couldn't do it with just the numerator, as there were no negatives yet in your structure. But all you had to do was turn it over. You could take the top fraction from the bottom, but to make up for breaking the rules you had to take that from the whole thing, expressed in its parts. And that gave you the correct answer. Plus, to appease the gods of rule, you also had to reduce the whole by one for good measure. Once you saw the move, it was instinctive and automatic.

It's a little hard to understand, just talking about it.
It's simple. To take, say, $4^7/_8$ from $8^1/_8$ you just reverse the fraction part of the subtraction and take $^1/_8$ from $^7/_8$ but remember to take away *that* from $^8/_8$, which was the original given, before fractions could come about, and so the answer is $^2/_8$ plus the four minus the 1 you have to take away for fooling around and there it is. The answer is $3^2/_8$, almost at a glance when you let your mind tumble that way. Seems simple enough now, and with later math it's just totally obvious, but in fourth grade I tell you it was like magic.

When did you get interested in poetry?
Eighth grade. A teacher, Blanche Harvey, read us "The Raven" and "Annabel Lee," and Poe's stories, all of which I loved. But what really got me going

was my mother's giving me *The Oxford Book of English Verse,* for my fourteenth birthday I think it was. I've never thought of it before, but *The Oxford Book of American Verse* didn't come till a couple of years later. I mean, my first take was that poetry was English, and I lived on an island. I mean, both ways, as that made where I lived an island away from where the poetry was, and also that poetry itself was an isolation, one I was ready to get lost in. So, that it was English was perfect. English Poetry, Oxford. That was where I wanted to be. A little Jude-like. Not in the book exactly, but there with it anyway. But someday why not, to be in the book, that would be nice. But also I mean I knew immediately I was, or wanted to be, always in that company. Or I always had been and never had realized it. I can believe that way in being born. A born poet. Isn't that just what any of us wants? To be a born poet.

Which poets did you read?
I read it all.

Which did you like?
Immediately I loved Skelton, Wyatt, Jonson. Donne, Marvell. I recited "To His Coy Mistress" at a church camp vespers, like a talent night program, one summer at Wooster College in Ohio. No one could believe it, that I was reciting so long a poem, or so suggestive a one, or even a poem at all. Actually I don't think anyone even got it, so it wasn't risqué. No one heard what it meant I don't imagine, and I was like hypnotized. But people were impressed to learn afterward that it was an old poem. No one had ever done a poem before.

You didn't pick up on Shakespeare or the Romantics?
Not at first. Shakespeare, yes. But at fourteen not the Romantics. I loved sonnets. So Shakespeare, and those songs, and lesser figures, like Daniel and Drayton, Sidney and Spenser, and the ballads—the first half of the book, up to 1650 about, is what I read through and through. I would read it on my sister's bed, with the door closed, memorizing many poems. No one looked for me there.

Did you write anything then? Any juvenile work?
Not for a few years. No poetry yet, but still I had the sense—it *was* a sense, almost like information arriving—that I could be one of these. But I don't think I wrote anything till I was sixteen or seventeen.

STEPHEN RODEFER   189

Do you still have that first writing?

No, not anymore. Well, maybe, perhaps in an attic somewhere, in Ohio or Buffalo. Something got put in a school paper, 1957 or '58, but I don't have it, a poem about spring snow.

When did you read American poetry and who did you like?

The next present, from my mother, was the companion *American.* I saw immediately Emily Dickinson. Before Whitman. It was easier to hear. But then at about sixteen Keats became my main love. That was the ideal. I adored Keats. "Ode to a Nightingale" was the standard for me. Then I noticed Hopkins and Thomas. I memorized "Fern Hill." Most of these I can still recite—that is, if I race into them, like your fingers on the piano keys, playing the Moonlight Sonata. I dreamt actually of finishing "Hyperion" so that everyone would believe it was a newly discovered manuscript. My first poem in real print was an answer to Hopkins in the Amherst Lit Mag—an *inversion,* as Jean Day told me recently, though I had never heard of such a thing at the time. But it was a natural.

Did you read anything else? Any prose?

With difficulty.

Poetry was an obsession?

Well, when my mother saw my new pleasure, she wanted to encourage my literary interests, like a great mother. So she told me I could charge some books at the book department of the big department store in Wheeling. Somehow I heard about Henry Miller, though not much other twentieth-century stuff, and I *wanted* to know about things modern. Anyway when I came home with one of the *Tropics* there was trouble. It was dirty on the first page and back it went—to the place under the counter from which literally the clerk had fetched it. No more books for me—none to be bought that is. Writing has seemed to have a slightly illicit dimension attached to it from the beginning.

Like my first real pen, a fountain pen given to me as a present. Probably at six or seven, I wrote a forbidden word on the box in which it came and it was taken away immediately. It may have been *fuck,* but I don't think it was that dirty. More likely *bastard* or something else. I had been called that at school and hadn't known what it meant. Thought it was *basket* at first. I shouldn't complain about my home life though. I led a normal young life, was happy, and encouraged. My father loved poetry. He had a signed Frost from his college days.

Do you feel your early literary influences are still with you?

Not much. Oh, some—obviously. I'd like to write as well as Keats or Shakespeare, or as scandalously and with as much humor as Henry Miller. Who wouldn't? But I don't think what I loved as a boy, or even in college, is that much with me—or I hope at any rate not too much with me.

Why not?

Well, any writer wants obviously to be taken seriously for himself, not just as some reflection or extension of something, an echo. Most of Dylan Thomas really seems pretty boring or inflated now, thank god. And Keats stopped working on "Hyperion" because he realized it was too much like Milton.

Do you find friendships with other writers to be important?

Yes, of course. That's one of the uses of any literary situation. But friendship *itself* is important. Writers naturally tend to have friendships with other writers. Same is true for movie stars, thieves, construction workers, and idiots. Obviously kinds attract.

Did you attend workshops early on?

None. I met a number of people at the Berkeley Poetry Conference in 1965. That's where I first saw Anne Waldman, Larry Goodell, Clark Coolidge, Ron Loewinsohn, Ted Berrigan, and many others. Hannah Weiner was there, Geoff Young, and I believe Ron Silliman hung about as a Berkeley student. We all went to that particular conference because it was just that kind of draw, which was really the New American Poetry. I was a student at SUNY Buffalo at the time, where Charles Olson was teaching. He was to be a featured writer at the conference, along with Jack Spicer, Robert Creeley, Gary Snyder, Allen Ginsberg, LeRoi Jones, Michael McClure, and others. It so happened that that was the summer of the Newark riots, and LeRoi Jones was transforming his identity to Amiri Baraka, dropping out of white culture. In fact, he ended up sending a telegram to Berkeley which said in effect that he wouldn't attend the white man's poetry conference. His lecture was to be entitled "Poetry and Murder," very dramatic. He had been teaching at Buffalo, with Ed Dorn, and we were disappointed he would not come. So you realized again that this poetry business was a bit of an isolating event.

Wasn't Robert Duncan there?

Yes, and Dorn also. There were two weeks of lectures, classes, and readings. It was one of the most intense exposures to poetry I've ever had in my life, and certainly the most informative. You went all day—class in the morning with Olson, say, or Gary Snyder or Duncan; then in the afternoons there would be one-shot lectures. Dorn gave that great lecture on the Shoshone Indians. Jack Spicer, who would be dead within a month, gave a lecture and read *The Holy Grail* straight through. It was amazing. We went to Gino & Carlo's in the evening, the bar where Spicer was a habitué. The submission basket for *Open Space* was literally on the bar.

I went out from Buffalo because I was in Olson's class, which got me a scholarship. David Franks from Baltimore, and Victor Coleman, who published my first book, from Toronto, and I drove out to California in my brother's V.W. I don't want to make it sound overly important, it just turned out that way. After all, there are poetry conferences going on all the time. But it seemed a particularly great moment.

Ginsberg was there also, wasn't he?

Yes, he had come from touring eastern Europe, where he had been elected King of the May in Prague, when there was that brief thaw before they got rid of Dubchek. That had been the first time they'd had the May Festival in Prague for decades, a medieval tradition. And Ginsberg, returning from Russia, showed up, and next thing you know he was elected King of the May. There's that great poem about it. He was expelled from the country directly after his election.

There was a real energy at the Berkeley conference because of things like that. Ginsberg coming there straight from Prague, Franz Kafka's city. Olson coming straight from Spoleto's Festival of Two Worlds, where Ezra Pound made his last public appearance. That was the first time Olson had seen Pound since St. Elizabeth's. So Olson showed up with his stories, and Ginsberg showed up with his, and it was an amazing time. Dick Baker was the administrator of the thing, now Roshi Baker. Tom Parkinson threw great parties in the Berkeley Hills. Ginsberg was disrobing, Duncan camped out in a toga, it was the first summer of the Rolling Stones. I remember Peter Orlovsky wiggling across the floor on his stomach, doing the Alligator to "Little Red Rooster." It was the threshold of an era.

What was Olson like as a teacher?

Well, I went to his classes for two years. A few of us took his classes a second time because literally it was difficult to figure out what was happening the first time around. And because you just wanted to be there. It was definitely a contact high.

A good document for Olson's teaching would be the tape of his last night's "reading" at the Berkeley conference. He goes on for two hours, *talking,* never finishing a single poem, hardly even starting one. People were getting nervous, while others loved it. Lew Welch was going nuts on the side trying to get him to stop talking and start reading. Even Creeley was trying to get him to pause and read a poem. But Olson would just reply something to the effect that poetry was politics, and this was a smoking caucus of poetry. For him it was a convention, and he was giving the closing address.

Olson had that wonderful and provocative habit of never seeming to finish any sentence. That's reflected in his poetry certainly, and in the fact that George Butterick has to finish the *Maximus Poems,* at least by ordering them.

He was a good teacher, then?

Olson was the most amazing teacher I've ever known. He was so energized and powerful. He was interested in *you* without being necessarily interested in what you were *doing,* if that can sound right. But still, almost miraculously, he had this great ability to promote in you your ability to do what only you could do, without ever wanting you to be like him, to know everything he knew, to read the books he read, though he'd of course insist that those were the only books worth reading.

Was this a creative writing class?

Oh no. There were little of that at that time at SUNY, or at least nothing of that kind involving Olson. Creative writing was John Logan. Olson's classes were called Poetics, and Myth and Literature. He'd spend two hours talking about parataxis or the pre-Socratics or the Sumerians, Whitehead or Lévi-Strauss or Merleau-Ponty. Or he'd talk about Dorn or Wieners or Snyder, people you had never heard of then (you must remember it was 1963). I had gone to Amherst where Robert Frost was the visiting canon and modern poetry courses ended with Auden and Stevens—William Carlos Williams was hardly mentioned.

Once, Olson spent half the semester saying we couldn't do anything because we didn't have the text. If only we had the book, he'd say, we could do it, but because we didn't we couldn't. Well, the book was *The Worship of Priapus* by Richard Payne Knight, who was a director of the British Museum early in the nineteenth century. Knight was a distinguished scholar and classicist who had a scandalous sideline—collecting the penises which had been knocked off antique statues. There were apparently whole secret storehouses in Naples of these things. *The Worship of Priapus* was based on phallic cults active in and around Naples literally for hundreds of years. It was an obscure nineteenth century tome, but Olson talked about it as if it contained everything we needed to know about the origin of the universe. But since we couldn't get it, we couldn't have the class, and he went on for weeks like this.

One day a few of us—Fred Wah, Andrew Crozier, Mike Glover, and I— made a trip to Cleveland to go to Jim Lowell's Asphodel book shop and to a then legendary bookstore that had a square mile of used books underground. It was totally dark, and you'd go from one room to another pulling on the light with a chain. Everything was completely dusty, no one had looked at the books for years obviously. We spent all day there and finally we found *The Worship of Priapus,* along with some early H. D. and Mina Loy, I remember. Needless to say, we jumped for joy and rushed back to class, as it were, triumphant. But it was too late, Olson said, too late and Payne Knight was wrong anyway.

Well, once you got to know Olson a little you realized soon enough that this was totally predictable behavior. Jeremy Prynne, who teaches at Cambridge, the poet, told me a similar story a couple years ago. Olson had asked him to turn up the sailing logs from Southampton to Gloucester. He had all the Gloucester material he needed for *Maximus,* but insisted he needed this additional information from the English end of it. Prynne went to some trouble to get this stuff from various old archives around Southampton; there were no xerox machines in those days and he went to great length apparently to get it all copied. When he sent it to Olson he got no response. Olson never used it, apparently; never really finally wanted it, perhaps. You see, Olson had this funny way of jumping time. When we walked in with the book, he didn't want it; when Prynne sent him the Southampton material, it didn't matter. He wasn't being catty, he had just entered another intellectual arena. And he could always concoct what he lacked. Or else he didn't need it.

Is that why people have faulted him for loose scholarship?
Scholarship isn't really the point. It's what he did with what he thought to be the case, rather than some failure to use correct information. What he made, rather than what he missed.

There are a lot of facts in Four Lectures. *Did you do research in Olson's sense?*

There is a lot of *information* in *Four Lectures*. But in-form-ation was just the point. It is there insofar as you gather it or retain it as you go along. In a way, isn't all sensation a kind of research? You are always editing what you do, or see, or where you move.

Is that what you mean in the preface to Four Lectures *when you say, "As should a book be as deep as a museum and as wide as the world"?*

I meant that once in touch with the experience of *the* world, you are inevitably involved with creating *a* world. I'm very sympathetic for instance with Williams's sense that Eliot was returning poetry to the classroom just at the moment that it was waking up to the local. On the other hand, I've always loved a lot of Eliot's poetry, and sometimes distrusted that animosity Williams showed towards it. I've always thought that the broadest way perhaps was to leave neither perspective out. That's what I was trying to get at in the Preface to *Four Lectures*. After all, one *is* always in a museum or a library if one is listening and recording and "reading," I mean just generally, the environment, the "entire" world as it exists around you every second. We are reading all the time—signs, horizons, the clouds, people on the street,—and some of this aspires to poetry. As slick and as awful as advertising is, sometimes it comes close: "Not Hormel, home-made." That's getting close to poetry, or at least to the figure of it. It's a text that can be studied, in the sense in which Longinus in *On the Sublime* studies it. I love also something Reznikoff said about Objectivism—to the effect that the writer does not write directly about his *own* feelings but about what he hears and sees; that he or she is limited to the testimony of a witness, and you express your feelings only indirectly by your selection of material, the way you construct it, and the musical dimension of the work. *Four Lectures* could be considered as a kind of postmodern testimony in that sense. The down and out, and the up and out, in another sense.

Some of the lines in the poem read to me like bumper stickers. "Paranoia is a carful." "Everything is based on beer."

I distrust that impulse and am a little frightened by it. If there is one thing that book is not, it's a series of one-liners. On the other hand, bumper stickers are interesting to me, as is any sign in the culture. As I was writing that poem, and even now when I look at it, I *can* see it almost as ribbons. I actually made a drawing of it once, and it seemed almost a Klee-like graphic of the poem. Sometimes I didn't give a damn what it said, but rather paid attention to the look and the sound of the whole curve.

I must say that reading *Four Lectures* now I have this purely formal attachment to it, quite apart from any question of reference. I sometimes think of it as an experiment in caesura, or an exercise in the comma. Or the sort of thing I think of as realism, the "new realism" as some people call it. I spent a lot of time moving those lines around, as well as writing them. But it's not collage. It's thread. A kind of a frottage of the brain as a city. Also, I saw the pieces as sonnets or like Donald Judd's boxes. Then someone asked me why fifteen lines, and I could only say that I didn't want them to be sonnets exactly. It was more the symmetry, the discreet measure of each box; yet I wanted the *flexibility* of the sonnet sequence. But to exceed it by a line.

You've called Four Lectures *a poem. So you see it as a single long piece then?*
I think I had in mind *Don Juan, Four Quartets,* Lautréamont, Ashbery's *Three Poems, When the Sun Tries to Go On,* lots of other things. When I started it I thought it would be far longer and be called simply Lectures. I see now that by calling it *Four Lectures* I more or less stopped it in some way. I have in fact finished a fifth section, and most of a sixth, but somehow the project seems closed now. The four sections seem like four movements, but I consider the whole thing one work. Sometimes when I read it I switch it around, I jump around within a particular section. The blocks *and* the lines can be modular.

I've only read the whole thing publicly a total of once, each section one time only at a reading. The most satisfying was a time when four people helped me, and we set up a very interesting situation. We stood in a row, but rather than going chronologically, we'd skip from person to person, always intentionally breaking any kind of pattern that would be forming. Further, every capitalized word was uttered by all four speakers. Then as a further *move* every reader had the choice of interrupting the previous speaker once per stanza. Anselm Hollo, Kit Robinson, and two other people did this with me, and it was very revealing. The whole thing had a funny sort of mix, an unpredictable particle physics. At other readings Carla Harryman, Ron Silliman, and Barry Watten have read parts of it. It's always interesting to have the other voices. Joanne Kyger once suggested that we do a radio play of it.

Something I've just finished is a prose work called *Among the Atomic Events,* which is a phrase of George Oppen's. Atomic events are the events in the laboratory wherein they record millions of photographs of what is going on in a nuclear reaction, which they scan then with computers. One event, or shot, in a thousand might be considered a legitimate atomic event, and then you've discovered a quark or something. The interesting thing, however, is that years later they go back and look at this material again and discover, with the advantage of a more advanced technology and new information, that there were atomic events they didn't know about the first time around. What this argues is that what you learn constantly forces you back into the past, which is the universe as we perceive it, to reassess what is there and what isn't. And the past is constantly changing. Readings of *Four Lectures* continually strike me as a similar retrospective discovery.

Why did you chose to make an index to the poem? It seems like a very odd gesture.
I included what I felt like including, then I stopped. In a way it uncovers a major gesture of the writing, to be honorific and satiric at the same time. What's funny and what's not has always been an amusing confusion in my mind, like the first line in *Lady Chatterley's Lover:* "We live in an essentially tragic age and we refuse to take it tragically." As a very young poet I was upset when people laughed at my work. I would think that they mistook the seriousness of it. But then if nobody laughed I'd think the writing was too dry. I have always been perplexed about this question of what is serious and what is light. They've usually seemed tangential to each other in my selection of them.

You enter L=A=N=G=U=A=G=E *magazine in a number of ways.*
You enter any language any way you can. Like any association. Any friendship. I suppose listing it in various ways was both doing what needed to be done in an index and making a point. L=A=N=G=U=A=G=E is a magazine with equal signs between the letters, and that's making an argument, isn't it. *Language* alone isn't a very interesting title for a magazine, but if you put an equal sign between the letters it's transformed into an argument about language itself—letters, weight, objectifications. One letter is as good as another, carries the same weight; you are making your writing out of materials which are as solid as blocks. I take that to be the argument of that title presented that way at any rate.

Think of it. Everything that we write is merely the rearrangement of the words in the dictionary. Here's the dictionary—now order these words in an interesting way. People have been doing it for thousands of years. Or even more absurdly—here are twenty-six letters. Rearrange them and see what you get. I hope that in part the index will begin to make you look at language in the way that some new writing proposes that you might.

What does language mean to you then?

It means what it says, in addition to what you think it means.

What is its purpose?

To heighten your perception and to give you pleasure. If it doesn't give you pleasure, what's the point? It seems that sometimes the bottom-level response to writing is "did you like it?" But I think that's a very real take after all. If you say that something pleases you without reservation, that carries great weight. I'm certainly interested though in more than just some sort of visceral response. I guess it goes back to the fascination of making, out of some found mess, some sort of momentary, stationary order that will reveal the nature of experience. That sounds grandiose, but that's the intent. To make out of an urban morass, that seems out of control, some kind of lucidity. Often we just go around feeling mistaken and lost, torn in several directions at once. One tries to incorporate, in writing, that experience, though I've often felt like painting or music might be better media for it.

How far can you hope to objectify language and still hope to give the pleasure you are talking about?

What I mean by objectification here is not some sort of mystical idea that a word is a thing, because it's not a thing. It's similar to the idea Robert Creeley emphasizes somewhere, that a poetry denies itself in any descriptive act, in any act which leads the attention *outside* the poem. There is a whole boatload of American poetry that wants to lead the attention outside the poem. Just go to the library or the bookstore and pick up poetry books at random. Hundreds of poems will begin, "I didn't think my father / remembered the flowers / that were put on the shelf / by the bed when I awoke / that irridescent day." The deeply felt American poem that comes out of a domestic context. What a friend of mine calls "stones and bones poetry." So what do you think about when you read that poem? Not the poem, certainly, or only badly so at the adjective before "day." Rather, you think about the *situation* the poet is "talking about." It's an assumption that seems contrary to every belief I have about what it is to make art. It's little better than watching television or reading greeting cards, and there are a lot of apparently important poets, if you read the *American Poetry Review,* who write that way. Now that's *non*-objectification of language.

Which isn't necessarily an argument against narrative.
Not at all. I think of *Four Lectures* as narrative, at least in the sense of narrative painting. I even think of it as a kind of prose. We have prose poetry, why not "poetry prose." It's a narration of what it means to be alive and sensate in the city. You can think of any writing as being a self-portrait, even when it doesn't speak about the author at all. You don't have to talk *about* yourself obviously in order to write about yourself. If you write about men leaning out of windows in shirt-sleeves above vacant lots where there are grimy newspapers, you seem to be talking about the world, while in fact you are identifying with a consciousness of fatigue and despair. If you churn out monograms in the face of a divergent world, clearly you are identifying with such a mechanism as could do that. What you see defines who you are, and to that extent I think of my work as a narrative of an odyssey through a cityscape which includes everything. Why argue difference if you cannot tolerate it?

I'm in my house, the radio is on, the telephone rings. It doesn't seem to me this's even nonlinear. I'm fixing breakfast, the phone rings, and suddenly I'm talking to nobody I've ever talked to before, who calls me daddy. I *am* a daddy, but I'm not her daddy; my number is one digit off. She is really confused when I tell her that but it's okay, she's just got a wrong number, and I'm developing a relationship with a stranger. But I have already mentioned my nonexistent daughter in print. As I walked into the living room to answer the phone, I've then displaced breakfast. I also forgot that I put a towel on the heater and now it's scorched. I smell it. When I pick it up I look out the window and see the guy across the street, I realize that yesterday I had neglected to talk to him about some neighborhood thing. So I catch him as he goes out the door and ask him if he'll be home later. By this time I have to go to the bathroom. Now all this is totally a "linear experience," maybe five minutes worth. Yet to see the segments it becomes totally strange. It must be what Heraclitus meant when he said we are estranged from that which is most familiar. We get so used to thinking we understand experience that we take it for granted, and sometimes actually miss it, we have such blinders on. In that sense it's not the new sentence so much as the new *sequence* that's being proposed.

So then objectification means entering fully into the poem.
Or into the world, into the consciousness of your particular experience of it. And language has a physical, three-dimensional reality. Its architecture is a metaphor for this phenomenon. The other aspect of this has become almost a commonplace now—that by "entering" into the work you somehow complete it. This can be overstated, and sometimes takes the slightly ridiculous form of simply reader-generated meaning. But there is a sense in which all modern art insists that the actual perception involved in taking it in is itself part of the work's intent. The Cubists tried to destroy the idea of one-point perspective, which had held sway since the Renaissance, because they realized that you don't walk around with one-point perspective. This is especially true when technology brings on a world of material that moves by at incalculable speed. You are in a train, looking out the window, and the telephone poles are whizzing by, the cows a little slower, and the trees in the distance seem to stand still for a while; you don't even see what's on the window, unless you're Jack Kerouac. All these things are happening at once. It's not an accident that Picasso and Braque are making those paintings at the same time that the French, the Italians, and the Americans are going up in airplanes and talking on wires; that Einstein is discovering relativity at the same time that Schoenberg is destroying notions of harmony. The first decades of this century are nearly incomprehensible on this score—the world changed more in twenty years than in the previous two thousand.

Along that line, a passage from Four Lectures *was wonderful: "What is brilliant becomes boring in the future's perspective." It says a lot about traditional verse.*
And about atomic events. Probably about some experimental writing as well. People are always claiming a form is worn out, then suddenly someone comes along and revitalizes it in a way that is really striking. Critics have been saying the novel is dead for years, then a brilliant novelist says no emphatically; or lyric poetry is dead, then a great lyric poet comes along and just sings. So I'm a little wary of all that.

You've mentioned language-centered writing. Do you see this as a phase, an attempt to work with language in new ways that is important from a theoretical point of view but not necessarily lasting?
I think a lot of people are working hard in a lot of ways, even within small groups which only *seem* homogenous. If you take a group of five or ten people and call them "Language poets," then look closely at their writing, you'll

see they are immensely different. There will be certain major similarities, but the differences are astounding, say, between Charles Bernstein's writing and Bruce Andrew's, or Steve Benson's and Peter Seaton's.

I think the whole idea of "language writing" is much like the "New American Poetry"—it's packaging. Universities do it, poets do it, publishers do it. It's a fetishization of product in order to get attention. You *have* to do this sometimes to identify yourself. For the purpose of getting attention but also for the purpose of knowing who you are and who someone else is, what you stand for and what someone else stands for. It's a kind of familial or tribal gesture that is totally understandable. Taken to its extreme, though, it leads to packaging a product so that everyone can need it and buy it. Not a very useful or even a very new gesture, but certainly a thoroughly American one. I'm intrigued by any language, writing which manifests its interest in itself. Certainly Donne or Hopkins or Dickinson or Stein managed this before any of us did.

In America we always like things to be new.
Sure. Look at Harriet Monroe's "New American Poetry" of 1917. *The New American Poetry*—that's a very offensive title in some ways. Like new car, new house, new wife, new book. "New" is, on that level, *the* American hype. Has been since 1492.

Do things have to be somehow new to draw in the reader? Or do you even think of a reader?
I certainly try never to write anything with a reader in mind. Or let me put it this way: I'm the reader. As I write I'm always reading, and I think of the act of writing almost like the act of reading. If I hear it, I write it down, then if I like reading it I keep it; if not I toss it out. The act of writing *is* the act of reading, because that's the second decision one makes, literally and literarily.

Confounding for me as a reader, after some of your "ribbons" in Four Lectures *I felt like I was thrown out of the poem.*
One wants to keep it going fast enough so that when you feel momentarily out you'll be drawn back in soon. Like the experience of living—you feel repelled, then you feel welcome. It's constant alternation. That was one of the interests in making the poem that length and in making the lines so long. When you are momentarily out, I hope it won't be long before you are back in, because it doesn't stop just because you do.

What about you as a reader?
Well, there are things there which now leave me out. There are things there which I no longer recognize—where they came from or what they refer to. But they still live. And I can be completely a reader with them.

Do you like those things when you come across them?
Sometimes. Other times not. On occasion it's embarrassing to learn later where I "got something," especially if its from a book I'd been reading six years before. The point, though, is that I can still be interested in the language even if I can no longer recall the background; that's what I'm after. If I don't know anything about Empedocles, still the words *limpid* and *Empedocles* would have an interest for me as a reader, or something like "Implicit nix." Children enjoy language on such a totally physical plane, where they almost bat it around like a ball.

Can we go back to your sense of a narrator? In Four Lectures *is the narrative voice female? Or is there more than one narrator?*
Well, it's not a narrative poem in any conventional sense, obviously. The fact that it begins "I was working in a factory, had seen Blow-up, and had a mini-skirt" doesn't mean that I'm identifying a female narrator, who then occasionally changes sex. There are obviously voice-overs in the poem, and I think of the real narrator as the airwave of the city. So I guess there is no narrator in the conventional sense. The narrator is the light bulb.

Is the city San Francisco more than any other?
I was living there and in Oakland when I wrote it, but I would hesitate to identify it as San Francisco. It just happened to be the place where I was being fed the city.

So the particularity of place is not a great concern.
Not really. I don't even think Gloucester is the polis in *Maximus*. It just so happened that Olson found himself in Gloucester and had that kind of interest in the world. He could have been as well in Raleigh, North Carolina, or Timbuktu. Philip Whalen suggests Gertrude Stein would have done all right if she'd have gone off to Kansas City rather than Paris. In some sense it's almost arbitrary where you find yourself. The conditions of the twentieth century have become so generalized, so implicitly shared, that it doesn't matter that you are in San Francisco, or in the *American* sense only slightly,

because often you are also in Africa, Asia, South America, New York, Albuquerque . . .

But you left Albuquerque.
Yes, I used to teach there.

And you can write better poetry in San Francisco?
Not at all. I'd never say that. I left New Mexico for a lot of reasons that had nothing at all to do with poetry, or only partly. You can write poetry in jail better than some places. And the university sometimes proposes itself as little better than a prison.

Can you tell me a little about your work process?
I work at my kitchen table. I live in a fairly small cottage, so I don't have a study or a desk. My books are on my kitchen table among my papers. Maybe that's why those mix-ups we were talking about occur, because breakfast, letters, bills, dreams, and writing are all collated together. *Four Lectures* might be a map of my kitchen table. Some of the messages are food, some are invoices of the mind, some letters from my friends, some notes and manuscripts. I work in what would look to most people like a cluttered environment, though it doesn't seem cluttered to me.

So you write regularly?
No. I really wish I had more discipline. I'm not one of those writers who churns it out. At the same time, when I do write I do it happily.

Why do you say you wish to be more disciplined?
Well, I just admire the habit of people like Robert Duncan, for instance. He said somewhere years ago that he gets up every morning and writes until eleven, then he goes to bookstores until one, goes home and takes a nap, talks on the phone for about an hour, and returns to his desk. I admire that kind of organization.

Novelists need that.
Yes they do. I've been trying to write some prose recently, some fiction, and I can really see how the habits I've developed over a couple of decades writing poetry are not good habits for writing long narrative fiction. But then again if you write every day you'd better develop, as Hemingway said, a good shit

detector. There is nothing worse than thinking that everything you put down is worth saving.

How much do you throw away?
I tried to figure this out once. I think I publish less than half of what I write. Basil Bunting told me once that he published less than 30 percent of what he wrote. Not only that—he destroyed the rest of it. I wish I could bring myself to do that. So it comes to your wanting to write every day to be productive. But the question looms, is production in and of itself "productive"? The history of this country seems to prove precisely that production is often *not* productive. If there is living proof of progress being retrograde, then we are it. Progress, like speed, sometimes seems to be just grinding its dentures.

Do you feel that you've settled into a style, or does your work keep changing?
My sense is that we must continually be reinventing the work as well as the world. I'm sympathetic to Zukofsky's idea that you write one poem all your life, but I also think that poem should have wildly different presentations. The mind casts up of itself vague and redoubtable fantasies of the real. And that is where consciousness and artfulness begin.

---

from *Four Lectures*

Pretext

Then I stand up on my hassock and say sing that.
It is not the business of POETRY to be anything.
When one day at last they come to storm your deluxe cubicle,
Only your pumice stone will remain. The left trapezius for now
Is a little out of joint. Little did they know you came with it.
When nature has entirely disappeared, we will find ourselves in Stuttgart.
Till then we're on the way. The only way not to leave is to go.
The gods and scientists heap their shit on Buffalo and we're out there,
Scavenging plastic trees. When nature has entirely disappeared,
We'll find ourselves in the steam garden. Evening's metonym for another
Beady-eyed engineer with sexual ideas, who grew up eating animals.

Do you like the twelve tones of the western scale? I prefer ninety.
I may work in a factory but I slide to the music of the spheres.
My job is quality control in the language lab, explaining what went
Wrong in Northampton after the Great Awakening. So much was history.

My father is a sphinx and my mother's a nut. I reject the glass.
But I've been shown the sheets of sentences and what he was
Really like remains more of a riddle than in the case of most humans.
So again I say rejoice, the man we're looking for
Is gone. The past will continue, the surest way to advance,
But you still have to run to keep fear in the other side.
There is a little door at the back of the mouth fond of long names
Called the juvjula. And pidgeon means business. It carries
Messages. The faces on the character parts are excellent.
In fact I'm having lunch with her next week. Felix nupsit.
Why should it be so difficult to see the end if when it comes
It should be irrefutable. Cabin life is incomplete.
But the waterbugs' mittens SHADOW the bright rocks below.
He has a resemblance in the upper face to the man who robbed you.
I am pleased to be here. To my left is Philippa, who will be signing for
   me.

from "Sleeping With the Light On"

I don't want to make a disclaimer beforehand but it wasn't raining in the
   capital.
Who's the woman with Attila? Don't all start at once but begin anyway.
More of what ensues when it is no longer the same. Half way between
here and God change place as in a novel, continuing to sing as though
it were verse. Pride doesn't speak. It kicks its foot out of the cradle
to disturb the mobile meant to hang over its slumberpoo like a waterfowl
on pilot. Out of paint make light, like a painter. Go far enough
so this phrase will become itself. One voice can't date address any longer.
The LYDIAN MODE. The chartreuse in the distance of the homerun.
A woman is dating an undertaker. She has a right. He wants her to lie
   down
beside the still. Birds are in the trees and they know it. They don't
drink. They consider the beauty of hills when they are on them and when

they are not. Something in nature that is definitely not coffee.

Comes a tide to make the clams open up, into the figment called dusk.

Jealous teachers poison their pupils; gooselivers, the favorite food of
  Mozart.

Are you a name artist? or just otherwise another writer whose main idea

of what to do in life is become famous. Better never to remember or to
  learn.

One's experience is hardly ever with one. O one hundred hours.

PERSONALITY is the persistence of others' sense of you,

taking you for something you are not, but in their minds there you are.

I am here to deal with English, not to be a mate in taxis.

Still testing your generation on the Drāno? Brian Eno simply isn't Not
  Vital.

Bridget Bardot gets to utter the *pièce de résistance* of all French cinema:

J'ai peur, and it's before Godard. Now I call that DARN innersting.

Warts are wonderful structures, which can appear overnight on any part
  of skin,

like mushrooms on a damp lawn, full grown and splendid in the
  complexity

of their particular cancer. Information rafts through the air.

An at bat. SOAPY NUTS. Just another extremely kissy baby destined to be

one more hardon scraping by. If you don't jelly up the ring, heaven will
  know

your kind. Is this thing on? Am I coming across some Monongahela or
  other?

Codex

That is the glebe and this is the glissando. The future is nothing

But a flying wing. You must make your case either with names or with
  an unfolding.

A position or a disclosure, a microbus. The corridor, the cascade, what
  stuck.

Glacier notes over the tops of hills. To be close again, as it was in the
  leanto.

Lengthen the line and increase the leading. These are the helloes of
  progress.

At the kitchen table the books are pored over, much as a neighbor will
  bum a cigaret.
The bungalow, radioed and occupied, has no other path to follow but the
  venture,
The undeniable yielding turmoil mapped out for us for life.
Somebody might ought cook someone a square meal. Life in our
  adulthood
Is mistaken for wanting completion. What it longs to do is continue
  being.
The BEES are sleeping beneath the pergola. At the end of each lesson is
  the vocabulary.
If one opening clouds, another will clear, so long as you both will
  breathe.
Where's a shovel or something, I say, what can dig, or a trowel?
  Language pointed
To its content. A crowd of people at the beach screaming "Tuna! tuna!"
  The evening
Breeze, trembling trees, the night, the stars. And there you are, in a
  manner of speaking.

So at sunset the clouds went nuts. They thought they were a text.
This language of the general o'erflows the measure, but my brother and I
  liked it alot.
I think I'll just pause long enough here to call God a bitter name.
Ripeness is all right but the lip is a couplet and nobody knows fuck-all
  about it.
The THREAD has always been bias. There are alternatives to purchasing
  goods
To recruit admirers. Right, but is it what Verdi would have wanted?
Nor is it enough to be seen by your youngers as having carried the
  tradition
To a good place. Given disasters everywhere, don't drink from the tap.
And for what reason make anything that is not for flight?
There are treatments to keep your retina from becoming detached but for
  what—
To see this? Why, there are things about Israel not dreamed of in the
  Bible.
How could I miss you when my aim is dead. The goal is sea sounds not
  yet writ.

STEPHEN RODEFER 207

All right. Enjoy the heads of your beaches. I'm not going in order
To get tied up on spec, but I wanted you to meet your fellow brains.
   Thank you,
People of destiny, for your brilliant corners. I like your voice. Look where
   it's come from.

11. Nathaniel Tarn

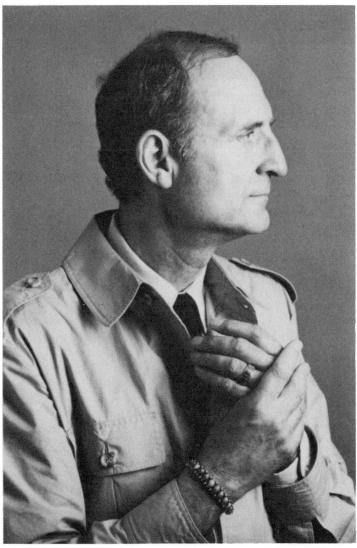

Photo by Nina Subin.

"Over the fragile sails your hands would make"

Nathaniel Tarn, born in Paris in 1928, was educated at Cambridge, the Sorbonne, Yale, London University, and the University of Chicago, where he received his Ph.D. in anthropology in 1957. He is a Mayanist and a specialist in the sociology of Buddhist institutions. He was general editor of Cape Editions and founding director of Cape Goliard Press between 1967 and 1969. He has taught at London University, the State University of New York at Buffalo, Princeton, Colorado, Jilin (P.R.C.), and the University of Pennsylvania, and for over ten years was Distinguished Professor of Comparative Literature at Rutgers. His many volumes of poetry include *Old Savage/Young City, The Beautiful Contradictions, A Nowhere for Vallejo, Lyrics for the Bride of God, The House of Leaves, Alashka* (with Janet Rodney), *The Desert Mothers,* and most recently *At the Western Gates.* In 1967 he published the standard translation of Pablo Neruda's *The Heights of Macchu Picchu,* and in 1975 edited *The Penguin Neruda.*

Of Nathaniel Tarn, Kenneth Rexroth has written that he "is one of the most outstanding poets of his generation, and as such very much a part of international modern literature—an excellent translator of several languages; a successful and imaginative editor; a scholar of wide range and depth in literatures of both the past and the present." Tarn himself has commented that "it does not seem possible to me, in this complex time, for a poet to fulfill himself or herself without that extreme attention to language and the craft for which, for better or worse, elite-addressed poetry is responsible. At the same time, the craft is mocked if it cannot also produce, perhaps in one product, perhaps in a variety of address, something available to whatever is left of the 'average reader.'"

How many books have you published?

Well, I keep counting them and always come up with different figures. It doesn't bother me much because the vitae one is forced to write are a pack of lies anyway. Also, it depends on what you count. I've got at least three books with only one poem in each. But I suppose I've published about twenty to twenty-five volumes, including translations and all the smaller nonsense.

Do you have a favorite?

I don't think so. The one I'm always most interested in is the most recent. But this can be problematic. My newest book, for instance, *At the Western Gates,* just out, really was supposed to be published about four years ago.

It's not a new work, and so I'm not overexcited about it, despite the publisher's beautiful job.

Did you find yourself drawn to writing first, or anthropology?
I started writing poems when I was five, so obviously there was something going on in that area quite early. But I didn't do anything much worthwhile until I was about thirty-five. I didn't actually publish a book of poems until 1964, so I came to publishing poetry late. The anthropology started almost immediately after my three years of English at Cambridge, when I was about twenty-one. From then on there was a lot of interweaving, but always with that conflict I've described in articles in *American Poetry* or *Conjunctions*. There is a tension in me between "the recording angel" and "the creative angel." On a number of occasions I've quit one and gone into the other. It's like being married to two women. There's a wonderful Alec Guiness film where he is a seacaptain with a wife in each of two ports; in the middle of his course he switches the photographs. That's the kind of tension I feel.

Where are you right now?
What I've just done is to leave the academy altogether to move for good to Santa Fe. I think my uppermost idea is to be a poet at this point. Just go back to being a poet, nothing more.

So the creative angel has won out.
Well, he/she has won, but it remains to be seen whether or not there will be any creative activity. You can't order these things. It could be that one feels one has won this great battle finally, then nothing at all comes. But you have to trust what has happened in the past, and usually whenever I've been able to get out from under the academic stuff things have moved along.

But anthropology obviously can be creative.
Sure. In fact, I have been involved since 1979 in a very ambitious project which will probably come to naught simply because it is too ambitious. I'd like to find a new language for certain kinds of cultural anthropology, a language which would neither be unjust to scientific procedures nor abdicate any of its literary potential. You can probably see that this is a very tall order indeed. The experimental texts are in various stages of composition. One of the wretched things about academic life is that you get a sabbatical and are off the leash for a year. I did this in 1979. The minute you come back, however, you are supposed to sit down and write it all up. Well, after

a year I had just started to touch the surface, and as I was plunged back into teaching and administration I more or less had to let the project lie. I'm not going to go right back into it just now, as I need to reshape and recenter. But in a year or two . . .

Well, how does that concern affect your use of language in your poetry?
It doesn't yet though I believe it will in time. There doesn't yet seem to be a clear causal connection of that type. The poetry just goes on developing in its own way, despite the gaps. Because something is not getting written doesn't mean that it's not happening underneath. I've always believed that poetry is an uninterrupted voice going on inside you, an internal source which never dries up, but which you are at various times more or less at liberty to listen to. When you have complete freedom to pay complete attention then that material can surface, and when you don't it can't. But that doesn't mean that it isn't going on and evolving in its own way.

The search for an anthropological language is obviously more conscious, more deliberate. It depends a great deal on what's already been done in the field, on various notions of literary methodology, textual exegesis, and so on. There is a complexity there which makes it a different project from the ongoing poems.

But maybe the two projects will meet at some point.
Perhaps. The sense I had when I started was that the language of anthropology had become an alienated language. What you've got is a highly technical jargon which is constantly tending to imitate the natural sciences, which are the model. So you get this incredible gobbledygook which is really of no use to either the informants or our society beyond the narrow academic requirements of the profession of anthropology. It becomes a matter of vested interests and it is incestuous.

The only exception, of course, is in the case of certain anthropologists who have always been thought to "write well." Evans-Pritchard wrote well, as did Robert Redfield. But that remains belle-lettristic, the sphere of *New Yorker* writing. It certainly does not go into the full extent of formalistic experiment that we've had since the schools of Moscow, Leningrad, Prague, Copenhagen. . . . Nobody is interested in that at all. So my idea will really be an effort at textual marriage, though as I say there is a great possibility that it is completely misconceived. I might be trying to marry a snake and a tiger. The space between the species may be so wide that it can't be done.

You mentioned a running poetic "voice." Is this a voice that is the intellect, or your experience, or rooted in childhood, or just what?
I just wrote a piece for Stanley Diamond ("*The Choral Voice*") which will appear in an anthology he is putting together of "anthro-poets," anthropologists who have discovered themselves to be poets, or whatever. I argued there that one place the voice was coming from was the dead. I said, incidentally, that this was fine in anthropological terms because a lot of anthropologists knew perfectly well that the people they studied would hold that it was coming from the dead. The general sphere of *los pasados.* When I wrote that particular piece I'd been reading James Hillman, who is a Jungian revisionist, and I'd been much impressed by his arguments. They are very strange in that they don't appear to follow a logical ordering, and yet in a curious way you do end up by feeling that there is a structure to the argument.

What does this mean exactly?
A whole range of things. That we talk from a whole range of selves. That poetry is not limited to this life; that there is the hypothesis of previous life and later life; that there is a noise coming from the universe constituted by an enormous number of sounds, of which the human voice would be a very small part. But to give a reasoned answer would need a book.

Would you accept the description of your work as visionary?
That would be very flattering, and obviously one would buy the ticket and go see the movie immediately. But it's another of these beautiful contradictions I seem to generate that I'm also intensely intellectual in most of my activities. I do believe in the reasoning mind as a wonderful tool. I'm fascinated by theory for its own sake, the manipulation and solving of problems related to symbolic systems. That's my original interest in anthropology—coming to a symbolic system totally fresh, despairing that it would ever make any kind of sense, piecing together the thing through months and years, finding finally a way of making sense of it. It is not necessarily a question of truth, but of viability in structural terms. That I've always found very exciting.

When there were intense debates in anthropology about Lévi-Strauss—whether he was right or wrong—my response was who the hell cares? This is the most intensely interesting mind of the twentieth century in anthropology, so let's just watch it do its thing. There will be plenty of time in later generations to sort all that other stuff out. I find it most unpleasant the way that fashion has accelerated like everything else in culture. We have a tendency to bury genius before it has an opportunity to drop into its own grave. Lévi-Strauss was given ten or fifteen years to do his thing, then suddenly he was out of fashion, no good, finished. Ridiculous.

So to come back to your question, the application of mind to the poetic archetype, and the word *mind* does seem to occur a lot in my poems, is very important to me. I would consider myself analytical, methodologically minded, and so on. Whether that takes me out of the visionary movie or not, I don't know. I'd hope not. After all, Blake thought intensely. A lot of people don't know what to make of William's intense system, but it is a system, beautiful and very complex. It's taken two hundred years to get people like Frye, Raine, and Erdman to give us a handle on the stuff.

It's interesting though: I took years and years to get to thinking clearly, by which I suppose I mean rationally. Mathematics, Latin, Greek were sheer torture. I like to read philosophy, though as we get down to our time, it gets so technical sometimes and so incredibly complex that I can only skim the surface. I would work by intuition, instinct, by analogical leaps: it took me years to be able to write an academic paper, slogging along from point a to point b to point c and making sure all the arguments were watertight. Now that I can do that, virtually in one draft, I am very anxious to give it up. You are rammed up against the conclusion that a poet is a very particular kind of animal after all . . .

What work have you done recently with translation?
I have not done any sustained work in translation for some time. This may be because I have been too busy for years to attend to *anything* important, or because I feel I have done my share, or because I have not met with anything I care deeply enough about. There may be something else: frankly, it is very irritating, when you have done translations, to have people harp on these to the exclusion of your own work. Of course, if you have translated someone very eminent or much in demand—like Pablo Neruda—this is understandable. However, if I find translations I much admire, I *am* curious about the translator and investigate his/her work. Few people seem to think of this.

Ideally, you should be in love with a certain poet in order to translate the work. Perhaps you should be young: the two tend to go together. You cannot do better, in youth, than to learn another language and then pay your debt to the Republic of Letters by doing something for it that others cannot do. (I have perhaps had more than my share of linguistic problems, first the hell of bilingualism—French/English—then the whole question of English English/American English).

I don't have too many theories about translation and usually refuse invitations to the interminable conferences people seem to hold about it. Like much else, it's something you do rather than talk about.

What about ethno-poetics?
There has been for some time a coming together of poetic and anthropological consciousness in our culture. Are you aware of the magazine *Alcheringa*? Now dead, alas. Well, Jerome Rothenberg was the initiator, though he had a lot of people around him interested in the same thing. He compiled a couple of very influential anthologies, particularly the first one—*Technicians of the Sacred*—in the late sixties. There were many points to the project, but for our purposes there were two primary goals. One was to bring current the translation of "primitive" and "archaic" poetries. They had gotten stuck in such places as the volumes of the Bureau of American Ethnology in Georgian, if not Victorian, English. Rothenberg's notion was to get the stuff translated by contemporary poets.

At the same time he wanted to show that many of the concerns of contemporary poets were identical to the concerns of these other peoples. This eventually gave rise to the whole notion of white shamanism, which native Americans and others have been very critical of. In some way, this idea of the poet as shaman descends from Baudelaire's sense of the poet as priest. God is dead, replaced by art. It also comes from an interest in Dada and surrealism, in such periodicals as *Minotaure* wherein poets and anthropologists were constantly being published side by side. Lévi-Strauss had connections with a number of poets. In the English-speaking world, you had Pound's interest in Frobenius or Eliot's in Jane Harrisson and the woman—I always forget her name—who wrote *From Ritual to Romance*. And you had the anthropologists interested in poetry and writing it: Ruth Benedict, Margaret Mead, Edward Sapir, Robert Redfield, dozens of them. The poetry was not very good. There is a whole network of these correspondences in the twenties and thirties. It was all in place a long time before Rothenberg, but he put it together for our time.

Will you comment on the political difficulties you alluded to?
Well, a number of people have pointed this out. To begin with, this "ethnopoetic" material is a subject matter which better not be faked or too much tampered with, for all sorts of reasons. Further, you get into the question

of whether or not the use of "primitive" materials is a rip-off. There is the vast question of under what conditions and terms you are making this material your own. There are a number of possible arguments here, not the least of which is the old saying that the true artist does not borrow but steals outright. If you do take something and make it entirely your own, believe in it fully, pay your respects to it, it must be a good thing for humanity. *But* on the other hand, it always seems to be the rich who take from the poor. The rich can afford to say, "Look at all this stuff lying about. Let's have a shot at it." It has to be more difficult for the poor to let go of their little piece, which is after all about all they've got. It's a complex argument, and it may not be for a couple centuries that this all gets sorted out. The tragedy, of course, is by that time the archaic peoples may have been eliminated. The whole stress of our so-called civilization has been to eliminate them. This goes right across the political spectrum, right and left.

What might follow here is the question of your own objectives in your poetry. Do you want to inform, or is it something more subjective?
Both. I'm very much a both/and person, as opposed to an either/or person. It seems like often people present me with what seems to be a very obvious alternative, but I don't see it as an alternative at all. Your question has a number of assumptions. Informing whom? The reader? Which reader? Subjective in what sense?

Well, it could be the reader, or yourself.
If I'm going to be honest about it, it must be to inform myself, simply in the sense that poetry is an exploratory device, and you are constantly learning about your own use of language, as well as your own unconscious. For example, there is an entirely different time frame in poetry, our ordinary concepts of time and space do not apply. You might for instance discover that you cannot lose or bury anything. You might think you've lost something, or be afraid of tearing a poem up. But in fact, the whole of your poetry's process is simultaneous, and if something has to come out, it will present itself for recognition again and again. Now, this kind of discovery has to be self-informing, though later you hope that someone else will tie into it. It's a mysterious process. You can write well, honestly, beautifully, according to your own ideas, and you won't find a reader in a hundred years. On the other hand, complete trash can find thousands of readers.

So in answer to your question, most people get their readers one by one. There is just no way of influencing the ocean of reception out there. Unless you begin perverting or simplifying your thinking, you've got to begin with the notion of production rather than reception. But this is the critic's business.

So you don't write for an audience.
I don't want to be that concrete about it, because it depends upon the occasion and the mood. I try to write a wide variety of poems. . . . This business of variety strikes me as more and more important. The contemporary poet is in an appalling situation. Virtually no one reads poetry: statistically the situation is absurd. Of the few who do, almost each individual has different requirements. How do you produce for such an atomized market? You can always do the old thing: ignore the market altogether, "follow your own vocation" and hope that the world catches up with you. If there is a world as we approach the state of total illiteracy! The other way, maybe more challenging, is to be faithful to your own voice but try to place it in various ranges. If it is a *rich* music, it should be able to play piano one day, cello another, tympany the next. Sonatas one day, quartets another, symphonies and oratorios the next. Blake is a good example here. He could write the *Poems of Innocence and Experience* (simple but by no means simplistic) and he could write the *Prophecies*. There is something for everyone here.

What do you mean by "total illiteracy"?
This goes a long way beyond the matter of poetry. My last few years as a teacher scared me stiff. We were graduating students who had cancer of the language. They could not read and did not; they could not write. The schools were feeding us people who were criminally underprivileged and had no notion that this was so. I am not even talking about elite knowledge now, I'm talking of a simple sentence in our language. This has been said often enough but I'm not sure the matter is being tackled. I see it as a major national emergency, perhaps—as our "culture" spreads—a major international one. It is very curious that we worry our guts out about parity in armaments for instance. If things go on as they are, there will be no one left to run this planet. They won't be able to read the instructions.

I used to believe that the American language was growing and evolving more than any other in the English community. The "Young America" of the sixties and early seventies seemed wonderful to me. Much of that energy seems to have dissipated. We now have acres and acres of New-Age blather, putting everyone to sleep while pretending to wake them; blissing everyone *out* while claiming to make them more aware. And here there is as much *corruption* of language (loss of edge, loss of energy, loss of *bite*) as in the more obvious places such as advertising, TV babble, and the rest of it. If poets *suffer* now, it has got to be in the *language,* no? I don't think *anyone* realizes how much one suffers in the language! To listen to some of the crap that comes out of commercials, that ocean of liquid excrement pouring out night and day, year in year out! It's worse than poison gas! You can't even listen to public radio anymore without that vomit. If you want *one* good reason why poetry should continue—literature if you will—switch on the radio or TV or one of our politicians. You have it right there, you don't need to go *any* further!

People get to thinking this is a matter of class. If you criticize the stuff, you are called elitist. I know a number of poets who have succumbed to this hoary old antiintellectualism. Somehow, if you talk this way, you are being antipeople. Well, I continue to distinguish between the *language of the people* (which has a magnificent history in this country) and the entrepreneurial language which consumer organizations are foisting on us as if it were the language of the people. It is not. Go out and listen to the people. There are some that have still not been brainwashed into talking like robots.

Some of this certainly does sound as if you write for an audience. And much of your poetry is certainly political.
Yes, but I would argue that I'm informing myself first and foremost about the strength of my opinion on a particular issue. I would hope that simultaneously the strength of that political feeling would communicate itself in the poem to somebody else. If you believe in what you are doing, it does follow that you hope that someone will receive it; otherwise, you are just going around in a fishbowl. For what?

On this question of reception, what are your reactions to Language poetry, in that much of it seems pretty inaccessible?
Everything about that work is fascinating, wonderful, worthwhile, etc., everything, that is, except the product itself. In the majority of cases which I have seen, I think this is true. This certainly does not mean that I'm not interested in this work; on the contrary, I read it avidly and I hope as carefully as I read anything else, I try to remain open to it, I keep going at it. It is very obviously of concern to people, and very obviously an important development. I welcome the emphasis on language, the return to the intellect, the stress on mind, the attack on consensus, the stuff on the reader as participating in the meaning of meaning (i.e., reception). I also welcome

not so much the so-called nonreferentiality—which I think is nonsense—but the attention to shades, shifts, disjunctions, interferences, alternations, polyvalences in models of referentiality, along a continuum from the orthodox to the highly experimental.

Further, I like the political stance of a number of these writers, although I believe it is often very naive. Marxism has gone a hell of a long way further than people like Silliman seem to have understood, at least when they began. However, they of course at the same time are becoming more sophisticated so that any critique obviously has to attend upon what they may develop. I like the stances on community, on feminism, and so on, though again in each case it's a little problematic. And they seem far from agreeing among themselves.

Anyway, all these theoretical concerns are fine—all the more so since they are precisely the concerns of the formalists on down, whose latest manifestation was French structuralism. To a certain extent we are very underinformed about history, and I don't think we fully realize how much the Language school is a rehash of arguments which have been going on in Paris and Paris satellites for the last twenty years or so. Or how much the programmatic behavior is drawn from the kind of "terrorism" characteristic of French schools, from surrealism on down to the *Tel Quel* group. Thus, while I welcome these theoretical concerns which strengthen the argument against the poem of the establishment, nevertheless the product in many ways is overintellectualized, as the French texts had been. The manipulation of referentiality often leads to such obscurity that the texts are fundamentally—and here I'm speaking of the poetry—unsatisfactory to me. In fact, the similarity to France of the last two or three decades is remarkable. The French it seems to me have managed to sink much of French poetry into the ground for the vast majority of its readers. Maybe the Americans are going to do the same thing.

So your feelings are mixed.
Yes. Now, there are some of those writers whom I'm far more interested in—Beverly Dahlen, Clark Coolidge, Michael Palmer, Michael Davidson, for instance—than others. And even amongst themselves there are various differences. Some are trying to back away from the label, and already the self-critique has begun, the breaking apart.

But you do see it as an important development?
Yes I do. It is one stage on in the game. What we had in the sixties and

the seventies was the "establishment" poem—what would be acceptable to the *New Yorker,* the Ivy League, and all of Her Britannic Majesty's possessions in this country—versus the so-called new poetry, which descended from Pound, H.D., Williams, and company, manifested in any number of schools. This was the opposition. Language poets come along and say, "Finish with this opposition, it's gone on too long, it's uninteresting. Let's move into Wittgenstein. Let's move into Marx. Let's move into Freud." To that extent, it's a step further.

But something is interesting here, and perhaps it hasn't been expressed enough. The concern with an "objective" poetry as opposed to a "subjective" poetry which you find in Olson, for example, is continued here. The Language poets have an interest in *text,* a poetry of objective treatment of language qua language which doesn't constantly throw us back into the personal sentiments of, say, a Mr. Kinnell, or a Mr. Merwin, or a Mr. Bly. There are two points here. One is that the Language poets pretend that there is only one enemy ("the workshop poem"), when in fact there is a whole other ground of people (Ken Irby, Armand Schwerner, Robert Kelly, Rosemarie Waldrup, Charles Stein, Leslie Scalapino, Mei Mei Bersenbrugge might be examples) working experimentally who seem not to accept the integral Language program or methodological approach. They would detest "the workshop poem" too. Also, when it comes down to the objectivity business, I feel once again like pleading for both/and rather than either/or. The whole of our culture is trying to make objects of us all the time; surely the ancient and traditional task of the artist to transcend this, to transmit interesting perceptions of the world, remains in that case valid and even radical. I came across some lines in Goethe the other day, at the end of a poem called "Vermachtnis": *"Denn edlen Seelen vorzufuhlen / Ist wunschenswertester Beruf"* : "for to devise patterns of feeling for noble souls is the most desirable of all callings." If that strikes many people as old-fashioned, too bad. I believe you leave off thousands of years of traditional responsibility at your risk and peril.

It is an extremely difficult problem, this last one. It is true that most egos or "personalities" resemble other egos and are therefore not, in structuralist terms, surprising. But that does not mean that from time to time there does not appear an ego that produces material which is sufficiently idiosyncratic to matter against the random noise. We still need to learn from such heterodox consciousnesses.

So do you work for that kind of voice? And doesn't that imply a kind of narrative?

I work for voice, yes, though I'm not sure about narrative. Someone was once kind enough to write that I do good long narrative poems. I've written those poems, but honestly I don't think of myself as primarily a narrative poet. Many of the nonnarrative poems, however, are perhaps so tight that they present difficulties to the reader. Our times are so difficult and so complex that maybe finally the only thing we can do is to subsist in the difficulties, the contradictions. For me this means that ideally a poet's range should be very wide. Sometimes the poems must be like markers buried deeply in the ground; other times they might be simple, even funny. This takes us right back to the start when you asked if I had a favorite book of my work. Each book is fundamentally different.

Of course, this last idea may be pure illusion. One of the fascinating things about creation is that you are constantly thinking that the voice is doing something new *at last;* later, though, you realize that it is all too familiar. But then it is because of that push that you keep going.

Going back to the visionary for a moment, you have always seemed to be interested in the "spiritual" or "religious" as well as the political. How do such terms as self/ego/personality *fit in here and what is their relation to "voice" exactly?*

Extremely tough question, but most important. Again, it would need a book. But let me try out a model. Let it be so that "gods"/"powers"/"guardians"—in so far as they are external to us—are, mostly, *place* together with the *nature* attendant on place (weather, climate, fauna, flora, etc.). As in all else, there are hierarchies: galaxies, planets, as well as countries, states, towns, villages. All of these have *voices* which must be attended to: the depth of attention is one index of spirituality. As beings, living in place, we neglect such voices at our peril. Let "ego" or "self" be a collection of stances, attitudes, orientations, passions which we "believe" ourselves to constitute, each ego or self moving through a world in which nature and culture are indissolubly intertwined. The collection has voices which, taken together, make up a "personality." These voices are cultural; they must be attended to on the same level as other persons' voices: *je est (toujours) un autre / un autre est toujours je.* Again, the depth of attention is the index of such "spirituality" as we may care to acknowledge.

So much for nature and culture. Where is the bridge? Let it be so that *depth of attention* itself is the bridge. Depth of attention is a unifying force, indissolubly melding together all single voices into a choral voice, place and being, live and dead, "human" and "divine." At such depth, the contradictions attendant on our normal time/place frameworks cease to appear as such. Let us call this depth of attention something like *presence*.

Each of us has our tools. For the poet, *language* moves the self to presence. It is the vehicle of ever deepening attention. But we must not hallow it as something *more* than a tool. The move to presence is altogether beyond any mode of exploitation and flows into a great ocean of sound where silence and the manifold voices are one.

Such a model complicates our attitudes to such topics as "subjectivity"/ "objectivity" in poetry, and many contemporary conclusions on such topics seem simplistic. Certainly, it takes us light-years beyond the "workshop poem" which can be left to deliquesce where it belongs.

As for the "religious," I guess you can see that I am not going to be very patient with any kind of formalized religion. Of the latter, my anthropological formation leads me to prefer the orthodox, the highly ritualized, the colorful, the mystical. This does not contradict what I said about impatience with formalized religion: let me stress that the *symbolism* involved in orthodoxies seems to me to deepen attention, whether it be mental or behavioral. Above all, I have the strongest distaste for the kind of blithe assumptions about personal saviors which run like riot through our country. The religious power which built this country now seems to me to have become the most crippling aspect of its mental life.

Do you see a kind of consistency through the years in your work?
Yes, I think so. If you have my feeling about the "inner voice" I suppose that follows. But too there is the sense that one is getting many different voices from various directions. In *Lyrics for the Bride of God* there are surely parts of the poem which come from different voices. Overall, though, there does seem to be a consistency, with a desire to broaden the range. I don't want to do the same thing over and over again.

Can we go back for a moment? Aren't the Language poets reacting to the workshop poem as much as anything else? And the American Poetry Review?
Whatever they are reacting to, they seem to me to be part of a problem which began with Modernism. It has to do with what I describe as the expectation of exegesis. A great deal of Modernism seems tied to a phenom-

enon in which the writer or artist moves into the university. You get a kind of ladder system in which no generation can defend itself, but has to defend the generation before it. I might be paid a very large sum to explicate X, who is the poet just before me, but I'm paid nothing to explicate myself. If I'm of any interest, it's the person coming after me who will be paid to explicate me, and so on down the line.

Now you may argue that, if reader response (reception) is as important as it is to the Language poet, he/she is going to claim that exegesis is an individual matter which cannot be regimented. This is fine for the rare free spirit, usually another poet. But, where there is *difficulty* or *obscurity,* the average reader will be led back to the professor, and the academy will reclaim its rights. Once more they will tyrannize over us with their canons. And once more, books of poems will be commodities.

In some curious way, I had a tendency to read Ron Silliman more than the others, and one of the extraordinary things to me is his incredible illusion that he is founding a literary community. The idea is that they are taking the book of poems out of the "commodity fetish" market, and that in some way their poems are more widely available than the average poet's. Well, are they? It seems to me that the reception/consumer aspect there is narrower than ever. The fact that we are manufacturing more and more poets through the mechanisms of the MFA means that the incestuous family is a very large one, but it remains incestuous. They are right on that point. But are the Language poets any less incestuous? Are there *nonpoets* on the street who are spending their time reading Language poetry? I don't think so. You may say that there is nobody on the street reading Olson, or Duncan, or anything at all, and to a certain extent that's true. But it seems to me that the funnel is narrowing more and more.

But isn't it possible that the "workshop poem" is a generic poem, the ego a generic ego? That the Language poets are simply trying to create in very small communities a shared code? Thus when Silliman talks about an audience he is not talking about people in the street, but rather Michael Palmer and Charles Bernstein?

Sure. One another. If that is what they mean by "community," ok, though there have always been "schools" and "movements." But then we get into the whole vast business of the hermetic. In the end it's very simple—poetry as a craft, if you think of it in terms of progress, has to get more and more complicated. Eventually a threshold is reached which creates a hermetic, incestuous situation which is immensely difficult to get out of. Once caught up in this—especially in the zero-degree political situation in which we find ourselves—you almost totally lose sight of reception. You lose sight of the original idea that the poet exists to produce things which will be of value to all of society, and at that point just what does "community" mean? *Interesting*, of course. I can bring to your attention very interesting communities of bird-watchers and model airplane builders. We are a nation of buffs—just look at the magazine racks. But where does the *overall* humanity fit into this? Then to top it off, one begins talking of Marxism, for God's sake! I may be very obtuse, and it's possible the whole thing is passing me by, but I just can't see it. It's like a brook pretending to be the sea.

Then the Marxism does bother you.
Not per se. And I certainly don't mean that the only Marxist poetry can be social realism. It's just that I cannot conciliate any Marxism I know of with that incredibly narrow band of "Language poets'" "community."

Moving back to the creative writing workshop, have you taught one?
Once, for two weeks only, thank God.

What do you think about the whole process?
I am profoundly divided on this. You've got to look at the thing in the context of the total culture. If our society reduces the cultural areas—Lévi-Strauss's idea that the artist will eventually live in a kind of national park, and be free to cavort there but not outside—we'll get a society without art. We are well on our way to this. If you think of universities as national parks, where people are free to be tied to their parking meters for four years outside the labor market and able to indulge in *culture*, then the survival of culture is obviously tied to the four-year-parking-meter system. Ergo, it's a good thing; otherwise, where else will you find it?

However, the fact that a thing is so doesn't mean that it's good. Obviously, any political take on this would seem to scream for the decentralization of culture. It shouldn't simply take refuge in the academy. At this point, one is tempted to say, "Go West young man. Get hold of your turkey sandwich. Go out and live." All the old messages. Stop fussing around in academic hothouses. So my feelings are mixed.

Have you taken creative writing courses?
No. And there, I've said it. But maybe that's why I feel, I suppose, that at

the heart of it the project is unnecessary. But then maybe there is no need to be taught anything, at least formally.

Though maybe the point isn't teaching writing as much as giving people, as you hinted, a place to hide out for a while.
Sure. From that point of view it's fine. I would personally, though, be fairly savage on this point. I once designed for the comparative literature department at Rutgers a possible writer's Ph.D. It was far more demanding than the literature Ph.D. The students did all of what the literature people would do, plus a number of extra tasks which were geared toward writers. It was postulated on the notion that the student from the start was someone who had taken the decision to be a writer, made a conscious choice, and a very difficult one. It was howled down by the comparative literature department. "Only English departments have creative writing branches."

What was the curriculum?
A very strong critical and methodological orientation in literary studies. Not the old chestnut about genres and periods, but solid theory from the beginning. Plus whatever a writer might seriously consider as curricula, very much in the spirit of Olson's *Bibliography On America For Ed Dorn,* or Pound's *ABC of Reading.* I guess I do believe that if you are going to be an academic, you should be an academic, period. In a sense there is something very half-assed about an artist in the university because on the one hand the system obliges him or her to be an academic while on the other the artist is always fighting out of the system. Then you end up with these wonderful assemblages of the great charismatic people, creative writing professors with their adoring students. A reservoir of graduate student friends and lovers. It's horrendous. At some of these programs it's as if people were drugged on SUNY or Iowa or wherever. Don't they realize that if they walked about a hundred yards they could actually *get out?* There are train stations and airports. There are roads. They could travel to Ohio, or Maine, or New Mexico. But they are bewitched.

My one real experience with this was at the University of Colorado's Writers' School one summer. It was fascinating. Apart from the fact that everyone wanted to be in your mouth, in your pocket, in wherever for twenty-four hours a day, the other extraordinary thing was that no one was writing about their immediate experience. You'd read manuscripts, then ask people for facts about their lives—it was like pulling teeth. Someone would be working in a town whose mainstay was, for instance, salmon fishery. Any question of salmon in the poem? No! Another was sitting all his life in orange groves. Was there a single orange in the poem? Nada! It was very weird. This was in 1973, and not a single person was talking about anything under his or her nose. *Love. War. Sex.* Some very worthy things. But one never had the sense that you got to know the people you were dealing with.

If I were to do this again, my temptation would be to talk about anything but writing—politics, anthropology, history of aviation. This might be painful for the people in the workshop who have paid to talk about their poems, but somehow it would seem more sane, and probably of more use.

Once, I was giving a class in modern European poetry. Some kids, whose creative writing teacher was on leave, joined my class thinking it was a creative writing class. They were all walking out. I said to one girl: "Hey, as a matter of interest, have you ever read Baudelaire, or Rimbaud, or Rilke . . . and so on." I'll never forget her reply as long as I live. "No," she said, "but nor do I want to before I get my own shit together." I can understand the feeling but it seems totally wrong to me. Like trying to be born without any kind of father or mother. I can understand that passion for a virgin birth, especially in our American context, but an art like poetry cannot survive if we don't first and foremost know our fathers and mothers. Just like our country will not survive if we don't finally manage to learn history. Or history in depth. What a godforsaken bore the eighteenth century can be if there is nothing behind it. But God, if we could only get back as far as that! Most of us seem to find *last year* antediluvian!

---

from *Old Savage/Young City*

Last of the Chiefs

I speak from ignorance.
Who once learned much, but speaks from ignorance now.
Who trembled once with the load of such knowledge,
trembled and cried and gritted his teeth and gripped
with his fists the ends of the arms of his throne.

Who once distilled this island in his green intestines
like the whale distils her dung gone dry called ambergris—
a perfume for faraway races

who wrecked us.

Only here and there, like lightning before the rain's whips,
like a trench along the deep, a thought such as I had:

in the belly of the whale there is room for such an island.

I laugh. I come now. I clear space. My name, my very being
is that: I clear space. I pass over them with my thongs, laughing,
that have died fighting the island-bellied whale, not prevailed,
turned at last their steels against themselves, lie in spasms,
their cheek and chest muscles like rock. I pass over them,
smoke them, whip them, revive them, send them out again.

Wise wind singer with a forked tail like white lightning
and your black pin eye. Paradise tern on her tail-long hair.

I am thankful. I accept. I take your offerings of pork lard
and the myriad flowers of the scissored palm leaf. I take.
I accept. But above all I thank you for the breasts in heaven
of my daughters of the island which is Nukahiva of the Marquesas

that you know as Herman Melville's green garden, his Pacific.

Some say he beautified this green back yard.
I speak from ignorance. I remember little.

from *A Nowhere for Vallejo*

"Yo nací un día
que Dios estuvo infermo,
grave."
          —LOS HERALDOS NEGROS

Conch shells at Mass
    alcaldes standing   golden cloaks
staffs tipped with silver
    alpaca lining   shield   flocks on their knees

priest dropping shards for the thousandth time
    of shattered language

the sacristan distributes herbs of grace
    and lights to the village elders

as   suddenly
        the church roof sails
            several feet into the air
the Sun opens its arms

the risen Host covers the face of the Sun like a kerchief
    and the wild thrones bellow
           dominations howl
archangels blare

              a poet   born
from the depths of the sea
        in Santiago de Chuco
on the scar of Peru

and female the soul of the absent one
and female my very own
till when shall we be waiting for
what no one owes us

People at the door outside
    press in against the temple
cheeks to their fathers' stones
        cave in like the walls of the sea

Sad destiny not to have ever lived but dead forever
    being dry leaf unknown to green
        orphan of orphans
           and
Mother I go tomorrow to Santiago
    to wet me in your benedictions and your tears

A child of seven
    ravished by the fiesta procession
especially the standard-bearer
    racing home to his mother

Mother I want to be the standard-bearer

Conch shells at Mass
   alcaldes gathered at the door
shrunk in the light of flash-bulbs
   a girl throwing petals on the vicar's head   he shrugs them off

I shall come back to Peru when not one stone is left standing

Flight from the Mountaintop

"Aber Freund! wir kommen zu späat. Zwar leben die Götter,
   Aber über dem Haupt droben in anderer Welt."
      Hölderlin

Running off the mountain:
            billow of air,
ground drops below peak,
multicolored sails swerving
            above the valley:
not us flying those wings
            but flown by them.
   (Tangle unravelled:
   the compelling
   drag on the bird . . . feet and legs in lime,
   beak in his own thick blood,
   needles sticking thru feathers,
      all that behind us.)
Now: arrows, spears, lances,
            columns, towers of air:
   victory headless at the crest,
   yet throat spouting song,
   stump bare and hardly bleeding.

      In their dreams men are
   (gods)
he had said,
   in reflection: SLAVES.
Ground is philosophy,
            the hospital—
but the air

six thousand feet above the valley:
you can't think of wreckage.
      In his flight
remembered the isle of light,
        how one morning
had borrowed father's wings,
strapping them on as if for combat, and had
neighbored the sun awhile in soaring lovelike
and free with birds, angels and all manner of
musical spheres, planets and meteors . . .

In their dreams (he had sd.) men were
    alike.
Dumb bums below, his life was bound up with
    in scalding slavery,
failed to recognize
his cataract out of that morning sky,
       blood like the lightest wine
dissolved in sun and aether.
       He could not have been
salvaged out of that air in any shape
recognizable to man, beast, god,
once he had started falling and
you could not have looked into his eyes
since the sun had taken them quite out.
    But his mind from then on—we are told
in his final speech—what a hoard that was
of incisive tools, and how well he knew
what he wanted around him and what
had to be trashed, like old shoes,
           outside his door.

2

"in the dream,
the glide descends in spirals
down to the extremity of my country

from which a ship will take you
                              to the farthest peninsulae
of all other imagineable countries.
It is a winter there
                    I had previously thought
                                        unfathomable."

"In deepest winter
          coldest things calm most.
Causing the mind to desist from raving and to still
inexhaustible choice that is making us all mad.
My gods how I pity you all in this iron age
and want silence now, from now on, always,
and shall not speak to you anymore, nor fly with you,
holding your hands in the sun, protecting your wings,
shielding the delicate wax on your shoulders
from his deadly bite."

"What it had occurred to me to say
concerned the birds of deepest winter in my country,
out of a north larger than memory,
perhaps full of mountains off whose peaks they flew,
which had now congregated for my eyes' pleasure
on the border black lakes of my country:
all that sludge on the lakes like sick thought
sensing its own destruction.
            The end as I had predicted
        (that silent end full of bombardments)
of intellect."

"Is not the metaphor of our indited clarity
that exquisite bird, part white, part black,
whose very head, the pattern of the head,
                is our question mark?
I forget (deliberately)
birds of one color,
even the great
          ghost-trampler of women,
or the black lout of the sea in all his forms,

who stands for the night of the sea in all his forms,
        and has no name, or,
if you will, a multitude, no matter. "

"—Your Majesty, my pilots sick today,
unfit for battle. They will not *think*
at the controls, they are dangerous.
I remember the country of the living,
        how they spoke in tongues,
the orders they gave, and the surrenders.
    I was granted today the order of silence.
    Already I don't remember speech.
Speech, I think, was like that very wide
                river behind my house
very beautiful in the cold air of winter,
            the blues especially,
carrying the perspective of all human beings,
            whether you looked
back to the source of the river, or down to the sea.
                It is time
perhaps to move inland and look for walls.
        A tower perhaps.
My wife, held back by her own husband always
    (an air-traffic controller)
might not get around to making it with me.
I don't know whether it will be possible to fly again:
    my flights may be long and impressive,
        but will not be visible anymore.
            Je suis hors concours.
These are the elegies, which is: a search for
the origin which does not belong to our deathless order.
And yet we are commanded to purify mankind
and the sentinel number I have posited as
characteristic of the nightly eras of the earth. "

3

And let me add
that if it were not for my own extreme sympathy with him:

I mean he who has delivered this poem to you this way,
I could not have spoken like this
nor begun to tell you
that in this America we now have
        a dreampath again, or spirit quest if you will,
departing every day from the mountain top—
                        billow of air underwing
        ground lost below height,
            altho it is not certain that anyone will look
at the finest flyers as they perform in the blue sky;
in the thunderhead sky with tones of copper or iron,
in the misted sky at zero/zero—
            whether they soar beyond the sun
        or collapse into the sea below
            or fix the shape of their outspread arms and legs
on the crumpled ground
                        (slaves to reflection),
        the middle of their bodies pulverised
                        by the effort of flight
and the order of angels closed for the time of this era
                    to any candidate whatsoever.

12. Diane Wakoski

Photo by Robert Turney.

"Listening for whatever there was to hear"

Diane Wakoski, whom Hayden Carruth has argued "has become in a very few years one of the two or three most important poets of her generation in America," was born in Whittier, California, in 1937. She received an undergraduate degree in English from the University of California at Berkeley, and has served as poet-in-residence at a number of major universities in this country, including the California Institute of Technology, the University of Virginia, and the University of Hawaii; since 1976 she has taught at Michigan State University. Wakoski's first book, *Coins and Coffins,* appeared in 1962; since that time she has published over thirty volumes of poetry and essays, including *Inside the Blood Factory, The Magellanic Clouds, The Motorcycle Betrayal Poems, Looking for the King of Spain, The Man Who Shook Hands,* and the complete *Greed.* Her awards include a Guggenheim fellowship (1972) and a National Endowment for the Arts grant (1973).

Diane Wakoski writes, "I think of myself as a narrative poet, a poet creating both a personal narrative and a personal mythology. I write long poems, and emotional ones. My themes are loss, imprecise perception, justice, truth, the duality of the world, and the possibilities of magic, transformation, and the creation of beauty out of ugliness. My language is dramatic, oral, and as American as I can make it. . . . Poetry, for me, is the supreme art of the individual using a huge magnificent range of language to show how special and different and wonderful his perceptions are. With verve and finesse. With discursive precision. And with utter contempt for pettiness of imagination or spirit."

In your essay on Anaïs Nin you mention that good writers have problems approaching middle age, that their lives become less eventful, less filled with tension, that the writing loses energy and organic shape.
I think when I wrote that I wasn't yet middle-aged. I was at that time deeply sympathetic with and fascinated by what I saw happening to middle-aged writers like Creeley and Levertov, who are both a little more than ten years older than I am. I know that a lot of people have felt, and I myself have felt, that Creeley was the poet of our time, but then when Creeley got to the point where *Pieces* was published his work got very uninteresting. When Levertov got totally involved with politics, and seemed to be writing bad political speeches instead of poems, I got disillusioned. I simply worked out a theory that I think is true; what it does is reflect the fact that most of us live what a Marxist would call a bourgeois life—not necessarily decadent, but bourgeois—and in that life pattern we do very adventurous things, if we do anything at all, when we are young, then sort of coast along through

the middle years. I see another aspect of that now that I'm middle-aged, that we are not merely coasting along, though it may look like that, but creating something new. I tend to think that many people have an early period that is really very powerful and a late period that's really very powerful, if they are lucky and live that long, and a middle period that is really pretty dull for other people. I feel that this theory has been validated in seeing Creeley's book *Later,* which is a wonderful book of poems. I think Levertov's very, very best book of poems is *Life in the Forest.* But both of them have gone back to earlier styles of writing while incorporating the material of their lives as they've progressed. Levertov is just as politically active as she was, but she's finally learned that her political poems are just not very good, that they are an act of conscience for her and an important thing in her life, but they aren't really what makes anyone interested in her as a poet. She continues to write them and even spends a certain portion of every poetry reading reading them, but she no longer believes, it seems to me, that that is the important part of her life. I saw the Creeley of *Pieces* as working his way through a kind of fascination with linguistic philosophy that had always been his fascination, but having come through it in a way that he can still write lyric poems.

How does this apply to your own work?
Certainly the theme of my poetry up through *The Motorcycle Betrayal Poems* is the search for perfect love/sex/romance in one's life, and how though one never finds it one must keep looking for it for that is the nature of the quest. I think after *The Motorcycle Betrayal Poems* books like *Virtuoso* and *The Man Who Shook Hands* seemed to bore people who were very interested in the overt search of the earlier book—though certainly *The Man Who Shook Hands* is certainly a story of that search continuing to an even more devastating reality, when your lover leaves in the morning and shakes hands with you. What began to evolve in my poems at that point is the counterpart theme, the theme of aging. It's really the same theme as love/sex/romance, as it's the search for some balancing of mind and body. Age will beat you as love/sex/romance beat you; there just doesn't seem to be any way to balance the body and the spirit—you choose either one or the other and then the one you don't choose beats you up and betrays you. If you try to balance them both you are in a constant juggling act, though maybe that's what my poems are about.

I know that there are people who feel disappointed that the theme of the search for love/sex/romance has turned into the search for some kind of peace with one's body in my work. Perhaps there is another reality we ought to think about, at least I think about it all the time, though I don't know how to write about it except with a kind of venom and anger. This is the fact that the American culture simply does not accept anything except youth and beauty, total sexuality. I constantly get responses from people at poetry readings that make me know that they disapprove of my talking about being middle-aged and aging. I get this from my colleagues all the time in Michigan. It's all right to age if you look like Jane Fonda or Gloria Steinem, but it's not all right to age of you look like most of us do. It's even less all right to talk about it or be miserable about it. One of my poems in a recent group of poems, "Saturn's Rings," is dedicated to Joyce Carol Oates. It's about how I've always wanted to win a Pulitzer Prize, and now that I'm middle-aged I realize that I probably never will. People either love the poem because they think it's very gutsy or it really, really, really makes them uncomfortable because you are not supposed to talk about wanting to win Pulitzer Prizes and not winning them. Just as you are not supposed to talk about no one wanting to go to bed with you anymore, or those kinds of things; that's not supposed to happen to you, and if it does it must mean that you are sick. You are supposed to age the way Gary Snyder does or somehow be doing aerobics. I'm not into doing aerobics and I just don't live in the woods. I just wish somebody would give me a Pulitzer Prize.

Why do you write then? Is it an attempt to create a career or is there some kind of inner necessity?
I don't think I had any concept that there was a career to be created. For one thing I started writing when I was very young. There is one thing that I feel often that I have to explain to people who are under twenty-five. When I grew up not everybody was middle class. More or less everyone is middle class now; by that I mean there is really a different level of economic reality that normal people experience now. The expectations that go with it are very much larger. I grew up under very poor circumstances. I lived with a working mother who worked all of her life, never had a pension, and still lives on her social security, which is about two hundred dollars a month. She lived on the edge of poverty all her life, supporting herself and a family. I grew up with the image that you worked very, very hard no matter who you were, that you never made money, and that there were the rich people and then the rest of the world. So I grew up longing to be a millionaire because that was the only way I could think of being anything different. It never occurred to me that you could make a career for yourself; I didn't see

anybody around me doing that. I knew that you could be a genius, but I thought that geniuses always starved, unless they were millionaires also. It never occurred to me that writing would do anything for me except give me one thing my mother didn't have—some kind of excitement or pleasure in her life. I knew that I had to work all my life at a forty-hour-a-week job that I hated. Again, it never occurred to me that even though I went to college that I could get better jobs. I went to college because I was excited about being in school and I was always a good student. I didn't realize that people get better jobs by going to college; in fact, my life has proven that— I've never gotten a good job because I went to college. So for me writing poetry, once I discovered it, was such an exciting thing to do that it gave my life some kind of meaning even if I was holding down a terrible job.

Again, because I grew up with a mother but more or less without a father it never occurred to me that a girl could get married and her husband would support her and that would be a good life. My mother had married and she still had to work. In some ways that may sound hard to you, but actually it made my life a lot easier. I didn't grow up with the sense that I would lose anything by anything I chose. And I didn't grow up with the sense of expectation that people have now. The only things I grew up having expectations about were the things that happened to geniuses—like winning a Pulitzer Prize. I see my own students now struggling with a very different sense of reality. They all live and have grown up in nicer houses than I have been able to buy for myself at age forty-five. They all have a standard of living now that I struggled to acquire at middle age. I don't know what I would do if I were faced with these current problems—the idea that if I took a business course I could earn a good living, or if I went to law school I could earn a good living, as opposed to writing poetry. Those things weren't choices to me. I was a person who read and loved to read, and who wrote, and writing every once in a while would bring me a check for ten dollars or whatever, and that was a big deal. I got personal satisfaction.

You also have to remember that I was in college from 1956 to 1960 at Berkeley, and that was just at the surge of the San Francisco Renaissance. Kenneth Rexroth had really made the whole idea of poetry reading into an interesting idea; this was when the Beat Generation was just coming along. The academic world did not seem like such a good place to be, except to people like me who were excited about going to college because no one in her family had ever been to college. Even to me college did not seem a means to an end, and all the San Francisco poets like Kenneth Rexroth and Robert Duncan were proclaiming that the only thing that happened to poets and poetry in academia was that they got buried alive. So there was no impetus to go to graduate school or do anything like that. In fact, my background fit in very well—you go out in the world and work at some crummy job, and then spend all your other time and energy working on your poetry. Your gratification comes from poetry readings and people responding to your poetry; it comes from getting together in people's apartments, drinking wine, and reading your poetry and talking about it. There is a sense of community, and your poems are all about how awful the world is and everyone agrees and you feel good. You don't really believe that there is any way to change that and thus poetry is a meaningful act. One of the things that became different in the sixties, though I'm not sure it was true, was the feeling that if you *did* something you could change the world. If you protested against the House Un-American Activities Committee maybe you could get that whole "McCarthy chasing commies" attitude changed. If you picketed, you could get the government to stop the war in Vietnam. I never believed that and so I never became political.

But isn't the very act of writing poetry a "political act"?

What I think art does, and this may be a controversial point of view, is that it takes over when human actions can't go any place else. So if there really is something that you want to stop, you should be out there trying to stop it, not writing poems and making posters, or whatever. When you know that nothing else can happen, when you know that nothing can reverse the half-life of plutonium, then you write "The Plutonium Ode." That at least is one final human gesture that has beauty and some kind of dignity. But if you really thought that you could stop nuclear war, then you ought to be running for senator, or doing whatever it is that would implement that belief. Poems are not going to do this. Art is what you do when you have no power over the practical details of your life.

And do you, or did you, feel this lack of power?

Yes, that's how art evolved for me. I had no power over the practical details of my everyday life. I had my brains and that's it. I didn't even have the belief that those brains could get me a good job. Maybe you'll see this as a defeatist or pessimistic point of view; I don't. I simply see it as accepting and understanding the world as it is. I guess I'm an old existentialist, and for me this vision has actually been a very optimistic one because I don't expect art to do more than it can and it gives me enormous satisfaction.

Earlier I was saying to Lee that while I've been on this trip I've given four readings—they've all been enthusiastically attended by people who seem to have been reading my poetry seriously and for some time. It has made me feel very good, but it has also seemed very odd to me, making me wonder if poetry is more alive on the West Coast than it is in the Midwest or the South, places where I've been recently. I don't know whether this is a flukey trip or what. But even if no one read my poetry I would still write it because it is that gesture of taking my life in my hands and doing something about it, in the way that is given a person like me who has that skill but no others. However, the pleasure of giving poetry readings where there is a responsive audience is immense. I'm sure that that has fed poetry, but I wonder to myself if we aren't going into a dark period now. From what I see of poetry students around the country, many of whom are very talented, is a total involvement in their own poetry without a sense of who is going to read it. I do not think that they are any more or less self-centered than I or my friends were. But it is just that they lack the sense of responsibility that if they want people to read *their* poetry, they have to read *other* people's poetry.

You see this in aspects of American life other than poetry, don't you—the "me generation," the great age of "self-help"?
Certainly I see this attitude in things other than poetry. We *are* moving into an age of self-help. You can write a book about self-help on any topic, get it published, and sell fifty thousand copies of it. But try to sell five thousand copies of a book of poems. . . . We are in a do-it-yourself age wherein people would rather play the flute badly than go hear a master—they would rather write their own crummy poems than read someone who is a great writer. I predict that for the next ten or fifteen years this is one of the things that we as artists and intellectuals will have to battle. I have nothing against all of us doing the most original things we can, but I despair of a world in which everybody feels like an expert and doesn't respect anyone else who is. It certainly means an age where everyone will write poetry and no one will read it. And it certainly means in some way a decline in those arts. Those are the times in history where things become secret and hermetic, and have their crazy realities.

My own grounding in poetry is so much that sense that poetry is written for other people to read; it *is* an act of communication. I would never write it and stick it in my desk drawer with the feeling that it's finished. I have to make an attempt for it to be published, or at least go out into the world to somebody to be exchanged. I feel that poetry is a way of communication and I need to feel that there is some kind of response. I used to write a lot of letters; I don't at this period in my life, but I probably will again. I like that sense of things going out and coming back. I'm delighted with the new journal *American Poetry* because I think this is a time when we need to have attention formally called to reading poetry and responding to it critically. Otherwise you have this huge number of poetry books being published as if they are going into the ocean, turning into soggy paper. Perhaps if there are more formal channels such as a magazine of criticism that is one way of making a small kind of reciprocity.

Do you see regionalism as an aspect of this kind of dark age feudalism you are talking about?
That's a good question. I think that maybe there are two sides to regionalism—a very healthy side, as well as the unhealthy side that I've been talking about. Let me meditate for a moment on the healthy side of regionalism.

One of the things that regionalism means to me right now is that we are finally, finally beginning to come of age artistically, critically, and intellectually as a cultural identity. We have realized that American poetry is, finally, something quite different from European poetry. The fact that it has been that way for a long time doesn't seem to have changed anything in the critical world, but I think that we finally have come to the stage where we can recognize that Whitman was the first American poet and that there is a tradition of poetry that comes out of Whitman. It can be described and discussed both historically and critically, and it is something very different from the European. This is one of the reasons that Europeans love Charles Bukowski's work so much—they see the Whitman tradition there and they love it. It's too bad Americans don't love it as much, but then you're never a prophet in your own backyard. It's finally time that critics started taking some kind of recognition of this. The Pulitzer Prize still goes to the Robert Penn Warrens of the world. There is Longfellow writing his "Song of Hiawatha" when Whitman is writing his "Song of Myself," and there's old Penn Warren updating it with Chief Joseph—you'd think anybody would be ashamed to write such a document in the 1980s, that anybody would be ashamed to publish it. But we are still there trying to imitate the European tradition. You'll still see James Merrill getting a Pulitzer Prize two or three times, twenty times, before Bukowski will get it.

But what I see in regionalism is a claiming of that American identity. A claiming of the local geography of it, a claiming of the writing that comes out of that geography, and of course a claiming of the very language. To the extent that that's done, and regionalism doesn't just worship bad local writers but in fact embraces what is powerful about the American language as opposed to the New England or the European tradition, then it seems to me very, very healthy indeed. I think that the kinds of writers that immediately get accepted on a more national level are not necessarily the best writers, but those who, metaphorically speaking, still have the English accent.

Now the other side of it I see as unhealthy is as follows: I spent about five months in Seattle, Washington; I was a visiting writer there for spring and summer terms. I really hated that place—not because of the rain, and the university was nice and there were some good students there. But there is an attitude in Seattle that is so provincial that it basically says that if you are from Seattle you are at the top of the line. They are defensive about everything from outside the Northwest, and they particularly push "Northwest writers." They create a kind of condition in the name of regionalism that is provincial and unprofessional. So that they had a truly terrible "little old lady poet"—a guy named Nelson Bently—teaching for years at the university who had no more right to be in that university than Ronald Reagan. It was because he was a Seattle "poet"; they didn't take into consideration that he was simply a terrible poet. I felt that my students had a hard time growing and developing any kind of sophistication, that it was a place that stunted you because it made you a king because you were there. You never had to learn competitive standards, and that is provincialism. That is the bad and ugly side of regionalism, as opposed to this other extremely healthy and rich side—this is the way we speak and I'm going to make an art of it. In fact, I'm going to make an art that is so beautiful and interesting that people from someplace else will be intrigued by it precisely because it has that uniqueness and that eccentricity.

What do you think is the impetus behind regionalism?

Well, the fact that we have such a huge country and such a large portion of our population is educated, so to speak, and therefore such a large number of people write books, that one of the impetuses behind regionalism has to be just a kind of human impulse to narrow things down. There is just no way that you can possibly *read* all the books of poetry published, even if you are a specialist and that's your job. So you simply start narrowing and choosing.

Then there are simply places with a stronger tradition. The fiction of the South has a firm place in the history of American fiction, and so I can imagine a southerner who just decides never to read anybody but Faulkner, O'Connor, and a few others, and feels safe in doing so. There is so much greatness there. But I don't really think, though, that you *are* safe in doing that. You have to constantly be selecting, but at the same time you just must keep yourself open. That is the challenge for any intellectual in any discipline. However, for so long this country was dominated by the European idea of art in painting, sculpture, music, poetry, criticism, that these regional movements had in some ways great vigor and health as simply as an attempt to balance things.

What is the difference in the vast sphere of influences that exist if someone chooses to look toward Russian writing, or American writing, or European writing to draw inspiration from? Why, just because we are Americans, do we have to focus on American writing?

We don't *have* to, but for a long time we hardly even looked at it, so it might be healthy. I'll simply speak as a poet. I don't think there is any way to be a great artist unless you totally embrace and embody your culture. Your art comes out of your, excuse the expression, roots. It comes out of what you've seen daily in your childhood, the language you've heard spoken around you. Every once in a while you'll discover a totally anachronistic artist who makes something out of a totally different scene, often because of exile or something else imposed upon him. But one of the reasons that it has taken so long to create a great American art and poetry, that there are so few people from the time of Whitman until the twenties or thirties, is that all those talented writers were looking to European cultures for the source of their energy. All I say is that the source of your energy is the ground you walk on. I don't mean that you should be uneducated. The whole point of going to school is so you learn about all those other things. But if you learn about them, fall in love with them, and forget about yourself, you can't become an artist—at best you'll become a scholar.

What about someone like Robert Bly, for example, who writes out of his culture, but certainly looks to Spanish and Latin American writers for inspiration?

What about him? Your source of inspiration can come from anywhere. Bly doesn't imitate their language in any way. Look, he isn't my favorite poet by any means, so I really wouldn't choose to talk about him. Still, Bly is the perfect example of an American poet trying very, very hard to use American myth, American culture, American roots, geography, and language as the matrix for his poetry. He may be deeply inspired by Spanish poets, but that doesn't make any difference. We are all inspired by all kinds of things—muse by definition is something that comes from outside. But the source of our writing energy must be American. Bly doesn't write in Spanish; he doesn't even do very good translations, I'm told, though I don't read Spanish. He ain't been well influenced by them. He has used their input as a kind of exciting event in his life.

I am not an isolationist. I'm not talking about averting your eyes when there is a European painting in the room, or not listening to Beethoven, or anything like that. I believe in education as much as I believe in anything in the world; that's what the first twenty years of your life are about—to stuff yourself as full of every diverse source of knowledge, information, art, etc. that you can. But if you are from New Mexico your writing is going to come out of being from New Mexico, and not from reading André Breton.

But what if André Breton is somehow more relevant than the chance circumstance of your place of birth?
Let me again just say one last thing on this subject. When you are twenty you may be very bored with your roots, and that's fine because you've got to move on from them. When you are thirty they will look more interesting to you, especially if you've gone somewhere else to live; in fact, you may not really be able to understand them until you have gone somewhere else. Then when you are forty you might actually even start being able to use them. So perhaps the kinds of things I'm saying right now aren't as useful to some of you as they might be to others of you. But the minute that you start thinking that an English accent sounds better than an American accent you are in trouble if you are an artist born in this country.

Do you believe in a collective unconscious?
I believe that Jung's theory is a good description of the universe, certainly as good as anyone else's.

Well, America is such a melting pot. Do you think that because some of us are only second-generation Americans that maybe we can find our roots here, in New Mexico for example, maybe even if we've only been here a relatively short time?
I don't think you have to *live* someplace. . . . Again, I think that we all have to cope with our lives as they are imposed upon us. It is when you turn your back on what's there that I think you lose your ability to be a

serious artist. It is when you learn to use what is most powerfully there that you become the greatest artist that you can be according to your destiny and what has been given you in terms of resources.

People's journeys are different. Ed Dorn is a good example, I think, of a poet who when he was young knew that he wanted to be a poet. He went to Black Mountain College for its brief existence, studied with Robert Creeley, became an excellent imitator of Creeley; I know this is a sweeping statement, but I'll stick by it—almost all of Dorn's early poetry is imitation Robert Creeley. It is beautifully written and interestingly written, and with the imagination of Dorn, but basically it is imitation Creeley. Then he goes to live for a long period of time in Idaho, leaves that life at about age forty, goes to England. He marries an English woman, and kind of wrecks his life in my opinion as he gets involved in drugs and listens only to rock music. But for some reason all his creative energies that he has stored up during all those long and boring years in Pocatello, Idaho, are really cooking. And what does he do? He writes one of the most original poems of our time, *Slinger.* What is he doing? He is writing the myth of the American West. And what has he done that no one else has done? He has taken the history of post-Descartian philosophy, phenomenology, and has written a poem embodying that philosophy. No one else has even thought of doing this before. Now he wouldn't have thought of this just staying at home in Idaho, but the only way he could write that original document—which to me is as original as any kind of Lévi-Strauss imaginings, or any of those other linguist/philosopher imaginings—was because he set up squarely in the myth of the American West. That to me is an example of how finally a poet who really educates himself, but doesn't ever let himself lose touch at least linguistically and imaginatively with his roots, finally uses his inheritance to write a totally original and magnificent poem.

I have a theory that many of the most important poets of the new American poetry, poets post-1945, are poets like Ginsberg who are in fact second-generation Americans. Precisely because this American culture has them coming to it assuming it not as new immigrants but the children of immigrants, or the grandchildren of immigrants, they had to struggle in an extra way with what the American language means and what this culture means. They can then write a poem like *Howl,* which in fact changes history, and redocument and reaffirm Whitman's *Song of Myself* as the *mainstream* in what is truly the new American poetry, not the European or New England. I'm not talking about pedigree. This is where you transcend regionalism. This is where regionalism becomes provincial—Bently is here so whatever he writes must be good. It's when a poet takes what is rich in his myth and his culture, and his sense of language that's different from another myth and culture, that he makes an original work out of it.

It's possible that most people won't do this when they are young. We have to in some way go through the Oedipal divorcing of ourselves. When I graduated from Berkeley I moved to New York City and that was a very, very important part of my life. It was in New York City that I started writing *The George Washington Poems*, started writing so much about being a westerner because I was aware of being a westerner living in the city. I was not unhappy being there, but it was a very important part of my happiness that I knew that I took the Pacific Ocean, I took the desert, I took all those things with me. It was that sense of landscape that made for me the slums of New York City inhabitable.

I am now living in the Midwest, and I've more or less finished *Greed,* or at least John Martin is going to publish the whole collected poem that I've been working with over the years. In part twelve, which was originally meant to be the last part but then was typically followed by a part thirteen, is over one hundred pages of prose and poetry, the persona Diane goes to the West to the desert to a meeting for the Society for Western Flowers. The meeting is presided over by George Washington, and all the characters from her poems—the motorcycle betrayer, the woodsman, and so forth— are all there. A masque is performed. It is my only attempt to write an allegorical play; it's called "The Moon Loses Her Shoes." There is conversation all through this about my journey as a poet, having come to a certain place where I have to start a new journey, an old age journey. The second half of the poem, then, is an awards ceremony for American poets presided over by Charles Bukowski, where I give awards to all of the poets who deserve them instead of the ones who get them. Each award is named after an American wildflower. This has been written for many years, but John Martin has not published it because he's afraid it is going to offend people, though it's not really very offensive at all. At the end of the poem I leave in my magical car that's being driven by a dalmation who wears Tony Lamas boots and seems like a typical character out of the West. I have my car pointed west. Further, there is a bridge poem that goes between parts twelve and thirteen called "Looking for Beethoven in Las Vegas."

How do these ideas carry over to what you are working on at the moment?
What I want to do now is begin a book-length poem which, like *Maximus* and *Paterson,* uses the city as focus and is about the West. By the way, as

an aside Olson wanted to call *Maximus* "The West" for a long time, though it's obvious that he wasn't writing about the West other than the West in terms of Greek civilization. I haven't decided yet whether I want that city to be Los Angeles, which could be the right city for me to choose in terms of roots, or San Diego, which is farther south but which I have a connection with because my father was in the navy and we used to drive back and forth there when I was young. There is a mythic sense of that connection for me. Or finally Las Vegas, which I never visited when I was young, but which to me seems like an almost archetypal American city that contains in an exaggerated form everything that is truly American.

I am living in the Midwest right now and feeling very frustrated, though I don't think that you have to live in the place that you write the poem. I'd prefer to. Part of the richness of *Paterson* comes from Williams having lived in the Rutherford-Paterson area all of his life, and all of that material from the historical society and all of that material from American history, all those letters that came to him, all happened in that area. Thus there is a sense of making the American poem and finding a new measure is all about from a place that he has experienced totally.

William Everson writes and speaks often about "eros and landscape." *Have you had some kind of dialogue with him on this subject?*
Not personally, though I admire him immensely. I think *Masks of Drought* is one of the best books of our time.

I'd like to change the subject. You have an interest in music—would you equate your poetry to any particular sense of music?
I feel uncomfortable with a lot of contemporary music that really in some ways parallels my poetry. A critic wrote, and actually I was very flattered, that reading my poetry was like listening to a piece of music by Philip Glass. While I admire Philip Glass, and I even like to listen to some of his music, I don't feel totally comfortable with it and I don't know whether my poetry is really that parallel or not. I deeply admire John Cage, but I think of him as an aesthetician rather than as a composer. I think it would be wrong to say that I sit and listen to John Cage music the way I listen to Beethoven, or that I get that kind of pleasure from it.

I think that I've probably got the same kind of divided feelings about contemporary music that some composers have about contemporary poetry— they admire it, but they'd really rather read Shakespeare. Maybe it's always slightly uncomfortable to be with a contemporary art form if you are an artist. Perhaps you are challenged and excited by it, but at the same time uncomfortable. We were just visiting John Martin, who is the publisher of Black Sparrow books in Santa Barbara, and was all evening playing Charles Ives for his pleasure. I am fascinated by Charles Ives's music, but I never play it for my pleasure. If I want to sit and *listen* to an Ives piece, I'll play a recording; and I'll go to a concert specifically if there is an Ives piece being performed. But it is something that I feel obliged to listen to, something I have an intellectual rather than emotional response to.

What about rock music?

I'm not really involved in popular music, though my husband is a Rolling Stones addict. I guess I see current rock as entertainment music for parties or something. Music for dancing. My husband, however, knows the lyrics of most Rolling Stones songs better than my friends who are Shakespeare scholars know Shakespeare's texts. He continuously has very esoteric explications of certain lines. I don't get interested in rock in that way at all. It doesn't seem to challenge me. I don't listen to it for pleasure the way I listen to Mozart for pleasure.

I have an odd relationship to music. I studied it formally. I've never been able to write with music as background; I need to have silence. But now I can't even read with music as background, and I do a lot of junk reading. I read lots of fiction, which I suppose is junk reading as opposed to something you have to concentrate on, like poetry. I read two or three murder mysteries a week; I've got a huge murder mystery collection, and I just acquired some more in Albuquerque today. And I try to keep up with contemporary fiction, so that maybe I read one new serious fiction work a month. I adore Victorian novels, so that I'm constantly reading and rereading Thomas Hardy, Anthony Trollope, and Jane Austin; I'm currently on a George Gissing kick. But I've gotten so that I can be reading a junk novel—like Trollope—and it bothers me to have music on. I simply cannot put it in the background. Maybe that's a good sign.

Do any contemporary fiction writers interest you much?

I'm just thinking about a book I read this month, which to me is an astonishing book and an author's second novel. A poet I've known for years and never been that excited about his poetry—Toby Olson—about ten years ago began writing fiction. He wrote a very experimental novel that's interesting but not terribly satisfying, called *The Life of Jesus.* But he has just published a novel called *Sea View,* which just won the P.E.N. Faulkner Award and is an extraordinary piece of writing. I hate "poetic novels," but this is a novel written by a poet which uses all the wonderful powers of description of a poet that people call "poetic" but in fact reads like a good novel. It's about a youngish couple in their thirties, the wife of whom has cancer and is obviously going to die. She is of Portugese origin, he is from Cape Cod, and they make a pilgrimage from the West Coast back to Cape Cod. He is a golf hustler. Now I never thought I could be in the least bit interested in golf, but I'm practically ready to learn how to play it after reading this book. There is a chapter that is like a long short story wherein Olson describes stroke-by-stroke a golf game when the husband is hustling these guys on an Arizona golf course. It is utterly incredible. At the same time he picks up a middle-aged Native American who is trying to get to this golf course, Sea View, on Cape Cod—the Native Americans of that area claim they have territorial rights to it. In the meantime, he has scored some laetril illegally from his old college roommate who has now become the most depraved drug dealer you can ever imagine. There is a scene when this Indian goes rattlesnake hunting on the desert that again is some of the most incredible description of the Southwest I've ever read. Here are all the great skills of writing merging with contemporary issues—dying of cancer, who owns what property in America, what does it mean to be connected with the land, popular athletics in our culture.

I love Margaret Drabble's fiction—there is nothing I haven't read by her. I of course also love Charles Bukowski. I think he's one of the few writers who does both fiction and poetry with equal aplomb; in fact they feed each other. It's possible the fiction would be less without the poetry, the poetry less without the fiction. Bukowski, if not unique, is pretty close to being unique in that sense.

I'm not terribly fond of avant-garde fiction. I like John Barth a lot, even when he is experimental. But again, there is that kind of traditional, Dickensian novelist who then applies native materials—I think *The Sot-Weed Factor* is a masterpiece, a book that comes as much out of our culture as is possible.

I don't read much short fiction. I used to read a lot of stories and I used to talk about how I thought the story and the poem were very similar to each other. I'm not sure that I now disagree with myself, but for some reason I find it less and less satisfying to read short fiction. I don't know if this just means that I'm in fashion because everyone claims it's hard to publish short stories now, though there have been recently a lot of young writers— Ann Beattie, Anne Tyler, Jayne Anne Phillips—who have gotten a lot of recognition through volumes of short work. Raymond Carver. This year's

O. Henry award book has a Carver story winning first place, and it's head and shoulders above the rest. Interestingly, that was the first Carver story I liked; I had read a book of his stories before and couldn't really see what all the excitement was about.

Could you, before you conclude, comment for a few moments on publication? You seem to have a rather bizarre history of publication.
Sure. I've never had as much luck with magazines as with book publishers. There always seems to have been a good publisher waiting there to accept a manuscript when I sent it out. I'm very troubled by the state of publishing today. There have to be at least 1,500 literary magazines, or at least it seems so; even if there are only 500, the number is enormous. I don't seem to be able to find one that I really like to read. Further, because of the large number of magazines, there doesn't seem to be two or three that people generally read, and thus again, as I alluded earlier, it seems as if you are just throwing your poetry out into the world to become soggy pulp.

I often have the experience of young writers coming to me—whether they are my students or people that I see when I'm giving readings—asking where they should send their poems. My general feeling is that it should be to the magazine that you *read*. But, as I was saying earlier, my general feeling is also that there aren't many that people read. I definitely think there is something unethical or immoral about sending your poems out to a magazine you don't even glance at. Here we go back to the do-it-yourself people. They want an audience, but they never want to be that audience. So maybe young writers should take it upon themselves to go to their libraries which, even after budget cuts, probably still take some literary magazines, and make it a week's project to read a single issue at least of each one of them. See if there are any of them that you really like.

It still seems premature to me to think of putting together a book manuscript when you've had virtually no poems published in magazines. Yet there is this kind of lacuna that exists of, well, it doesn't really mean anything to publish in magazines. I had no hesitation fifteen years ago, or even ten years ago, saying to young poets that they should send their poems out, and when they've had fifty or sixty in magazines then that is time to put together a book manuscript; what this means is that if they are good and interesting poems, one or two people will have seen your name one or two times—and that is what makes a potential audience for a new book of poems. My theory is that the reason new books of poetry can only exist these days if they are prize-winners is that there is no other way to keep things straight. If you've never heard of the person, but he has won a prize given by so-and-so, then you figure it's fine. I think this is a crazy situation. There is more opportunity for people to be published than ever before in history, and yet it seems to mean less, and it seems to require that you make rules for yourself that are based on a personal code of some kind of integrity. So if you could subscribe to two or three magazines and read every issue of them, then it would be much more meaningful for you to get your poems published there.

Speaking of awards, Carolyn Forché has published two fairly slim books of poems, and has won two major awards. I've read that you don't think too much of her work. Can you comment on this?
Well, in her first book of poems there is maybe one really good poem, the one about her grandmother's garden, which I saw in an earlier version when she was a student and I helped her rewrite. I still think it's her best poem. *Gathering of the Tribes* is, what can I say, a first book with one good poem in it; it's not what I'd ever pick as a prize-winning book, though on the other hand it deserved to be published as a young writer's work. The second book of poems seems to me to capitalize on the sensationalistic life that she has led. As one reviewer recently said of *The Country Between Us,* if you look at the poems that are not about El Salvador they look like any other poems that come out of a college writing workshop program about the experiences that a middle-class person has—that Forché is capitalizing on the sensationalisitc attitude towards a popular event, and whether or not she is actually homosexual she capitalizes on that.

Lee has told me about a new review apparently trashing Carolyn Forché in the most recent *Sulfur,* though I haven't seen it yet. Eliot Weinberger is a very elegant writer so I'm sure it's done with great finesse. I feel guilty, though, about that kind of reviewing, that total trashing of someone. I don't think Forché should be trashed—all the people who worship her should be trashed. She is just a beginning poet with a certain amount of talent. She is not worthy of the kind of attention she is getting, either politically or poetically. I find that irritating and annoying.

But you yourself have spoken about the "drama" of the poet's life . . .
No, the drama of the poem. I have said again and again that a poet's poems are as interesting as *he* is. That means what goes on in his *head.* I do not think you have to go to El Salvador and sit at the general's table to meet an interesting person. In fact, I think you'd have to be a moron to have that experience and *not* make it sound interesting—you'd have to be a very bad

writer. This is just what I'm saying: when Forché has ordinary experiences to write about she doesn't do anything extraordinary with them. There are adventurers and there are writers. Carolyn may become a very good writer; it's hard to say. Probably she is more interested in politics than writing right now, so she certainly isn't in a good stage of her life for becoming a better writer. But who knows what will happen? She is intelligent, and she is a decent human being. In a way, it seems unfair to trash her when it is really people with no imagination who are willing to accept these adventures as a substitute for poetry who are at fault.

I want the excitement to come out of the page, through imagination and language. There is nothing wrong with personality cults that we create in this country because in some ways they are fascinating in themselves; yet there is such a small platform for poetry, and poetry is such a rich thing, that to waste it on the Carolyn Forchés is foolish and sad.

Isn't this sensationalizing of the life rather endemic to American poetry? Look at James Dickey.

I don't really get that mad about these things any more, though Dickey is another good example. When I was at Emory James Dickey came to read for a mere $1,200 because his normal fee of $3,500 was being paid by a medical convention for him to talk to doctors about the making of the film *Deliverance*. Of course he is worshiped in the South, particularly at Emory. You have probably all heard Dickey read, or have heard tapes of him, or have at least heard about his readings. He is a fantastic showman. But one of the things that has always griped me about Dickey from the very first time I heard him at the YMHA in New York in the early sixties is that he gives an hour-long poetry reading that is fifty-five minutes of Dickey talking—and he is brilliant—and five minutes of poems. This is exactly what he did at Emory, and it was one of those events that every single person in the English department went to and it was packed. He is a true storyteller in the southern style, and he even read his children's poem, which was disgusting, and the audience lapped it up. Afterwards I realized that they had been to an elaborate talk show, just like television, and they had been given permission to think it was poetry. They were entertained. The chairman of the English department walked out with me and said, "That's the most inspiring poetry reading I've ever been to." I'm not totally stupid so I didn't say anything; I just smiled. But I realized that even chairmen of English departments don't really like poetry. The terrible thing is that Dickey is a wonderful poet, but there is no way that you'd ever have known it from that reading. Instead, it was a talk show for people who like to think they like poetry but really hate it.

Carolyn Forché's readings are the same thing. They are for people who love politics, and would like to think that they like poetry. So the ⌐ is the talk, the getting into the ambience of the thing, but very little poetry. If you go home and get something from reading the poems, hurray, more power to you. I hope they last.

Don't get me wrong. I'm a lover of poetry readings and I do think they can be great events. But they should be great events of *poetry*. I have heard great poetry readings where the audience was with the poet in some way that was exciting and magical, but it was with the poetry, not the personality. For example, I went to Buffalo to give a reading at a little college about two years ago, and I found out just by accident that the Jung society was meeting there for the weekend and that Robert Duncan and Robert Creeley were giving a reading together. Well, I thought that this would be an historic event, so I changed my plane reservations and stayed over an extra two days so that I could go to the reading. I'm not sorry—it probably was the greatest poetry reading I've ever been to in my life. There was an audience full of people who loved poetry and the archetype, but most of whom did not write poetry; that is, an audience we all love, long for, and very seldom get to have. All the people in the audience, if they were not familiar with Creeley or Duncan, at least were poetry readers. It was a large audience of three to four hundred people, in a motel rather than a university. And you had to pay to get in. Now it could have been terrible. As you know Creeley is capable of giving a poetry reading where he mumbles through the whole thing and you can't understand a word, you have to be an afficionado to enjoy it. Duncan is capable of getting started off on a tangent and forgetting the poetry. They also are very competitive in their own quiet little ways. Who knew what would happen?

It was just, however, one of those perfect occasions. Creeley was sober— though I guess he's always sober now that his life has improved—and he didn't mumble. He didn't just chose eccentric poems to read; he really chose a retrospective view of his great poems, as well as some new things. He read for about forty minutes, a substantial amount of time, and the whole audience was with him. Then there was an intermission, after which Duncan came on. Again, it was not an eccentric reading. Here is Duncan who hasn't published a poem for about twelve years, someone who has a great body of work, but he didn't just pick the new things. Instead he chose work like "My Mother Is a Falconress," which is his greatest poem, and other early poems, working his way up to some new poems which sounded remarkable. It was a breathtaking event. It was nothing like a crowd for a rock band, where you are kind of breathing in time and mesmerized; it was an intelligent, thoughtful, listening crowd responding to the language.

I know, then, that poetry readings *can* be great events. We substitute these James Dickey talk shows and Carolyn Forché El Salvador shows for these great events. I feel sorry because we don't have that many readings. At my college we are lucky if we have a few hundred dollars a year for poetry readings, and I'm lucky if I can drag a few people to come to them. I see this all over the country. I just don't think *that* time should be wasted on politics or anything else. It belongs to poetry.

To the Lion

I am the girl who visits the sun,
east of destiny and west of destruction,
who comes in the rain to remind you of tomorrow
and the silken trees.
I am the girl broken out of stone.
You have broken me from stone.
Lion, brush the tears from my face.

I am the girl you will never forget
because forgetting me is forgetting your own name.
It is a chain. We all love somebody else,
the lion, the sun; even the rain loves somebody
else. We know it. We know it.
We are foolish.
Lion, brush away the tears.

I am the girl, waiting for you to speak,
to open your eyes and let the words
fall out in my hands
like broken stone. I am the girl
who would not know what to do
if the words came true,
if stones tumbled in her hands.

I am the girl
who is speaking with words
and knows words will never break stone.
Lion brush away my stone tears.

I am the girl who, for a moment, has found silence
a blessing, thankful for stone
and its confines,
and I am the girl who has broken the silence of stone
to speak
and in so doing
has sealed her voice behind fallen rocks
forever.

Summer

he slid out of the skin, leaving it
like a dried lima bean hull,
white and papery on the road.
his body inched along
the highway,
rippling its new red colors
bits of brown
like stones
seemed strewn along each arm and thigh.
it was a strange transformation
which had been coming.
the moon had warned him flipping like a fish in the sky,
a bowl of sweet cream left overnight emptied itself to the snake
living under the hearth.
when the time had come the old skin had shucked off
crackling. no pain
no pulling. he slid his wet body into the sun,
he was dry now
and brown.
the ocean rushed through his head; he heard the crabs

moving sideways on the bottom
and the fish
shouting
with their fins.

For the Girl with Her Face in a Rose

This tapestry which I've never seen
woven in 1901
depicts your wish of self,
disembodied,
the face floating in a giant
florabunda,
the seeker near your rose-enclosed lips,
listening for your voice.
Perhaps this is wisdom.

My own wish cannot be seen in any
weaving
but in the flesh itself
of calla lily,
pale curled flowers with their yellow
pollen-covered fingers
on which no one ever slips
a golden ring.

The wish to be alive
at my own death
which I would want never to come
except as the season's apple, plum,
corriander, pansy,
leek, corn.

I would give up any voice,
even the whisper on these pages
if I would not have to die.
If even
I could age until I fall away from my bones

like the sticky apricots
under late summer's buzzing tree.
Not even the wish
to be young and fresh
and eternally a flower.
Rather, not to die.
Not to suffer pain.
Not to lose my breath.

To the Young Man Who Left the Flowers on My Desk One April Afternoon

I accepted them.
                    It was the graceful
thing to do, even though I knew
they weren't meant for me:
Far, far too lovely they were—
half blue, wild tolling blue
as lucent and yielding as new
melon flesh and dew, dew on their lips;
half demure, demure and elegant
white rose, sleeping beauties quiet
and masked against any beast.

I cannot say what they meant
to us all, coming at the time
when they did. It was love,
and we opened our hearts,
so much evil having recently skulked about.

They were left, I know, for another girl—
perhaps the afternoon-nymph with unwilting
grace and enormous blue eyes,
so much like those wild, fragrant first flowers
whose heavy perfume I could smell all night,
or maybe it was the white-limbed
marble Greek, smooth as cool Chablis,
whom I found to be so like
those silent tea roses that I gasped

to see perfection in a thing still young;
and yet the flowers pleased me most of all
because I am plain,
and beauty means so much . .

so very much to me.

Civilization

I admire all the brave and robust people who live on shoestrings,
somehow crafting interesting meals out of dollar bills,
drinking passable wine for a quarter,
building houses out of old telephone poles and getting featured in *Better
   Living*.
They go to Europe and meet the most interesting people and
somehow earn a refund,
go to the opera in thrift store drapes and get photographed for
the society page.
Somehow, they work twenty hours a day, never sleep, have the most
beautiful children,
get lots of sex, write novels in their spare time, tune their own
cars,
and like Mildred Pierce bake 100 pies every day, even the day
their ten-year-old
dies of pneumonia in the hospital.

I have always been poor, and never managed well.
I took taxis when I was tired and thus had no money for food
halfway through
the week. The mediocre wines on my table cost as much as
emerald necklaces,
and I always look like I live on welfare.

I suppose this will sound like self-pity,
but I think it is only facing facts and not liking that reality.
The language of pain is difficult to transmit;
it is the glorious nature of civilization to reject suffering.

13. Anne Waldman

Photo by Cynthia MacAdams.

"Everything run along in creation till I end the song"

Aram Saroyan has written that, "Of all the poets of my generation, none has done more than Anne Waldman to bring poetry before the public at large." Waldman's activities on behalf of poetry have been numerous, from her decade as director of the Poetry Project at St. Marks church-in-the-Bowery in New York City and her co-founding (with Allen Ginsberg) of the Jack Kerouac School of Disembodied Poetics at Naropa Institute in Boulder to her service as "poet-in-residence" with Bob Dylan's "Rolling Thunder Review" and her countless readings and performances.

Waldman was born in Millville, New Jersey, in 1945 but grew up on Macdougal Street in New York's Greenwich Village. After graduating from Bennington College, she returned to New York to direct the St. Mark's Poetry Project until 1978, when she moved to Naropa Institute, where she currently serves as co-director. Her numerous books include *Baby Breakdown, Fast Speaking Woman, Journals & Dreams, Make Up on Empty Space,* and *Skin Meat Bones,* and she has edited *The World* and *Angel Hair* magazines, as well as *The World Anthology* and *Talking Poetics from Naropa Institute* (with Marilyn Webb). She has made many recordings of her work, including selections for John Giorno's "Dial-a-Poem" series, and recently has released a 45-rpm single, "Uh-Oh Plutonium!" produced by Hyacinth Girls Music in New York.

I'd like to begin by talking about some ways I've been working in the last five years or so, which might be of interest to you as writers. I've discovered recently that I'm working in parallel areas, and the poems manifest in a number of ways. There are situations in which you set up an environment or atmosphere for your discipline and the poems simply arrive. When I first started taking myself seriously as a writer I wrote at night as that was the only time I could set aside, the only time when things settled down enough to allow a psychological space to work in. Some of you may have more regular work habits, writing an hour or two a day every day, and this is of course good discipline. It can be frustrating if the poem doesn't gel. Often I'll write a couple of lines then have to put them aside because they are not working, but simply through the discipline you create an invitation for the energy to come to you. By making "poetry time" you sharpen your faculties for the poem. William Carlos Williams spoke of this. Because he was a doctor he often wrote late in the day. He has talked about being exhausted from working yet exhilarated by the time he'd set about writing, that the best work occurred in a tense state. Fatigue is an anesthetic and lets the body go to an unimportant place, making room for the poetry.

So, the poems are coming spontaneously?
Yes. As one would say, they become gifts. They don't seem to be consciously sought after in the sense of working out a sonnet, but you've created a conducive atmosphere. You must have experienced this—you don't know where the thing has come from, yet have put aside the time for it.

Next, I find that I have this way of consciously making poems, like a film maker, working with images and arrangement, somewhat like collage or cut-ups.

Like William Burroughs?
Well, Tzara is really credited with the invention of the cut-up, but one could say that any number of poems are really cut-ups, or at least collage-like pieces where you bring in many different voices from your reading or listening. But it's making the work. You are consciously sitting down and "making." With the cut-up à la Tristan Tzara, you sit down with a newspaper and literally cut up the lines, put them in a hat, shuffle them, lift them out one by one, and assemble in a purely chance operation. That's an extreme of what I'm talking about, of course, but I find that there is another kind of work where I use journal writing, especially dream journal writing. To draw on that raw writing—a dream, an overheard conversation, a quote from something I'm reading, notes from talking to someone, or even pictures—is fascinating to me. So I consider this second way I'm working to be more architectural, consciously shifting, building, and arranging language.

So in effect cutting up your journal?
That's it in part. In fact I find that exercise very useful, as you are working with something that has already come out of you. The wonderful thing about cut-up is the element of surprise—you never know what it is that you are going to bump up against next. William Burroughs and Byron Gysin are interested in this kind of surprise. *The Soft Machine,* an early book, is largely cut-up, and more recently the two have published a book called *The Third Mind.* "The Third Mind" actually refers to this other thing that comes in as you are doing the cut-up. They were doing collaborative cut-ups, so there were two minds at work, then there was this third mind that seemed to manifest in the work. If you try the experiment you'll see that there seems to be something else at work there, some kind of organizing principle.

You should try it. Take someone else's work, like Rimbaud. I've recently been working with poet Arthur Sze at the Institute of American Indian Arts in Santa Fe, and often we'll take something like a Denise Levertov poem and reorder it, just to get inside the work, to get inside her consciousness and her conscious decision about where to stop a line, where to put a comma, where a new thought will begin. You actually get in touch that way with your own mind grammar.

Is the "third mind" another way of thinking of the "muse"?
Well, there is a similarity I suppose, at least in terms of an energy principle, but somehow cut-up is a different kettle of fish. The cut-up muse is less a personal muse. We all have muses—yours could be a child, a lover, a location—but I find that they are always shifting. The third mind seems somehow less transitory.

Jerome Rothenberg has a translation of a shamaness which reminds me very much of what you are talking about, what you do in Fast Speaking Woman.
Maria Sabina. *Fast Speaking Woman* did originate out of that first category, of spontaneous poetry. It has a very obvious simple structure—I'm a this woman, I'm a that woman—and "woman" was very much in the air at the time, as women were starting to get in touch with their energy, their power. I'd written "She Chant" which was very similar. It also has a simple chant structure, and is basically oral, something that can be reworked from the bottom up, for example. I had traveled to South America and was keeping a journal, and one day the poet Michael Brownstein brought me a record of Sabina chanting in the Mazatec tongue in a ritual situation. The young Mazatec women are guided through the night in a mushroom-ingesting ceremony, and the shamaness guides through her chanting through this unknown terrain. I incorporated some of her lines, maybe the most seminal ones—"I'm a rock woman, I'm a tree woman, I'm a wind woman"—certainly the most elemental. Then in the poem I took off with "I'm a silk scarf woman, I'm a woman with tantrums, I'm a no-nothing woman. I know how to work the machines!" whatever. It was easy and natural. Michael McClure later wrote a poem entitled *Man of Moderation,* which is his male version of the poem, which is quite amusing.

What about a third type?
Well, I'd always worked with forms a lot. In college writing situations you are called upon to write sonnets, or imitate a Keats ode, and so forth. As a young writer I wanted to get away from that, although being able to work

with forms and English literary tradition always seemed to be a great asset. At some point later it seemed to me, however, that working in forms like the sestina, the canzone, and the pantoum (which originally was a Malayan probably sung form of four lines per verse) were interesting in terms of discipline. In the case of the sestina, for example, you start with six words basically, and you have to use these words in six verses in a varying pattern as end words. There is a coda at the end wherein you use all six words in three lines. What happens is that those words have to undergo a lot of strain, and you can tell when you are making up something just for the sake of the word. But other times the words become almost invisible, and that is when one of these forms will work, when the structure becomes invisible and yet you know there is a lovely architecture there.

The work with forms can inform the first category, if you become well versed in it. I had been trying and trying to write a successful pantoum about having a new child. Suddenly, in the middle of the night this poem in the voice of a baby came through in the pantoum form. It took very little conscious manipulation, but the form was one that I had been working with for some time, and I'd written a few unsuccessful pantoums. Maybe the fact that it was in the voice of the baby made it work, a simpler and natural repetition.

So obviously you can write a poem in traditional form drawing on your dreams or your journals, but it also seems to be a distinct way of working. Sometimes the energy of the day suggests the discipline of a sestina, and there is simply a different approach than with the poem that is going to arrive magically or through cut-up.

What about simple open-form poems?
That's the fourth kind, a kind of poetry that is open-ended, more discursive, and seems to border on prose. This seems to be a kind of getting in touch with thinking patterns, and those tend to be longer lined. That's the kind of work again that can come out of journals as that's the kind of writing one tends to do there. This also involves, however, a refinement, actually making the poems. Then there's the "snapshot" poem—simply writing what you see, hear, etc. No projections. So-called objectivist.

Do you teach all these approaches at Naropa?
Yes. In fact I just finished up an intensive ten-hour workshop, two hours one night then the next day an eight-hour stretch. We tried all kinds of experiments—cut-ups, working with music (Satie, Mozart, jazz), visual im-

agery (a random collection of postcards). I also suggested at one point that students work with the seven most used words in the language (*the, of, and, to, in, that*) in terms of musical rhythms. We worked with sensory ideas— five words related to touch, five related to smell, etc., working with twenty-five words in five-line clusters. So in a way one can invent one's own forms. All these possibilities overlap anyway.

Might you differentiate a bit more from the last type of poem you mentioned and the first?
Sure. Let me read you a passage from a piece entitled "Coup de Grace". This work, which runs about five pages, seems to be playing with phrases, poetry bordering on prose:

> You say you know what's up, what's what, what is or isn't true, what's a modicum or midge of delight. A very small being. Well, you need beauty to go on with the truth part, or hand in hand or hand over head or head over heels in love with him. You'd need it. Sure. And sure a trace. Sure a quarry is the heart. Excavation. Open season. To open the season here and nourish the surer part. Inmissable friends. Inadmissable facts to find a cure place, a safe place to live with great store for feeding, great schools, outlets of all kinds for every pudendum nail blind drain towel rack bulb spring washer plug. Not to be a piker about shopping but all the time wanted the glorious objects to glow you with their radium dials, not enough to make you ill. You want to see them chemistries, the tiny tit magics of the alchemical world, of the astrological world. You want to see the elements in their element. . . .

And so on.

Do you hear what I mean? It's not a poem, exactly, and it's ongoing. I was working with the sound and more proselike grammar of the phrase like "Well you'd need beauty to go with the truth part hand in hand, or hand over head, or head over heels in love with him." So it's somewhere possibly between what we usually call poetry and what we usually call prose. Does it really matter *what* it is, in fact? Or, "How can the family make a gesture to the sidewalk we would all understand." Prose. "Would it be daughter to mother, father to daughter, son to mother, sister to brother. The family needs caulking. The family needs ockum. The family is in a continual flux of birth, old age, sickness, death, and ducking. Can a horse take responsibility? Can it rake? Does it dance? Sure, a sheen of her aura dispels the gloom. Sure, you keep brushing your hair and the world shines. The novitiates are all of them in a soup. Soup de grace."

The form is that this is actually addressed to someone. There's a you in there. I keep coming back to that. "You say you know what's what." "You" be this or that. A monologue-rant almost. It ends with, "Tell me, friend, if dollar diplomacy is working in those faraway places. Do you shy away from the frequent hostage-taking? Can'st be thyself and true."

The play there seems similar to what Language poets are doing.
Yes, there is the resonance of play here, and I'm interested in various of these approaches. I've been playing with experiments which seem divorced of personality or usual meaning. This poem does play and invite the language. There are also a lot of jokes there. At the same time there is a trajectory of emotion and a trajectory of address. So I guess there might be more "meaning" here than some of the Language poets would favor. But then we should avoid pigeonholing. Within that group there are a lot of different writers working in very particular ways, and when you actually read the work you see the differences immediately.

Might you go back to a discussion of forms for a moment?
Sure. Let me read a sonnet. It's an overdone form perhaps, and yet one of Philip Sydney's sonnets triggered one of my own. What the sonnet does is kind of spit something out and come to some kind of illumination or summary at the conclusion. It is basically a small circular song. This is called "Two Hearts":

> She's got my heart and I've got hers
> It was fair, we fell in love
> I hold her's precious and mine she would miss
> There never was anything like this
> Her heart in my brain keeps us one
> My heart in her guides thoughts and feelings
> She loves my heart for once it was hers
> I love hers because it lived in me
> I once wounded her, it was misunderstanding
> And then my heart hurt for her heart
> For as from me on her hurt did sit
> So I felt still in me her hurt hurt, it
> Both of us hurt simultaneously and then we saw how
> We're stuck with each other's hearts now.

So it's got some musical sound, but is very different from the older sonnet, especially in the lines:

> For as from me on her her hurt did sit
> So I felt still in me her hurt hurt.

I love the play of "her," "hurt," and "heart."

And the chant?
Well, actually you could say that the oral work is another area, like *Fast Speaking Woman*. I've got a piece called "Skin Meat Bones":

> (singing)
> I've come to tell you of the things dear to me
> And what I've discovered
> Of the skin meat bones
> Your body waking up so sweet to me   skin
> Dawn light brings   skin
> I'm in hungry repose   meat
> It's getting close to motion
> Oh skeleton   bone

The poem arrived as "Skin Meat Bones." It seemed enough in one way, but I went further into it. It became a meditation on those three notes, as well as those three realities. Skin being a kind of surface, meat a little deeper, bones inside. But I guess that poem is really of the first category, of a spontaneous, magical gift. I woke up after some dream in which a friend of mine had green skin, and when I woke up the light was a particular way and he did have green skin. I heard these sounds in my ear, and also my body. It was a very physical experience as well.

You've mentioned Sidney. Who were other writers who influenced you when you were a younger writer?
I'd gotten a fairly decent and the usual liberal arts education as a literature student. I read a lot of the classics in college, and of course I was in awe of Blake, Yeats, and others. When I got out of school and decided that writing was something that I wanted at the center of my life I had to forget everything I'd been taught about literature for a while—so as not to be overwhelmed. So there seemed to be a kind of innate confidence in this dumb approach. Some writers need to be nurtured in groups; others work very well in isolation. Personally, I was happy to be in a community of New York writers.

I was reading a lot of John Ashbery, Frank O'Hara, a lot of other New York poets. Being from the area, I guess I was identifying with their states of mind, rather than the particulars.

Anyway, I'd read an O'Hara poem and see that there was a connection to Mayakovsky the Russian poet; then that might take me to Apollonaire, who wrote walking-around Paris poems, like the wonderful "Zone." Soon I began to feel a lineage, through connections and leaps. Diane DiPrima would send me to H.D. I'd read H.D. and that would lead me to Sappho. That kind of thing. Charles Olson would set me on to looking at Mayan hieroglyphs. There would be these wonderful resonances as poets have always been involved with civilization and history and mythology. I wasn't consciously modeling myself on anyone, though, which is what your question implies. O'Hara was very freeing because he presents details of his personal life, throws his friends into poems, what he's eating, reading, seeing. Poems I was writing from my apartment on St. Mark's Place were like that; I could just look out the window and get off into the details. Anything seemed possible and interesting for the poem.

Lately, I've been staying with things over a period of time, writing longer pieces. There is a poem in *Makeup on Empty Space* called "Incantation" which is rather long. Right now I'm working on another entitled "Science Times" that is similarly meditative, which is in twelve-line verses and at this point runs about fifteen pages. After you've been writing for fifteen or twenty years you count on your stamina, your addiction.

Speaking of meditation, have you had formal training in a spiritual discipline?

I have one basic practice of shamatha-vipassana meditation as well as a Vajrayana practice. *Shamatha* means peace and *vipassana* means awareness in the Sanskrit. The technique is simply to sit in the meditation posture and follow the breath. An attempt to see all mental events as thoughts, which refines your mental awareness and clarity. It's useful in anything you do in your life, even washing dishes—a kind of panoramic awareness. Certainly this parallels the writing discipline, but I don't use the buzzwords of basic Buddhist practice in my writing, and would advise any student of writing to be careful of that or of any other abstract vocabulary which is too big and fuzzy. You must be careful of the abstractions, and in fact the whole point of meditation is to put you in touch with the particulars instead of living in a fantasy world where you are three steps back and a hundred steps in front of yourself. We are always going like that, racing around and victimized by our thinking, our projections. When you just stop, sit down, and follow your breath there is nothing going on. You aren't putting things into motion, churning up more "stuff."

So this is useful in my life. But obviously writing could be your meditation practice as it refines your sensibility, you become discriminating. You watch how your mind is working. You see how the world is not all that solid, and "you" who are not all that solid either, is usually thinking it up (projecting).

In developing an oral poetics, what kind of theories have you been drawing on?

I don't pay attention to too many theories when I'm working. It seems very simple, human, a basic tradition arising from psychological and heartfelt necessity in all cultures. I remember being at an ethnopoetics symposium with the big battle going on—what came first, the oral tradition or the written? How do we date from? But originally dance, music, and poetry were inextricably combined. Along the way they got separated out and we ended up with the muses, the categories of epic poetry, lyric poetry, dance, and so on.

Well, there seems to be a need to tell stories. Everyone speaks narrative continuously.

I would agree with that somewhat. There is also another idea which I talked about once with Gary Snyder. You'd write a narrative which begins in prose and when your character needs to express an emotion, some great love or lament, the narrative breaks into song. So the whole narrative would be a combination of the two, but with distinct shifts.

We've got a Shamanic poetics class coming up at the Naropa Institute, and there we are going to look at all kinds of anonymous texts. Actually, I favor those kinds of texts because they seem to be less personality or ego involved. It's a more communal and shared experience. We'll try to get to that quality in human beings which needs to manifest in that way. Traditionally, these kinds of works are like the daily newspaper for the Copper Eskimo. In their chanting sessions they'll sing about what is going on, what they've just done. There seems to be a need in a communal situation to come up with some account of the things that are happening day to day.

You've mentioned Naropa a few times. Might you tell us a bit about it? Is it a school for poets?

Sure. It's not just a school for poets. The primary departments, in terms of

B.A. degrees, are psychology, poets and writing, music and dance, dance therapy, Tai Chi, Buddhist Studies, and an M.A. program in psychology. It is a liberal arts school with a contemplative backdrop. It is inspired by Buddhist psychology, though not all the people who are there are Buddhist; in fact, we've recently had a Catholic priest in residence.

In 1974 I was invited out to Boulder with Allen Ginsberg and Diane DiPrima by the founders of Naropa who wanted to get the art disciplines existing there on a permanent basis. We had done some teaching but were basically so-called non academic poets, and the idea of starting a poetics school was amazing to us. Since that time, of course it's been changing and evolving. I've been co-director with Allen from the start, and sometimes I leave and sometimes he leaves; I just spent the last three years in New York, visiting Naropa during summers, for example. Now I'm back, and he will visit in spring and summer. Our summer program is especially powerful, with a lot of wonderful guest faculty. It's a very rigorous, eight-hour-a-day program, with writing workshops and other classes. Last summer we had Robert Creeley, William Burroughs, Allen Ginsberg, Amiri Baraka, and Diane DiPrima, who are more or less adjunct faculty. This summer Jerome Rothenberg, Bernadette Mayer, and others will be there, and we are planning a one-world poetics conference, which will present a lot of traditions.

At the heart of the program is a one-to-one interview situation, where you meet privately with the faculty. It's basically designed for writers, but there is a lot of other activity as well. It's an intensive combination of study and writing.

And what is the Jack Kerouac School of Disembodied Poetics?

When Allen and I were looking for a title for our school, we wanted something flashy and playful. We fought over whom we should honor. I kept wanting to make it the Gertrude Stein School. Allen had no problem with that per se, but he felt that it didn't cover enough, that a lot of people couldn't identify with it. Kerouac seemed more appropriate. Kerouac studied dharma and has in fact a huge, unpublished tome called *Some of the Dharma;* he was very interested in Buddhist psychology, as well as his own Catholic tradition. He had, basically, a spontaneous, open, and disciplined mind. Kerouac was also someone both poets and prose writers could agree on.

Okay. So we decided on the Jack Kerouac School and I kept wanting to add something that would be curious, something outrageous. "Disembodied" in the sense that we were conjuring up all kinds of energies. At Naropa we are currently going through the accreditation process and becoming more like a real school with academic standards. The administration wants to phase out the "School of Disembodied Poetics" title in favor of something like "Department of Writing and Poetics," but we are trying to hold on to it, especially in the summer program. It has a colorful history.

We also wanted to have chairs; the Emily Dickinson Chair of Silent Scribbling, the Frank O'Hara Chair of Deep Gossip, and so on. We had a fantasy about what the school could become, that we'd get grant money and bring in people from all over the world. Poets teaching in other languages. It's been ten years and that really is a short period of time for a visionary project like this one. At the beginning it was suggested that we view it as a hundred-year project.

And wasn't there some unpleasantness, the "Naropa Poetry Wars"?
Yes, we've had wonderful scandals. The "poetry war" was really like a family squabble in the poetry community. The perpetrators were Tom Clark, Ed Sanders, and Ed Dorn, with Allen Ginsberg and myself no doubt overreacting. We were close friends, and we are close friends again. There were a lot of misunderstandings, and those have been resolved, but the central issue is still very open and provocative: rugged American individualism versus some kind of more disciplined working of mind or practice. Actually, Tom and Ed were really calling into question the whole relationship to the Tibetan Buddhist teacher. Bill Merwin had been a Buddhist student (and still is), but had a complicated run-in with a particular teacher (Trungpa Rinpoche). The whole relationship in any discipline between teacher and student is powerful and problematic. You give up a lot to find out a lot. In America, one's distrust of authority is very real; one is naturally incredibly suspicious of any kind of spiritual hierarchy.

In England, the connection to Buddhism is stronger. The English recognize the thousands of years of history of a major and important and intelligent religion. But here the Zen tradition or Tibetan tradition is relatively recent, and to see students with shaved heads, as in the case of Zen, is still weird to people. About five years ago there appeared Clark's and Sanders's books, and the conflict became very exaggerated. Tom is more of a muckraker, and he was carried away going after the "story." I appreciate his passion and anger in a way. Now he writes me friendly letters and recently wrote a good review of *Makeup on Empty Space* and a rave of Ginsberg's *Collected Poems*. Actually, people tend to think the drama is still going on, but on a personal level it has healed over.

Is Trungpa still at Naropa?
No, he's living in Nova Scotia now. But he still travels to Boulder.

Do you consider him a teacher?
Yes. I find his books on Buddhist dharma very trustworthy. Developing a relationship with a so-called root teacher, however, is very difficult, as the teacher can become very heavy-handed. Ideally, a teacher is a mirror of you— your neurosis, your wisdom, your potential. But you really have to know what you are getting into. Because the teacher is there to root out your neurosis, to cut your "trips" often in a direct and powerful way. It has to be a conscious decision, made with caution and skepticism. What concerned Ed and Tom was that the students of Buddhism in Boulder might be just another brainwashed sect. They simply did not understand the tradition it represented, which is atheistic and highly intelligent. There is no worship of a deity, and nothing is going to "save" you but your own mind. The teacher helps you to understand your own mind.

What about politics? It seems to me that in the sixties there was with a poet like Ginsberg a much fuller embrace of the political.
Well, take Diane DiPrima for example, a very political poet. She's a student of Trungpa's and is very much involved with alternative healing practices. In fact, she told me recently that for her the other work has become as important as the poetry, a way for her to channel these concerns. I find truly political people are working in a more one-to-one situation, rather than working with old generalizations. We all had compassionate ideals, but often we would be more than a little sloppy in our rhetoric and in our own lives. We've learned that we must work with our own minds to transform our neuroses before we can comment on or help anyone else's.

Allen is very public, a diplomat, a culture figure. His recent *Collected Poems* has made him even more visible. So anything he says or expresses what's on his mind, what he's up to, is picked up on. He recently gave a *Time* reporter a demonstration of Tai Chi and that made it into the magazine. That's in a way a political act. Tai Chi is an awareness discipline that can uplift and help de-pollute the world.

And you are active in the anti nuclear scene.
Yes, in Boulder there is a very active group I'm peripherally involved with. They get thorough and reliable information out to people. And I'd recommend that all you writers become members of the P.E.N. Club and get on

that mailing list; that you find out about the repression going on throughout the world, the various writers and artists who are in jail for their beliefs. Or Amnesty International. Those organizations are very effective. Or the Union of Concerned Scientists. What you end up doing is writing a lot of letters. This often demands more of people than demonstrating twice a year. Do it all! The important thing is to be effective, not just mouth off. The issue of torture and repression throughout the world is an urgent one to address, just as the nuclear issue is. As writers you can express this effectively.

Might you direct these notions to your work in Makeup or Empty Space? Is "Makeup" itself a political poem?
That poem takes off from the idea in Buddhist psychology that the feminine energy tends to manifest in the world, adorning empty space. What we see in the world, the phenomena, is created by feminine energy. For me, the idea of makeup as a literal making up of the empty world, the idea of giving birth became then central in this meditation. In a lot of Buddhist and other practices often what you do is create a visualization of something, then empty it out so that it is never fixed or solidified. We've all experienced phenomena that way. We've all walked around feeling as if we are in a dream state, as if everything has an illusory quality, and this points out for us the impermanence of our existence. Form is emptiness—it's quite provocative and wonderful.

So I'm putting makeup on empty space in this poem. The poem itself is makeup. I begin with my own face, putting on eyebrows. Then I move to adornment, encircling myself with necklaces and bangles on my wrist. Then a more personal situation, undressing "you." I was working with particulars; at one point there is a drive up a canyon which was a literal situation of dangerous icy roads. All part of the makeup on this groundless ground.

I've got many more what you'd normally think of as political poems than that—poems addressing certain kinds of issues—but I think of this piece as having a political expansiveness as well.

But obviously less specifically political than "Plutonium Chant."
Sure, in the sense you mean. That came out of a demonstration at Rocky Flats where I had to come up with a protest on the spot. It basically says, "We'll all be glowing for a quarter of a million years. Teeth glowing, underwear glowing, pages of words glowing, microfilm glowing, nails knuckles glowing," and so on. I took it and turned it into a pop song ("Uh-Oh Plutonium!"), made a record which was popular for a time, and I was able

to perform it. It's political in that it has a clear message, but it is meant to be humorous too, and danceable and accessible.

You mentioned earlier that the teacher was a mirror for the student. I'm wondering if you see a teacher in your poetry.
Yes, I learn all the time from my own writing, as we all do. You put something down that you weren't, at least on one level, consciously aware of. I can see things after the fact in my poems that have emerged fully naively, and I hope I learn from them.

Can we go back to your earlier discussion of inspiration? Is there a poem in Makeup *which is an example of a "gift"?*
I'd say that the last poem, "Incantation," although it was written over a long period of time, definitely came that way. "Make-up on Empty Space" itself also came rather magically.

Is there any particular kind of form that these spontaneous poems take?
Not really, though I've had poems come to me in traditional forms as well as open forms. The "Baby Pantoum" poem I spoke about earlier was one of those. It was a very special experience in the way that the form itself became invisible as I was working on it. I have a sestina in *First Baby Poems* which came close to the same experience. I was pregnant and in a Buddhist seminary. I was going crazy. I couldn't eat the food, so the words I picked were *soda cracker, calcium,* chateaux (at Lake Louise where I was), *path, waterfall,* and *meditators.* So this was something I set up in advance, but it came after a time again almost spontaneously. Everything fell into place.

Still, it seems to me in reading your work that the gift poems most often are open-form poems that have an oral dimension.
Like "Skin Meat Bones," which I mentioned earlier. Yes, these categories *do* overlap. That poem in particular was for me like a key into reality, seeing everything as skin, meat, bones.
 Do you find these categories useful? I began to think of my poetry this way because it behooved me as a teacher working with writing students to actually look at these processes and get a grasp on them. Hopefully, this doesn't simply make them hollow, but richer possibilities. Again, in *Makeup on Empty Space* I have two dialogues. This form comes right out of Sydney, Donne, and Yeats—the idea of a dialogue that is—though of course theirs are written in meter and rhyme and mine is open form.

So then even in the two dialogues there is the sense of the importance of oral poetry?

Well, it's always been there. Certainly in the last two decades we've seen the resurgence of the poetry event or reading as a viable experience. Coleridge and Wordsworth would read to each other, or Charles Dickens would read from his novels impersonating his characters, but it has only been recently that we've seen the poetry reading evolve as an art event per se. And even so there is not a well-developed audience. Most people would rather go to a play or a movie. Still, obviously for most poets, the public reading is important. The two dimensions of the poem—the page and the voice—go hand in hand. I'm also extremely attentive to how the works look on the page.

In that way, Gertrude Stein's work has been very important to me. The various stages she went through, seeing poetry as basically nouns, prose as basically verbs, etc. Setting those very concrete tasks for herself. She would actually turn nouns into other parts of speech. And the repetition! I find her wonderful to read aloud, although she wasn't writing with that in mind particularly. Today we have such questionable reading habits, reading as we do primarily for information. We want the hard stuff, things we need to know in some sort of solid way. Most people don't seem to read for pleasure or illumination. I've been teaching the Romantics and my students can't get into the poems easily. I read aloud to them from *Don Juan*—octava rima, very bouncy—and the poem became more alive for them. So there is a great service and delight in the oral presentation.

So it's not one or the other.

Exactly. And you also have to be careful not to get carried away with the personality of the poet, which is a problem in the oral dimension. I'm very happy to be alive with my work, to be able to read it aloud and get it "across" that way. Some of the work, as I've said, comes to me musically, and a piece like "Skin Meat Bones" is simply inert on the page. On the other hand, a long, more meditative piece like "Incantation" is a piece I'd like people to read themselves and see on the page. But it's wonderful that the oral performance situation makes some of us somewhat like traveling circus people. This is especially pleasurable because of the interaction with other poets, since we're often isolated in the actual doing of the work. When you get out you feel there is a wonderful community that has evolved all over the world. You look up the poets and get a meal, a bed, an argument. This sense of community and support, even though we each may have a particular aesthetic bias, seems important these days. There's a Sanskrit word for spiritual community: *sangha*. It resonates for me with the word *song*.

Queen

My sandpaper husband who
wears sackcloth when I don't behave
says Come sit on rattan, woman
Your will is as brittle as glass
Your mad mouth is untamable
& your heart is always in another country

Your ears are radar stalks
Your eyes magnetize yardmen
& when you sing you shake the house
AHHHHH AHHHHH AHHHHH
My wife is a burning house

My silky husband who tends the garden
whose arms shake like branches in a storm
complains I'm a slugabed on his time
He says Wake up woman of sleep & cream
Wake up & sweep back your flickering night-lids

Your hands are leopardesses
Your shins are Cadillacs
Your thighs are palaces of tears
When you weep the house rises
My wife is the Indian Ocean rising

My husband of sacred vows
has October weather in his voice
He says Come to bed, amorous woman
Your ancient desk is covered with leaves
Your tardy poem can't be coaxed
But will come to you like a Queen.

Drugs

Addressing tonight the young men the young women of tender
passage, speaking out of a stereo place, a double barrelled
feeling for your skin your arms your eyes your hips your lips
your legs, legs that buckle turn to me quivering, eyes not
focused, arms spindly and shot through, glitzy fear haunts
you, aura the color of the street. Not a beach not an alpine
slope not a radiant bower. Not a causeway not a moonlit
forest. Broken I say, and scattered in a fratricide
arrangement of the deranged senses and murdering of women
too. But it is the face that comes apart as the apparati
crumble, prostrate on the stoop or up in that family
apartment, that fancy apartment. In one second we all
feel we live forever. I never know what time it is! Clocks,
radios, TVs break down. Long lines wear down the spirit.
The idol who this artist wrought falls to the ground as if
to a grave. Early graves I see my neighbor frothing and
bound in a strait jacket carried to the attendant ambulance.
Ambulare: to walk free on one's own steam. A moral speech,
yes a mortal one, and a mighty fleet is storming you with
its prevarications. You say Leave me alone, you say you
hate the mighty harmonies.

You forget what I just said to you. You repeat yourself.
You whine. You try to fasten the sweater unsuccessfully
not like the youth who knows his own con. Concommitant, con
vivace, tender feelings to take a specific shape and continue.
Complete metabolic transfusion in which my infant logic plods
stupidly along. It won't ever stop, ignorant one, to listen
or ever refuse the likes of me in the replenishing hells or
halls, no bare feet, no firedrills, prone, face down in mud.

Sit beside me again, sit to people the lonely universe, and
break the adamantine chains that strap you down. Not the
situation I leave you here, squabbling under the window to
fix their bodies right, get them straight. I say Rites of
Passage, I say it's missing, and bow my head. And how you
will end up not knowing the universe is evident. Incandescent
splendor, my smart clothes: cocaine. The greatest affirmer,

coke, the smokescreen of all the attitudes, coke, and everything's
okay, yeah, in my wallet, in my power play, my rendevous
with braintalk, my little box is tight.

The heroines of whom you are the kick for, who takes you
deeper home. Junk, a point I get to beyond which I'd never
go for no man no woman no saint no idea no manifesto no
poetry no one's mother no plan or scheme to get rich no
lover no lover's beauty no prophecy flecked with fire and
brimstone. Scabs line the sidewalk, walking quickly for
the stroller's speed to be transmitted, a fast clip by the
leer or jeer or hassle and drown one sorrow in a drink.
Drink making me emotional, or quaalude, that weak sister.
If I could be Thersites-tongued, if I had that lucid scaly
tongue I would wag at you, I'd snap and bark and scoff and
bite. A pack of hounds to plead this sentiment, for it is,
you know, my surface sentimentality makes me mad, me a loon.
O dear speeder, speed-reader, speed-beater. Tonight I am
singing for the swift-neck tension I get in my brain stem,
high under Miss Green under a beneficent lamplight before
the supreme task (grandiose my powers) is done.

Task to set the thoughts unassailably down. I am my own
assailant with a canister of tear-gas in one hand, my
cobra protection implement in the other. Sisters, I say,
go armed.

But I wanted to tell you my approval smacks of what won't
go over as a kiss, an embrace, what can't be interpreted
as how I love you, because when you fall back, lump of
desire, limp of head, the lights go out all over New York.

You speak, and when you are speaking you speak to the speaker,
you are hearing the speaker, the hearer is the speaker, he
speaks to hear his speech to hear his mind roll on . . .

The speech is a history, the story of some people, the laughter
of some people, how the people nudged each other, the speaker
is the centrifugal force to propel the speech to all who
will stay here, listening. He speaks in a story. He won't
listen but comments on the speaking, on the fast tone of
the speaker. I need more pills! I need more history, history!

Hectic and demanding is my habit. Hectoring me like a shrew,
like a shadow, like a dumbshow, like an out-of-towner. I am
walking to no Eleusis.

Silky shadow to deeper than a hum the pain.

I cushion the mugger's quality of pillow of guilt. He's an
old-timer, burnt sienna, who puts in him those holes in him.
How enters the bloodstream, how rushes, how draw back, pull
up the reins. Horsie, whoa!

So. Go on. So. No. Go on. I say go on. I say no, go on.
I say You live in my garden-heart. I say no creature of habit
be. There's beauty sensible like a fine torso, like torso
of fine baby-man. I need to be mothering. I need to be
mothering my art, go on.

Crack in the World

I see the crack in the world
My body thinks it, sees the gaping crack in the world
My body does it for me to see
Blood flowing through the body crack
Body, send your rivers to the moon
Body twists me to the source of the moon
It turns me under a wave
It sets up the structure to make a baby, then tears
it down again.
Architecture of womb-body haunting me
Someone is always watching the ancient flow
It doubles up my mind
Ovum not fertilized
I see the crack in the world
Thoughts intersect in the body
He must not keep me down
Let me go my way alone tonight
No man to touch me
A slash in me, I see the slash in the world tonight
It keeps me whole, but divides me now

Out on land, to bleed
Out on street, to bleed
In the snow, blood
This is a South American song
Scent of oleander
Or this is a cactus song
Sing of a blood flower a rose in the crotch
O collapsible legs!
My body enchanted me to this
It is endometrium shedding
I am compressed in the pressure of my heart
It is life pursuing the crack in the world
Between worlds
Between thoughts
A vacant breath
Works won't do it
Ovum not fertilized
The man hasn't done it
I cover every contingency
the catty one
or puritan walking in a fecund world
Words sing to me of endometrium collapse
Words go down to my belly
Back swelling, to put my body next to the earth
This is periodic
It comes at the full moon
Let me go howling in the night
No man to touch me
Don't fathom my heart tonight, man
No one wants to be around this factory,
this beautiful machine
but I shun your company anyway
My flexible body imagines the crack
Body with winds
See the crack in the universe
The curse, glorious curse is upon me
Don't come to my house
Don't expect me at your door
I'm in my celibacy rags

My anthropocentric heart says there's
a crack in the world tonight
It's a long woman's body
It's a break in the cycle of birth & death
It's the rapid proliferation of cells
building up to die
I make up the world & kill it again & again
I offer my entrails to the moon
Ovum not fertilized
Architecture haunting me
Collapsible legs you must carry the world
You get away from me
You keep your distance
I will overpower you with my scent
of life & death
You who came through the crack in my world
You men who came out of me, back off
Words come out of the belly
Groaning as the world is pulled apart
Body enchanted to this
Body elaborated on this
Body took the measure of the woman
to explain the fierceness of this time
walking on the periphery of the world.

Acknowledgments

All poems reprinted by permission of the authors.

Clark Coolidge: "From *Quartz Hearts*," *Quartz Hearts* (San Francisco: This Press, 1978): "From *mine*," *mine: the one that enters the stories* (Berkeley: The Figures, 1982); "Brass Land I Live In," *Solution Passage* (Los Angeles: Sun & Moon Press, 1986).

Theodore Enslin: "Ballad of the Goodly Company: Birds," *To Come To Have Become* (New Rochelle: Elizabeth Press, 1966).

Clayton Eshleman: "The Lich Gate," "Equal Time," "For Aimé Césaire," *Hades in Manganese* (Santa Barbara: Black Sparrow Press, 1981); "Fracture," "Manticore Vortex," *Fracture* (Santa Barbara: Black Sparrow Press, 1983).

William Everson: "First Winter Storm," *The Residual Years* (New York: New Directions, 1948); "A Canticle to the Waterbirds," "The Way of Life and the Way of Death," *The Veritable Years* (Santa Barbara: Black Sparrow Press, 1978); "Blackbird Sundown," *The Masks of Drought* (Santa Barbara: Black Sparrow Press, 1980).

Thom Gunn: "On the Move," "Touch," "Rites of Passage," "Moly," *Selected Poems* (New York: Farrar Straus Giroux, 1979); "Bally *Power Play*," *The Passages of Joy* (New York: Farrar Straus Giroux, 1982).

Kenneth Irby: "The Grasslands of North America," "Strawberry Canyon Poem," *Catalpa* (Lawrence: Tansy Press, 1977).

Tom Raworth: "You Were Wearing Blue," "South America," "Logbook page 372," "The Moon Upoon the Waters," "Magnetic Water," *Tottering State* (Berkeley: The Figures, 1984).

Ishmael Reed: "I am a Cowboy in the Boat of Ra," "The Conjurer," *Conjure* (Amherst: University of Massachusetts Press, 1972); "The Katskills Kiss Romance Goodbye," "Loup Garou Means Change Into," *Chattanooga* (New York: Random House, 1973).

Michael Palmer: "To Robert E. Symmes 1933," "Seven Forbidden Words," "The Flower of Capital," *Notes for Echo Lake* (San Francisco: North Point Press, 1981); "Dearest Reader," "Book of the Yellow Castle," *First Figure* (San Francisco: North Point Press, 1984).

Stephen Rodefer: "From *Four Lectures*," *Four Lectures* (Berkeley: The Figures, 1982).

Nathaniel Tarn: "Last of the Chiefs," *Old Savage/Young City* (London: Cape, 1964); "From *A Nowhere for Vallejo*," *A Nowhere for Vallejo* (New York: Random House, 1971); "Flight from the Mountaintop," *The Desert Mothers* (Greneda, Miss.: Salt-Works Press, 1984).

Diane Wakoski: "To the Lion," *Discrepancies and Apparitions* (Garden City: Doubleday, 1966); "Summer," *Inside the Blood Factory* (Garden City: Doubleday, 1968); "For the Girl," *Saturn's Rings* (New York: Targe Editions, 1982); "To the Young Man," *Virtuoso Literature for Two and Four Hands* (Garden City: Doubleday, 1975); "Civilization," *Cap of Darkness* (Santa Barbara: Black Sparrow Press, 1980).

Anne Waldman: "Queen," "Crack in the World," *Skin Meat Bones* (Minneapolis: Coffee House Press, 1985); "Drugs," *Makeup on Empty Space* (West Branch, Iowa: Toothpaste Press, 1984).

Bibliography

CLARK COOLIDGE. Poetry: *Flag Flutter and U.S. Electric* (New York: Lines, 1966); *(Poems)* (New York: Lines, 1967); *Ing* (New York: Angel Hair, 1969); *Space* (New York: Harper & Row, 1970); *The So* (New York: Boke, 1971); *Moroccan Variations* (Bolinas: Big Sky, 1971); *Suite V* (New York: Boke, 1973); *The Maintains* (San Francisco: This Press, 1974); *Polaroid* (New York: Boke, 1975); *Quartz Hearts* (San Francisco: This Press, 1978); *Own Face* (Lenox: Angel Hair, 1978); *American Odes* (Bolinas: Tomboctou, 1981); *A Geology* (Elmwood: Potes & Poets Press, 1981); *Research* (Berkeley: Tuumba, 1982); *Mine: The One That Enters the Stories* (Berkeley: The Figures, 1982); *Solution Passage: Poems 1978–1981* (Los Angeles: Sun & Moon Press, 1986), *The Crystal Text* (Great Barrington, Mass.: The Figures, 1986). Other: *To Obtain the Value of the Cake Measure from Zero,* with Tom Veitch (San Francisco: Pants Press, 1970); *Smithsonian Depositions & Subject to a Film* (New York: Vehicle Editions, 1980).

THEODORE ENSLIN. Poetry: *The Work Proposed* (Ashland, Or.: Origin Press, 1958); *New Sharon's Prospect* (Kyoto: Origin Press, 1962); *The Place Where I Am Standing* (New Rochelle: Elizabeth Press, 1964); *This Do (and the Talents)* (Mexico City: El Corno Emplumado, 1966); *New Sharon's Prospect and Journals* (San Francisco: Coyote's Journal, 1966); *To Come to Have Become* (New Rochelle: Elizabeth Press, 1966); *The Four Temperaments* (Privately printed, 1966); *Characters in Certain Places* (Portland, Or.: Prensa de Lagar Wine Press, 1967); *The Diabelli Variations and Other Poems* (Annandale-on-Hudson: Matter, 1967); *2130–6131: Poems 1967* (Cabot, Vermont: Stoveside Press, 1967); *Agreement and Back: Sequences* (New Rochelle: Elizabeth Press, 1969); *The Poems* (New Rochelle: Elizabeth Press, 1970); *Forms, Part One: The First Dimension* (New Rochelle: Elizabeth Press, 1970); *Views 1–7* (Berkeley: Maya, 1970); *The Country of Our Consciousness* (Berkeley: Sand Dollar, 1971); *Forms, Part Two* (New Rochelle: Elizabeth Press, 1971); *Forms, Part Three* (New Rochelle: Elizabeth Press, 1972); *Etudes* (New Rochelle: Elizabeth Press, 1972); *Views* (New Rochelle: Elizabeth Press, 1973); *Forms, Part Four* (New Rochelle: Elizabeth Press, 1973); *Sitio* (Hanover, New Hampshire: Granite, 1973); *In the Keepers House* (Dennis, Mass.: Salt-Works Press, 1973); *With Light Reflected* (Fremont, Michigan: Sumac Press, 1973); *The Swamp Fox* (Dennis: Salt-Works Press, 1973); *The Mornings* (Berkeley: Shaman/Drum, 1974); *Fever Poems* (Brunswick, Maine: Blackberry, 1974); *The Last Days of October* (Dennis: Salt-Works Press, 1974); *The Median Flow: Poems 1943–*

1973 (Los Angeles: Black Sparrow Press, 1974); *Synthesis 1–24* (Plainfield, Vermont: North Atlantic, 1975); *Landler* (New Rochelle: Elizabeth Press, 1975); *Papers* (New Rochelle: Elizabeth Press, 1976); *Ranger I* (Richmond, Calif.: North Atlantic, 1978); *The Fifth Direction* (Markesan, Wisconsin: Pentagram, 1980); *Ranger II* (Richmond, Calif.: North Atlantic, 1980); *Two Geese* (Markesan: Pentagram, 1980); *Opus 0* (Shorewood, Milwaukee: Membrane Press, 1981); *Markings* (Shorewood: Membrane Press, 1981); *In Duo Concertante* (Markesan: Pentagram, 1981); *Axes LII* (Willimantic: Ziesing Brothers, 1981); *Processionals* (Grenada, Miss.: Salt-Works Press, 1981); *A Man in Stir* (Markesan: Pentagram, 1983); *Songs w/out Notes* (Grenada: Salt-Works Press, 1984); *Music for Several Occasions* (Shorewood: Membrane Press, 1985). Other: *Mahler* (Los Angeles: Black Sparrow Press, 1975); *The July Book* (Berkeley: Sand Dollar, 1976). Editor: *The Selected Poems of Howard McCord 1961–1971* (Trumansburg, New York: Crossings Press, 1975).

CLAYTON ESHLEMAN. Poetry: *Mexico and North* (Privately printed, 1962); *The Chavin Illumination* (Lima: La Rama Florida, 1965); *Lachrymae Mated* (New York: Caterpillar, 1966); *Walks* (New York: Caterpillar, 1967); *The Crocus Bud* (Reno: Camels Coming, 1967); *Brother Stones* (New York: Caterpillar, 1968); *Cantaloups and Splendour* (Los Angeles: Black Sparrow Press, 1968); *T'ai* (Cambridge, Mass.: Sans Souci Press, 1969); *The House of Okumura* (Toronto: Weed/Flower Press, 1969); *Indiana* (Los Angeles: Black Sparrow Press, 1969); *The House of Ibuki* (Fremont, Michigan: Sumac Press, 1969); *Yellow River Record* (London: Big Venus, 1969); *A Pitchblende* (San Francisco: Maya, 1969); *The Wand* (Santa Barbara: Capricorn Press, 1971); *Bearings* (Santa Barbara: Capricorn Press, 1971); *Alters* (Los Angeles: Black Sparrow Press, 1971); *The Sanjo Bridge* (Los Angeles: Black Sparrow Press, 1972); *Coils* (Los Angeles: Black Sparrow Press, 1973); *Human Weddings* (Los Angeles: Black Sparrow Press, 1973); *The Last Judgment* (Los Angeles: Plantin Press, 1973); *Aux Morts* (Los Angeles: Black Sparrow Press, 1974); *Realignment* (Providence: Treacle Press, 1974); *Portrait of Francis Bacon* (Sheffield, England: Rivelin Press, 1975); *The Gull Wall* (Los Angeles: Black Sparrow Press, 1975); *Cogollo* (Newton, Mass.: Roxbury, 1976); *The Woman Who Saw through Paradise* (Lawrence, Kansas: Tansy Press, 1976); *Grotesca* (London: New London Pride, 1977); *On Mules Sent from Chavin* (Swansea: Galloping Dog Press, 1977); *Core Meander* (Santa Barbara: Black Sparrow Press, 1977); *The Gospel of Celine Arnauld* (Willits, Calif.: Tuumba Press, 1978); *The Name Encanyoned River* (Providence: Treacle Press, 1978); *What She Means* (Santa Barbara: Black Sparrow Press, 1978); *A Note on Apprenticeship* (Chicago: Two Hands Press, 1979); *Nights We Put the Rock Together* (Tiburon: Cadmus, 1979); *The Lich Gate* (Barrytown, N.Y.: Station Hill, 1980); *Hades in Manganese* (Los Angeles: Black Sparrow Press, 1981); *Visions of Fathers of Lascaux* (Los Angeles: Panjandrum, 1983); *Fracture* (Los Angeles: Black Sparrow Press, 1983); *The Name Encanyoned River* (Los Angeles: Black Sparrow Press, 1985). Editor: *A Caterpillar Anthology* (New York: Doubleday, 1971). Translator: *Residence on Earth* by Pablo Neruda (San Francisco: Amber House, 1962); *State of the Union* (with Danis Kelly) by Aimé Césaire (Bloomington: Caterpillar, 1966), *Seven Poems* by Cesar Vallejo (New York: Grove Press, 1968); *Spain, Take This Cup from Me* (with José Rubia Barcia) by Cesar Vallejo (New York: Grove Press, 1974); *Letter to Andre Breton* by Antonin Artaud (Los Angeles: Black Sparrow Press, 1974); *To Have Done with the Judgment of God* (with Norman Glass) by Antonin Artaud (Los Angeles: Black Sparrow Press, 1975); *Artaud the Momo* (with Norman Glass) by Antonin Artaud (Santa Barbara: Black Sparrow Press, 1976); *Battles in Spain* (with José Rubia Barcia) by Cesar Vallejo (Santa Barbara: Black Sparrow Press, 1978); *The Complete Posthumous Poetry* (with José Rubia Barcia) by Cesar Vallejo (Berkeley: University of California Press, 1978); *Notebook of a Return to the Native Land* (with Annette Smith) by Aimé Césaire (New York: Montemora, 1979); *Antonin Artaud: 4 Texts* with Norman Glass (Los Angeles: Panjandrum Books, 1982); *Aimé Césaire: The Collected Poetry* with Annette Smith (Berkeley: University of California Press, 1983).

WILLIAM EVERSON. Poetry: *These Are the Ravens* (San Leandro, Calif: Greater West Publishing, 1935); *San Joaquin* (Los Angeles: The Ward Ritchie Press, 1939); *The Masculine Dead* (Prairie City, Illinois: The Press of James A. Decker, 1942); *X War Elegies* (Waldport, Oregon: Untide Press, 1943); *The Waldport Poems* (Waldport: Untide Press, 1944); *War Elegies* (Waldport: Untide Press, 1944); *The Residual Years* (Waldport: Untide Press, 1944); *Poems: XCMXLII* (Waldport: Untide Press, 1944); *The Residual Years* (New York: New Directions, 1948); *A Privacy of Speech* (Berkeley: The Equinox Press, 1949); *Triptych for the Living* (Berkeley: The Seraphim Press, 1951); *An Age Insurgent* (San Francisco: Blackfriars Publications, 1959); *The Crooked Lines of God* (Detroit: University of Detroit Press, 1959); *The Year's Declension* (Berkeley: University of California, 1961); *The Hazards of Holiness* (Garden City: Doubleday, 1962); *The Poet Is Dead* (San Francisco: The Auerhahn Press, 1964); *The Blowing of the Seed* (New Haven: Henry W. Wenning, 1966); *Single Source* (Berkeley: Oyez, 1966); *The Rose of Solitude* (Garden City: Doubleday, 1967); *In the Fictive Wish* (Berkeley: Oyez, 1967); *A Canticle to the Waterbirds* (Berkeley: Eizo, 1968); *The Springing of the Blade* (Reno: The Black Rock Press, 1968); *The Residual Years* (New York: New Directions, 1968); *The City Does Not Die* (Berkeley: Oyez, 1969); *The Last Crusade* (Berkeley: Oyez, 1969); *Who Is She That Looketh Forth as the Morning* (Santa Barbara: Capricorn Press, 1972); *Tendril in the Mesh* (Np: Cayucos Books, 1973); *Black Hills* (San Francisco: Didymous Press, 1973); *Man-Fate* (New York: New Directions, 1974); *River-Root* (Berkeley: Oyez, 1976); *The Mate-Flight of Eagles* (Newcastle, Calif.: Blue Oak Press, 1977); *Rattlesnake August* (Northridge, Calif.: Lord John Press, 1977); *The Veritable Years* (Santa Barbara: Black Sparrow Press, 1978); *Blame It on the Jet Stream* (Santa Cruz: The Lime Kiln Press, 1979); *The Masks of Drought* (Santa Barbara: Black Sparrow Press, 1980); *Eastward the Armies* (Aptos: Labyrinth Editions, 1980); *Renegade Christmas* (Northridge: Lord John Press, 1984); *In Medias Res* (San Francisco: Adrian Wilson, 1984). Other: *Robinson Jeffers: Fragments of an Older Fury* (Berkeley: Oyez, 1968); *Archetype West: The Pacific Coast as a Literary Region* (Berkeley: Oyez, 1976); *Earth Poetry: Selected Essays and Interviews* (Berkeley:

Oyez, 1980); *Birth of a Poet: The Santa Cruz Meditations* (Santa Barbara: Black Sparrow Press, 1982); *On Writing the Waterbirds and Other Presentations: Collected Forewords and Afterwords* (Metuchen, New Jersey: Scarecrow Press, 1983). Editor: *Novum Psalterium PIIXII* (Los Angeles: Countess Estelle Doheny, 1955); *Cawdor/Medea* by Robinson Jeffers (New York: New Directions, 1970); *Californians* by Robinson Jeffers (Np: Cayucos Books, 1971); *The Alpine Christ* by Robinson Jeffers (Np: Cayucos Books, 1973); *Tragedy Has Obligations* by Robinson Jeffers (Santa Cruz: The Lime Kiln Press, 1973); *Brides of the South Wind* by Robinson Jeffers (Np: Cayucos Books, 1974); *Granite & Cypress* by Robinson Jeffers (Santa Cruz: The Lime Kiln Press, 1975); *The Double Axe* (with Bill Hotchkiss) by Robinson Jeffers (New York: Norton, 1977); *American Bard* by Walt Whitman (New York: Viking, 1982).

THOM GUNN. Poetry: *Poems* (Oxford: Fantasy Press, 1953); *Fighting Terms* (Oxford: Fantasy Press, 1954; revised edition, New York: Hawk's Well Press, 1958); *The Sense of Movement* (London: Faber & Faber, 1957); *My Sad Captain and Other Poems* (London: Faber & Faber, 1961); *Selected Poems* with Ted Hughes (London: Faber & Faber, 1962); *A Geography* (Iowa City: Stone Wall Press, 1966); *Positives* (London: Faber & Faber, 1966); *Touch* (London: Faber & Faber, 1967); *The Garden of the Gods* (Cambridge, Mass.: Pym Randall Press, 1968); *The Explorers* (Crediton, Devon: Gilbertson, 1969); *The Fair in the Woods* (Oxford: Sycamore Press, 1969); *Poems 1950–1966: A Selection* (London: Faber & Faber, 1969); *Sunlight* (New York: Albondocani Press, 1969); *Moly* (London: Faber & Faber, 1971); *Poem after Chaucer* (New York: Albondocani Press, 1971); *Moly, and My Sad Captains* (New York: Farrar Straus, 1973); *Mandrakes* (London: Rainbow Press, 1973); *Songbook* (New York: Albondocani Press, 1973); *To the Air* (Boston: David R. Godine, 1974); *Jack Straw's Castle* (London: Faber & Faber, 1976); *The Missed Beat* (Sidcot, Somerset: Gruffyground Press, 1976); *Games of Chance* (Omaha: Abattoir, 1979); *Selected Poems 1950–1975* (London: Faber & Faber, 1979); *Talbot Road* (New York: Helikon, 1981); *The Passages of Joy* (New York: Farrar Straus, 1982); *The Menace* (San Francisco: Man Root, 1982); *Fighting Terms: A Selection* (Berkeley: Bancroft Library, 1983). Other: *The Occasions of Poetry: Essays in Criticism and Autobiography* (London: Faber, 1982; revised edition, San Francisco: North Point Press, 1985). Editor: *Poetry from Cambridge 1951–52* (London: Fortune Press, 1952); *Five American Poets* with Ted Hughes (London: Faber & Faber, 1963); *Selected Poems of Fulke Greville* (London: Faber & Faber, 1968); *Ben Jonson* (London: Penguin, 1974).

KENNETH IRBY. Poetry: *The Roadrunner* (Placitas, N.M.: Duende Press, 1964); *Kansas/New Mexico* (Lawrence, Kansas: Dialogue Press, 1965); *Movements / Sequences* (Placitas: Duende Press, 1965); *The Flower of Having Passed through Paradise in a Dream* (Annandale-on-Hudson: Matter Press, 1968); *Relation* (Los Angeles: Black Sparrow Press, 1970); *To Max Douglas* (Lawrence: Tansy Press, 1971; enlarged edition, 1974); *Archipelago* (Berkeley: Tuumba Press, 1976); *In Excelsis Borealis* (Np: White Creek Press, 1976); *Catalpa* (Lawrence: Tansy Press, 1977); *From Some Etudes* (Lawrence: Tansy Press, 1978); *Orexis* (Barrytown, N.Y.: Station Hill Press, 1981);

A Set (Lawrence: Tansy Press, 1983). Editor: *Seventeenth Century North America* (with Robert Callahan) by Carl O. Sauer (Berkeley: Turtle Island Foundation, 1980).

MICHAEL PALMER. Poetry: *Plan of the City of 0* (Boston: Barn Dream Press, 1971); *Blake's Newton* (Los Angeles: Black Sparrow Press, 1972); *C's Songs* (Berkeley: Sand Dollar, 1973); *Six Poems* (Los Angeles: Black Sparrow Press, 1973); *The Circular Gates* (Los Angeles: Black Sparrow Press, 1974); *Without Music* (Santa Barbara: Black Sparrow Press, 1977); *Alogon* (Berkeley: Tuumba, 1980); *Notes for Echo Lake* (San Francisco: North Point Press, 1981); *First Figure* (San Francisco: North Point Press, 1984). Editor: *Code of Signals: Recent Writings in Poetics* (Richmond, Calif.: North Atlantic, 1983). Translator: *Relativity of Spring* (Berkeley: Sand Dollar, 1976).

TOM RAWORTH. Poetry: *Continuation* (London: Goliard Press, 1966); *The Relation Ship* (London: Goliard Press, 1966); *Haiku* with John Esam and Anselm Hollo (London: Trigram Press, 1968); *The Big Green Day* (London: Trigram Press, 1968); *Lion, Lion* (London: Trigram Press, 1970); *Moving* (London: Cape Goliard Press, 1971); *Penguin Modern Poets 19* with John Ashbery and Lee Harwood (London: Penguin, 1971); *Tracking* (Bowling Green: Doones Press, 1972); *Time Being* with Asa Benveniste and Ray DiPalma (London: Blue Chair, 1972); *Pleasant Butter* (Northampton: Blue Pig/Sand Project Press, 1973); *An Interesting Picture of Ohio* (Privately printed, 1973); *Back to Nature* (London: Joe DiMaggio Press, 1973); *Act* (London: Trigram Press, 1973); *Ace* (London: Cape Goliard Press, 1974); *Bolivia: Another End of Ace* (London: Secret, 1974); *Cloister* (Northampton, Mass.: Blue Pig/Sand Project Press, 1975); *That More Simple Natural Time Tone Distortion* (Storrs: University of Connecticut Library, 1975); *Common Sense* (San Francisco: Zephyrus Image, 1976); *The Mask* (Berkeley: Poltroon Press, 1976); *Sky Tails* (Cambridge: Lobby Press, 1978); *Four Door Guide* (Cambridge: Street Editions, 1979); *Heavy Light* (Colchester, Essex: Transgravity Press, 1979); *Nicht Wahr, Rosie?* (Berkeley: Poltroon Press, 1980); *Writing* (Berkeley: The Figures, 1982); *Tottering State: Selected and New Poems, 1963–1983* (Great Barrington, Mass.: The Figures, 1984). Other: *The Minicab War* with Anselm Hollo and Gregory Corso (London: Matrix Press, 1961); *Betrayal* (London: Trigram Press, 1967); *A Serial Biography* (London: Fulcrum Press, 1969); *Sic Him Oltorf!* (San Francisco: Zephyrus Image, 1974); *Logbook* (Berkeley: Poltroon Press, 1977); *Cancer* (Berkeley: Turtle Island, 1979). Translator: *From the Hungarian* with Valarie Raworth (Privately printed, 1973).

ISHMAEL REED. Poetry: *Catechism of D Neoamerican Hoodoo Church* (London: Paul Breman, 1970); *Conjure: Selected Poems 1963–70* (Amherst: University of Massachusetts Press, 1972); *Chattanooga* (New York: Random House, 1973); *Secretary to the Spirits* (New York: Nok, 1977). Other: *The Rise, Fall, and . . . ? of Adam Clayton Powell* as Emmett Coleman, with others (New York: Bee-Line, 1967); *The Free-Lance Pallbearers* (Garden City: Doubleday, 1967); *Yellow Back Radio Broke-Down* (Garden City: Doubleday, 1969); *Mumbo-Jumbo* (Garden City: Doubleday, 1972); *The Last Days of Louisiana Red* (New York: Random House, 1974); *Flight to Canada* (New York: Random House, 1976); *Shrovetide in Old New Orleans* (Garden City: Doubleday,

1978); *God Made Aslaska for the Indians* (New York: Garland Press, 1981); *The Terrible Twos* (New York: St. Martin's/Marek, 1982). Editor: *19 Necromancers from Now* (Garden City: Doubleday, 1970); *Yardbird Reader* (Berkeley: Yardbird, 1972); *Yardbird Lives!* with Al Young (Berkeley: Yardbird); *Calafia: The California Poetry* (Berkeley: Yardbird, 1979).

STEPHEN RODEFER. Poetry: *The Knife* (Toronto: Island Press, 1965); *After Lucretius* (Storrs: University of Connecticut Press, 1973); *One or Two Love Poems from the White World* (San Francisco: Pick Pocket, 1976); *Safety* (San Francisco: Miam, 1977); *The Bell Clerk's Tears Keep Flowing* (Berkeley: The Figures, 1978); *Plane Debris* (Berkeley: Tuumba, 1981); *Four Lectures* (Berkeley: The Figures, 1982). Translator: *Villon* (Placitas, N.M.: Duende Press, 1976).

NATHANIEL TARN. Poetry: *Old Savage/Young City* (London: Cape, 1964); *Penguin Modern Poets 7* with Richard Murphy and Jon Silkin (London: Penguin, 1966); *Where Babylon Ends* (London: Cape Goliard Press, 1968); *The Beautiful Contradictions* (London: Cape Goliard Press, 1969); *October* (London: Trigram Press, 1969); *The Silence* (Milan: M'Arte, 1970); *A Nowhere for Vallejo* (New York: Random House, 1971); *Lyrics for the Bride of God: Section: The Artemision* (Santa Barbara: Tree, 1973); *The Persephones* (Santa Barbara: Tree, 1974); *Lyrics for the Bride of God* (New York: New Directions, 1975); *Narrative of This Fall* (Los Angeles: Black Sparrow Press, 1975); *The House of Leaves* (Santa Barbara: Black Sparrow Press, 1976); *From Alashka: The Ground of Our Great Admiration of Nature* with Janet Rodney (London: Permanent Press, 1977); *The Microcosm* (Milwaukee: Membrane Press, 1977); *Birdscapes, with Seaside* (Santa Barbara: Black Sparrow Press, 1978); *The Forest* with Janet Rodney (Mount Horeb, Wisconsin: Perishable Press, 1978); *Atitlan/Alashka: New and Selected Poems* with Janet Rodney (Boulder: Brillig Works Press, 1979); *The Land Songs* (Plymouth: Blue Guitar Books, 1981); *Weekends in Mexico* (London: Oxus Press, 1982); *The Desert Mothers* (Grenada, Miss.: Salt-Works Press, 1984); *At the Western Gates* (Santa Fe: Tooth of Time, 1985). Editor: *Con Cuba: An Anthology of Cuban Poetry of the Last Sixty Years* (London: Cape Goliard Press, 1969); *Selected Poems: A Bilingual Edition* by Pablo Neruda (London: Cape, 1970); *The Penguin Neruda* (London: Penguin Books, 1975). Translator: *The Heights of Macchu Picchu* by Pablo Neruda (London: Cape, 1966); *Stelae* by Victor Segalen (Santa Barbara: Unicorn Press, 1969).

DIANE WAKOSKI. Poetry: *Coins and Coffins* (New York: Hawk's Well Press, 1962); *Discrepancies and Apparitions* (Garden City: Doubleday, 1966); *The George Washington Poems* (New York: Riverrun Press, 1967); *Greed: Parts One and Two* (Los Angeles: Black Sparrow Press, 1968); *The Diamond Merchant* (Cambridge, Mass.: Sans Souci Press, 1968); *Inside the Blood Factory* (Garden City: Doubleday, 1968); *Thanking My Mother for Piano Lessons* (Mount Horeb, Wisconsin: Perishable Press, 1969); *Greed: Parts 3 and 4* (Los Angeles: Black Sparrow Press, 1969); *The Moon Has a Complicated Geography* (Palo Alto: Odda Tala Press, 1969); *The Magellanic Clouds* (Los Angeles: Black Sparrow Press, 1970); *Greed: Parts 5–7* (Los Angeles: Black Sparrow Press, 1970); *The Lament of the Lady Bank Dick* (Cambridge: Sans

Souci Press, 1970); *Love, You Big Fat Snail* (San Francisco: Tenth Muse, 1970); *Black Dream Ditty for Billy "The Kid" Seen in Dr. Generosity's Bar Recruiting for Hell's Angels and Black Mafia* (Los Angeles: Black Sparrow Press, 1970); *Exorcism* (Boston: My Dukes, 1971); *This Water Baby: For Tony* (Santa Barbara: Unicorn Press, 1971); *On Barbara's Shore* (Los Angeles: Black Sparrow Press, 1971); *The Motorcycle Betrayal Poems* (New York: Simon and Schuster, 1971); *The Pumpkin Pie* (Los Angeles: Black Sparrow Press, 1972); *The Purple Finch Song* (Mount Horeb: Perishable Press, 1972); *Sometimes a Poet Will Hijack the Moon* (Providence, Rhode Island: Burning Deck, 1972); *Smudging* (Los Angeles: Black Sparrow Press, 1972); *The Owl and the Snake: A Fable* (Mount Horeb: Perishable Press, 1973); *Greed: Parts 8, 9, 11* (Los Angeles: Black Sparrow Press, 1973); *Dancing on the Grave of a Sone of a Bitch* (Los Angeles: Black Sparrow Press, 1973); *Winter Sequences* (Los Angeles: Black Sparrow Press, 1973); *Trilogy* (New York: Doubleday, 1974); *Looking for the King of Spain* (Los Angeles: Black Sparrow Press, 1974); *The Wandering Tatler* (Mount Horeb: Perishable Press, 1974); *Abalone* (Los Angeles: Black Sparrow Press, 1974); *Virtuoso Literature for Two and Four Hands* (Garden City: Doubleday, 1975); *The Fable of the Lion and the Scorpion* (Milwaukee: Pentagram Press, 1975); *Waiting for the King of Spain* (Santa Barbara: Black Sparrow Press, 1976); *The Man Who Shook Hands* (Garden City: Doubleday, 1978); *Trophies* (Santa Barbara: Black Sparrow Press, 1979); *Cap of Darkness* (Santa Barbara: Black Sparrow Press, 1980); *Magician's Feast Letters* (Santa Barbara: Black Sparrow Press, 1982); *Collected Greed* (Santa Barbara: Black Sparrow Press, 1984); *Why My Mother Likes Liberace* (Tucson: Sun Gemini Press, 1985). Other: *Form Is an Extension of Content* (Los Angeles: Black Sparrow Press, 1972); *Creating a Personal Mythology* (Los Angeles: Black Sparrow Press, 1975); *Towards a New Poetry* (Ann Arbor: University of Michigan Press, 1979).

ANNE WALDMAN. Poetry: *On the Wing* (New York: Boke, 1967); *Giant Night* (New York: Angel Hair, 1968); *O My Life!* (New York: Angel Hair, 1969); *Baby Breakdown* (Indianapolis: Bobbs Merrill, 1970); *Up through the Years* (New York: Angel Hair, 1970); *Giant Night: Selected Poems* (New York: Corinth, 1970); *Icy Rose* (New York: Angel Hair, 1971); *No Hassles* (New York: Kulchur, 1971); *Memorial Day with Ted Berrigan* (New York: Poetry Project, 1971); *Holy City* (Privately printed, 1971); *Goodies from Anne Waldman* (London: Strange Faeces Press, 1971); *Light and Shadow* (Privately printed, 1972); *The West Indes Poems* (New York: Boke, 1972); *Spin Off* (New York, 1972); *Self Portrait* with Joe Brainard (New York: Siamese Banana Press, 1973); *Life Notes: Selected Poems* (Indianapolis: Bobbs Merrill, 1973); *The Contemplative Life* (Detroit: Alternative Press, 1974); *Fast Speaking Woman and Other Chants* (San Francisco: City Lights, 1975); *Sun the Lond Out* (Berkeley: Arif, 1975); *Journals and Dreams* (New York: Stonehill, 1976); *Shaman* (Boston: Munich, 1977); *4 Travels* with Reed Bye (New York: Sayonara, 1978); *To a Young Poet* (Boston: White Raven, 1979); *Countries* (West Branch, Iowa: Toothpaste Press, 1981); *Makeup on Empty Space* (West Branch: Toothpaste Press, 1983); *First Baby Poems* (New York:

Hyacinth Girls Editions, 1983); *Invention* (New York: Kulchur, 1985). Editor: *The World Anthology: Poems from the St. Mark's Poetry Project* (Indianapolis: Bobbs Merrill, 1969); *Another World* (Indianapolis: Bobbs Merrill, 1971); *Talking Poetics from Naropa Institute* with Marilyn Webb (Boulder: Shambala, 1978); *Nice to See You: Homage to Ted Berrigan* (New York: Coffee House Press, 1985).

Index

Michelangelo Buonarroti, 24
Micheline, Jack, 176
Miller, Henry, 77, 190–91
Monet, Claude, 130
Mondale, Walter, 136
Monroe, Harriet, 74, 201
Monroe, Vaughn, 187
Morgan, Dale, 115
Morris, Robert, 12
Morrison, Jim, 170
Morrow, Brad, 33
Mozart, Wolfgang Amadeus, 31, 187, 248
Murray, David, 167

Nabokov, Vladimir, 117
Neruda, Pablo, 24, 45–46, 52
Nietzsche, Friedrich, 137
Nin, Anaïs, 235

Oates, Joyce Carol, 172, 237
O'Connor, Flannery, 243
O'Hara, Frank, 133, 267, 270
O'Hara, John, 169
Oliver, Ray, 90
Olson, Charles, vii–viii, 22, 42, 51, 53, 57, 76, 108–10, 112, 116, 140–41, 157, 191–94, 202, 220, 223, 225, 246, 267
Olson, Toby, 248–49
Oppen, George, vii, 24, 30, 196
Oppenheimer, Joel, 167
Orlovsky, Peter, 192
Ortiz, Simon, 171

Padgett, Ron, 157
Pagels, Elaine, 72
Palmer, Michael, viii, 12, 219, 223
Parkinson, Thomas, 75, 192
Pasternak, Boris, 116–17, 130, 192
Perkins, Carl, 186
Phillips, Jayne Anne, 249
Picasso, Pablo, 200
Pinsky, Robert, viii
Plath, Sylvia, 26, 95
Plato, 167
Plymell, Charles, 111
Poe, Edgar Allan, viii
Porter, Cole, 170
Pound, Ezra, vii–viii, 22, 41, 51–52, 57, 95, 138, 172, 192, 215, 220, 225

Powell, Bud, 53
Powell, James, 90
Prince, Richard, 98
Prynne, J. H., 151, 157, 194

Redfield, Robert, 212, 215
Redgrove, Peter, 50
Reich, Wilhelm, 54
Reverdy, Pierre, 119
Rexroth, Kenneth, 65, 77, 117, 119, 210, 238
Reznikoff, Charles, vii
Rich, Adrienne, 172
Rilke, Rainier Maria, 14, 22, 51, 127, 129, 195, 226
Rimbaud, Arthur, 12, 14, 88, 226, 261
Rinpoche, Trungpa, 270–71
Rivera, Diego, 171
Robinson, Kit, 13, 152, 196
Rodney, Janet, 210
Roethke, Theodore, vii, 69
Roosevelt, Theodore, 26
Rosenthan, Irving, 109
Ross, Alan, 162
Rossini, Gioacchino, 187
Roth, Philip, 169
Rothenberg, Jerome, 53, 215, 262, 269

Sabina, Maria, 262
Samperi, Frank, 23
Sanders, Ed, 270
Sandburg, Carl, 77, 169
Sapir, Edward, 215
Sappho, 267
Saroyan, Aram, 12, 260
Sartre, Jean Paul, 100, 172
Satie, Eric, 263
Sauer, Carl, 108–10
Scalapino, Leslie, 220
Schiller, Johann von, 132
Schöenberg, Arnold, 200
Schubert, Franz, 187
Schwartz, Delmore, 131
Schwerner, Armand, 220
Seaton, Peter, 201
Shakespeare, William, 52, 71, 76, 93, 96, 100, 189, 247
Shapiro, David, 130
Shoemaker, Jack, 142
Sidney, Sir Philip, 189, 265, 273